Separation and Reunion in Modern China

In this original and highly readable book, Charles Stafford describes the Chinese fascination with human and spiritual 'separation' and 'reunion'. Drawing on his field studies in Taiwan and mainland China, he gives a vivid account of raucous festivals of reunion, elaborate rituals for the sending-off of gods (and of daughters), poetic moments of leave-taking between friends, and bitter political rhetoric about Chinese national unity. These idioms and practices of separation and reunion – which are woven into the fabric of Chinese daily life – help people to situate themselves in historical communities, and they also help to explain the passions aroused by the possibility of national division. The discussion of everyday rituals leads into a unique and accessible general introduction to Chinese and Taiwanese society, culture and politics.

CHARLES STAFFORD is Senior Lecturer in Anthropology at the London School of Economics and Political Science. He is the author of *The Roads of Chinese Childhood* (1995).

Separation and Reunion in Modern China

Charles Stafford

CAMBRIDGE
UNIVERSITY PRESS

PUBLISHED BY THE PRESS SYNDICATE OF THE UNIVERSITY OF CAMBRIDGE
The Pitt Building, Trumpington Street, Cambridge, United Kingdom

CAMBRIDGE UNIVERSITY PRESS
The Edinburgh Building, Cambridge CB2 2RU, UK   www.cup.cam.ac.uk
40 West 20th Street, New York NY 10011-4211, USA   www.cup.org
10 Stamford Road, Oakleigh, Melbourne 3166, Australia
Ruiz de Alarcón 13, 28014 Madrid, Spain

First published 2000

Printed in the United Kingdom at the University Press, Cambridge

Typeset in Times New Roman 10/12pt [VN]

A catalogue record for this book is available from the British Library

ISBN 0 521 78017 9 hardback
ISBN 0 521 78434 4 paperback

For my parents and my sisters

Contents

Acknowledgements

I am indebted to the many people in Angang and Dragon-head (and more generally in China and Taiwan) who have shown me unfailing hospitality and kindness during my various periods of residence there: they truly forced the topic of this book upon me. (My research was funded primarily by the Wenner-Gren Foundation, the Luce Foundation Taiwan History Field Research Project, and the Chiang Ching-kuo Foundation.) Over the past few years, I've discussed my growing interest in the 'separation constraint' with many colleagues, students and friends: Yen Yueh-ping, Goncalo Duro Santos, Stephan Feuchtwang, Steve Sangren, Raymond Firth, Maurice Bloch, Rita Astuti, Janet Carsten, and a great many others. In the middle of completing her dissertation on the anthropology of Chinese 'writing', Yen Yueh-ping kindly helped me locate some of the Chinese-language sources to be found in chapters eight and nine; and she also checked my (sometimes ragged) translations. I've presented material from this book to a number of seminars and workshops. In particular, I'd like to thank participants in the workshop on 'The anthropology of separation and reunion in China', which was held at the London School of Economics in May 1999. I am grateful to the two readers for Cambridge University Press, who gave the manuscript a highly sympathetic reading, and provided many insightful comments. Finally: I've dedicated this book to my parents (who have recently celebrated their fifty-second wedding anniversary), and also to my two sisters. Rather like the 'unruly son' of Chinese lore, I seem to have vanished off to a different place; but perhaps this book will serve as some kind of 'return', however modest.

Introduction: an anthropology of separation

> After the separation of death, one can eventually swallow back one's grief; but the separation of the living is an endless, unappeasable anxiety.
>
> Tu Fu, Tang dynasty poet (eighth century AD)[1]

> When two friends or relatives meet who have been separated from one another for a few weeks or longer, they greet each other by sitting down, one on the lap of the other, with their arms around each other's necks, and weeping and wailing for two or three minutes till they are tired. Two brothers greet each other in this way, and so do father and son, mother and son, mother and daughter, and husband and wife. When husband and wife meet, it is the man who sits on the lap of the woman. When two friends part from one another, one of them lifts up the hand of the other towards his mouth and gently blows on it.
>
> A. R. Radcliffe-Brown, *The Andaman Islanders*[2]

This book ends with a local matter, so-called: the passions aroused by the potential reunification of Taiwan with mainland China.[3] Dangerous territory! But it begins very differently, with a 'universalist' hypothesis: that the existential constraint of death (which anthropologists since Frazer have repeatedly discussed), is merely a subset of the existential constraint of separation (which anthropologists since Frazer have arguably . . . well, *obscured* – and thus in some ways ignored). Of course, as I'll explain below, anthropologists *have* dealt with separation in many complex senses: as an aspect of cultural psychology, as a near-universal feature of rituals, as an old problem 'made new' by the era of global displacements, and so on. But they've arguably failed to grasp the centrality of separation as a human dilemma in its own right. This is unfortunate, to say the least, for separation experiences (best viewed, I'll suggest, from a realist perspective, i.e. one which at least starts by taking its object literally) have crucial social and psychological effects. They are, in short, productive. Be that as it may, between my 'universalist' beginning and my 'localist' ending – both of which are likely, although for completely different reasons, to be controversial – I'll hopefully be on safer ground. (As Deng Xiaoping once famously remarked: 'When crossing a stream, grab onto the stones.') Using ethnography

1

from Taiwan and mainland China, I'll describe, bit by bit, the Chinese fascination with separation and its counterpart, reunion. This is in order to illustrate, by the end of the book, how the elaboration in China of a universal constraint – separation – helps set the stage for, and arguably even intensifies, the highly contentious Chinese politics of unity.

It happens that in China processes of separation and reunion, epitomised in moments of parting and return which involve both the living and the dead, are often a matter of great concern. In fact, at times it seems that going away and coming back again are even *more* significant, vis-à-vis certain kinds of relationships, than any fixed state of being together. My evidence for this is of various kinds, but was mostly collected during anthropological fieldwork in two different localities: one in rural north-eastern mainland China and one in rural southeastern Taiwan. There – that is to say in both places – in everyday social encounters and conversations, in formal rules of etiquette and politeness, in celebrations of calendrical festivals, in rituals of kinship and of the life-cycle, in procedures for dealing with gods and with the dead, in ideas about food and eating, in notions related to doors and social space, in classical poetry and literature, and even in heated (and sometimes 'enchanting') political rhetoric, the Chinese fascination with separation and reunion is made manifest time and again. Of course, these manifestations occur in different contexts, and the Chinese terms and expressions used in relation to them are captured only roughly by the English terms 'separation' and 'reunion'.[4] However both the manifestations and the terms do share some striking family resemblances. For instance, 'greeting' (*jie*) and 'sending-off' (*song*) guests is often a complex and sometimes even convoluted matter in China, while the elaborate 'greeting' (*jie*) and 'sending-off' (*song*) of ancestors and gods is at the very core of Chinese religious life.

Of course, the stringing together of examples of this kind may be misleading and even productive of category errors, not least through helping us conflate Chinese and Taiwanese ethnography. But it also helps generate some compelling arguments, because Chinese practices and idioms of separation and reunion, when viewed together, imply a coherent way of thinking about *all* human and spiritual relationships – which are always seen to be in flux, in a very fundamental sense, and therefore repeatedly subject to partings and returns. This, in turn, has concrete implications for Chinese historical consciousness. For to grow up in China is, by definition, to have one's life, and one's personal emotional history, punctuated by the informal and ritualised separations and reunions which are realised in all families and communities over time. These help people situate themselves in relation to other people, in relation to places, and in relation to the flow of time and events. In short, they contribute to the sense Chinese people have of themselves as subjects in history.

But not – of course! – in a simple or straightforward way. To cite only one (yes, predictable) complication: the public elaboration of leave-takings in China seems, in many circumstances, inversely proportional to the emotional closeness of the attachments in question. More trouble is often taken over separations from distant associates and honoured guests, than over those from close relatives and friends. The physical departure of the latter often even passes unremarked, in part, as I will argue, because separations of this kind are made to seem *impossible*. Meanwhile, as one might expect, even 'impossible' separations (e.g. between fathers and sons) are sometimes very desirable indeed, while others (e.g. between parents and daughters) are seen, however unwanted, to be socially necessary. Owing to these and other complications, an argument along the lines I propose is undoubtedly difficult to substantiate. But I hope that in this book I will at least succeed in making comprehensible my viewpoint and in conveying the interest and importance of a subject which was more or less forced upon me by Chinese friends.

And I must stress: it was never my intention to study separation and reunion, as such. Instead, I've gradually formulated it as an area for research over a period of years, through linking together certain of my reactions to fieldwork in Dragon-head, a farming community in north-eastern China, and in Angang, a fishing community in southeastern Taiwan.[5] It struck me, for example, that people in Angang and Dragon-head seemed very disinclined to bring certain public 'reunion' banquets to an end, by way of contrast with ordinary meals which they usually seemed happy enough to race through. I noticed that when I left these two places, even temporarily, certain kinds of people made a fuss over my departure, whereas everyday partings between friends and kin seemed almost wilfully abrupt. I was surprised to learn, while living in Angang, that a great many occasions in Chinese popular religion relate directly to, and even derive their primary meaning from, the arrival and departure of deities and other spirits. (To be honest, I was surprised to learn that these spirits moved at all, having assumed that they were simply *there*.) I also realised, while living in Dragon-head, that passages and entryways such as doors and gates – spaces for 'sending-off' and 'greeting' which are almost always architec-turally elaborated or decorated in some way – are often important and problematic during rituals and social events. I learned that the word for such entryways, *men* (door/gate), can be used to designate, among other things, a 'family' or 'clan'. Later, a friend drew my attention to the existence of an entire genre of Chinese classical poetry related directly to the emotions of 'sending off' (*song*), a genre which to this day provides friends and acquaintances with appropriate 'words of parting' (*bieci*). These diverse social realities – prolonged meals, emotional leave-takings, expensive rituals, elaborate doors, sentimental verses – are easily observable in China and Taiwan, and they all share a traceable connection. That is, they all relate in some way to the problem of separation. But how specifically Chinese is the matter to which these realities have drawn my attention?

Separation as a universal constraint

Anthropologists are meant to be professionally fascinated with cultural variation, but in fact they often dwell on aspects of human experience – such as birth, reproduction, and death – which *transcend*, at a fundamental level, cultural and historical variability, and which all human societies must deal with in some way. Of course, this qualification ('in some way') lies behind many long-standing anthropological debates about the limits of cultural variability, as well as some newer ones influenced by cognitive and evolutionary science. I don't intend to rehearse these matters here (for a useful overview see Brown 1991), nor am I personally interested in fishing expeditions for new universals. But the existence of common constraints across diverse cultural environments clearly does help to explain, on a very basic level, certain shared human realities. It helps us grasp, for example, why *underlying patterns* of things as seemingly 'private' as emotions (cf. Myers 1988), or as 'culturally-specific' as rituals (cf. Bloch 1992), are found instead to be widely distributed in human populations. These distributions are a function of our common natural history; and while this doesn't necessarily diminish the strangeness of what happens in other times and places, it does underline the fact that what would seem truly strange would be a time or place in which such constraints did not exist – e.g. where people did not die.

This brings me back to separation. The aim of this introduction is to suggest that separation, which anthropologists have generally *not* taken to be a common or universal human constraint, should be so taken, and also to suggest that it is amongst the most important of them all. Let me state my general premise as simply as possible. All human beings of course engage in social relations of various kinds, however it is presumably quite rare – given the spatial, temporal, and cultural realities in which most people in most societies live – for the entire set of any one person's relations to be physically present simultaneously, much less for any length of time. Instead, those with whom we are socially engaged (including parents, siblings, lovers, spouses, children, neighbours, friends, enemies, and so on – however culturally defined) arrive and depart throughout our lives, in some cases many times in a single day. The resulting separations may be momentary or permanent, mundane or dramatic, longed-for or deeply regretted, and obviously they are culturally patterned. But repeated *physical* separations in various forms – including, ultimately, in the form of death – are surely an inevitable feature of human life; and, as I will discuss in a moment, they surely everywhere stand in a complex relationship with various forms of *emotional* and *social* separation and distance. These facts, which may seem obvious, or even trivial, deserve further consideration, as does the possibility of their universal distribution. For the unavoidable reality of separation – and perhaps especially in its most 'simplistic' material (or realist) forms – can present human beings with exceptional, at times wholly intractable, dilemmas.

Awareness of separation and awareness of death

But in what contexts, and at what stages in the human life-cycle, do these dilemmas become salient? As I'll discuss in a moment, many psychological theories have given a central place to infantile 'attachment' and 'separation', and to the role of these processes in human emotional development. Briefly, they hold that infants develop a sense of self partly through encounters with persons who become, for them, key objects of attachment and desire, and who are present and then absent in both literal and much more abstract senses. While mastering their considerable distress at separation, children begin to measure their own *autonomy and dependency*, and thus to comprehend human relatedness.

Now this perspective implies that children should be aware of, and in fact skilled in, certain issues which arise from the separation constraint quite early in life – and arguably long *before* they are aware of the kinds of constraints on which anthropologists have primarily focussed their collective attention. Here a telling comparison may be drawn with the awareness of death, to which separation is closely linked in emotional terms. Psychological evidence (to be discussed below) suggests, surprisingly to my mind, that for most young children death is *not* especially salient as a conscious concern or explicit anxiety. One possible explanation for this is that they do not yet fully grasp the relevant concepts. As the cognitive scientist Susan Carey notes, a range of cross-cultural evidence suggests that children's awareness of death moves through three developmental stages (Carey 1985, cf. Slaughter et al. 1999). In the first (up to approximately age five), death is normally 'assimilated to the notions of sleep and departure', and its emotional impact derives from seeing it as 'a sorrowful separation and/or as the ultimate act of aggression' (Carey 1985: 60). To die is 'to live in some other place . . . from which one cannot return' (Slaughter et al. 1999). The second stage is transitional; in this, children grasp the finality of death, but they still see the 'causes of death as external to the dying person' (Carey 1985: 61). Only in the last stage (which begins around age nine or ten), is death understood to be a process which is both internal ('organic') and inevitable (1985: 64). In sum, while young children have an early awareness of the concept of death, they tend at first to conflate it with sleep *and separation*, and only gradually do they comprehend it in biological/organic terms. (Carey suggests this can only happen once they are cognitively equipped to comprehend it, i.e. once they are equipped with an intuitive 'biological theory' which makes death comprehensible.)

Leaving aside issues of cognitive development, as such, this material of course leaves open many interpretive questions, including the question of what it *means* to say that a ten-year-old, or indeed an eighty-year-old, living in a particular social context, 'now understands death'. This matter has been addressed, at least indirectly, by Renato Rosaldo in his discussion of death, 'positionality', and the accumulation of experience. Rosaldo describes his own incomprehension, *as an adult*, and over a period of many years, of claims by senior men among the Ilongot (of the Philippines) that their head-hunting activities were a translation into enraged action of the grief felt upon the death of loved ones (1993: 3). But he says this 'powerful rage' *did* finally become comprehensible to him following the sudden accidental death of his wife during fieldwork (1993: 3). Reflecting years later on this traumatic event, Rosaldo observes that 'ethnographic knowledge tends to have the strengths and limitations given by the relative youth of field-workers who, for the most part, have not suffered serious losses and could have, for example, no personal knowledge of how devastating the loss of a long-term partner can be for the survivor' (1993: 9). Emotional inexperience (which in this particular instance might easily extend into old age) has methodological implications for anthropology; but Rosaldo's more general point is that the relationship of *everyone* to death – and to any culturally conceived category such as 'death' – is inevitably transformed with age and experience (1993: 16–21).

Awareness or comprehension, in this sense, is undoubtedly a life-long task; and just as a child might begin to process the separation constraint early in life, so they might begin to process the death constraint. But evidence suggests that for most young children – and is the same not true for most young adults? – death remains a *relatively* unfamiliar and incomprehensible matter, and one which is routinely conflated by them with separation. This process of conflation moreover takes place precisely during the time of life when separation is arguably their *central* existential (or psychological) concern. Given the growing anthropological interest in children as producers rather than inheritors of cultural forms, the developmental priority of the separation constraint is potentially of considerable significance. But this is not simply a matter of 'child psychology'. For when adults eventually grapple with key emotional dilemmas, including both the problems of love (i.e. the emotions of romantic attachment) and the problems of death (i.e. the emotions of grief and mourning), they arguably do so via their previous, i.e. infantile, grasp of separation. But in order to explain this – and before discussing anthropological accounts of separation – I must make a brief psychoanalytic detour, starting with Freud.

The psychology of separation

In psychology and psychoanalysis, it is routine to take separation and absence as defining features of human relationships, rather than as epiphenomenal. The basic issues are neatly illustrated in Freud's famous, oft-cited, discussion of *fort* and *da* in 'Beyond the Pleasure Principle' (and we might well ask why so many commentators have been *struck* by this simple passage):

[The boy] did not disturb his parents at night, he conscientiously obeyed orders not to touch certain things or go into certain rooms, and above all he never cried when his mother left him for a few hours. At the same time, he was greatly attached to his mother, who had not only fed him herself but had also looked after him without any outside help. This good little boy, however, had an occasional disturbing habit of taking any small objects he could get hold of and throwing them away from him into a corner, under the bed, and so on, so that hunting for his toys and picking them up was often quite a business. As he did this he gave vent to a loud, long-drawn-out 'o-o-o-o', accompanied by an expression of interest and satisfaction. His mother and the writer of the present account were agreed in thinking that this was not a mere interjection but represented the German word *'fort'* ['gone']. I eventually realized that it was a game and that the only use he made of any of his toys was to play 'gone' with them.
    One day I made an observation which confirmed my view. The child had a wooden reel with a piece of string tied round it. It never occurred to him to pull it along the floor behind him, for instance, and play at its being a carriage. What he did was to hold the reel by the string and very skilfully throw it over the edge of his curtained cot, so that it disappeared into it, at the same time uttering his expressive 'o-o-o-o'. He then pulled the reel out of the cot again by the string and hailed its reappearance with a joyful *'da'* ['there']. This, then, was the complete game – disappearance and return. As a rule one only witnessed its first act, which was repeated untiringly as a game in itself, though there is no doubt that the greater pleasure was attached to the second act.
    The interpretation of the game then became obvious. It was related to the child's great cultural achievement – the instinctual renunciation (that is, the renunciation of instinctual satisfaction) which he had made in allowing his mother to go away without protesting. He compensated for this, as it were, by himself staging the disappearance and return of the objects within his reach . . . The child cannot possibly have felt his mother's departure as something agreeable or even indifferent.

How then does his repetition of this distressing experience fit in with the pleasure principle? It may perhaps be said in reply that her departure had to be enacted as a necessary preliminary to her joyful return, and that it was in the latter that lay the true purpose of the game. But against this must be counted the observed fact that the first act, that of departure, was staged as a game in itself and far more frequently than the episode in its entirety, with its pleasurable ending. (Freud 1955: 15–16)

This anecdote forms part of an essay in which Freud discusses the compulsive repetition of what are presumably unpleasant experiences (e.g. when people repeatedly dream of traumatic events). Such repetitions are controversially interpreted by Freud as manifestations of an unconscious 'death instinct',[6] but also as attempts to replace a passive response to 'unpleasure' with mastery. Of course, in Freud's scheme the prototypical experience of 'unpleasure' is the inevitable *failure* of infants to achieve their early libidinal goals. Such rejection experiences, he suggests, are compulsively re-enacted by neurotics, but also to some extent by everybody else – e.g. by infants in their games. Freud thus uses the *fort/da* game as a simple illustration of how the 'reality principle' (a realistic acknowledgement of the obstacles to pleasure) works in conjunction with, and to some extent helps one to master, the 'pleasure principle' (the instinctive desire to maximise pleasure and minimise unpleasure). In his anecdote, the mother's ability to physically walk out of the room clearly stands for something much more complex: her real or imagined emotional 'distance', i.e. her ability not to be mastered by her son's desires. But the *crisis* is provoked by her literal departure. And it is striking that the temporary resolution of the crisis is a symbolic or conceptual one: for Freud this is precisely the birth of symbolism! The child, rather than protesting against something which he cannot in any case control, instead symbolically replays the unpleasant experience and makes it his own.

Freud notably describes this as a great *cultural* achievement, a characterisation of a scrap of child's-play which perhaps needs some explanation. Recall that for Freud the problem of separation from the mother is really a subset of the more general problem of the Oedipus Complex. In a later essay, Freud discusses the significance of typical early childhood dilemmas – including the non-availability of the original 'object-choice', the mother – for subsequent emotional states, *and* for the child's developing ability to master his own desires. According to Freud, this ability is achieved, in part, via the internalisation of external obstacles:

The child's parents, and especially his father, were perceived as the obstacle to a realization of his Oedipus wishes; so his infantile ego fortified itself for the carrying out of the repression by erecting this same obstacle within itself. It borrowed strength to do this, so to speak, from the father, and this loan was an extraordinarily momentous act. (1995: 642)

Why momentous? In part because the mastery of desire – or, to return to *fort* and *da*, the mastery of physical/emotional separation from the mother – is, for Freud, crucial to normal human development. But also (thus Freud) because the father-inspired mastery of desire stands behind all of man's great cultural achievements, and behind his sense of social propriety. As Jessica Benjamin puts it: 'Obedience to the laws of civilization is first inspired, not by fear or prudence, Freud tells us, but by love, love for those early powerful figures who first demand obedience' (Benjamin 1990: 5). Obstacles to desire (including physical distance from its object) are therefore *socially productive*; and 'separation anxiety', in a very extended sense, is thus an important link between Freud's psychology and his sociology.

Needless to say, a great many questions have been asked of Freud's 'obvious interpretation' of the *fort/da* game, and of his psychological and sociological theories in general. But I've cited him in order to illustrate a certain influential *view* of the development of human emotions and subjectivity, in which early separation and object-loss plays a central, indeed defining, role. But how should separation itself be conceived? Given human imaginative capacities, what exactly is *meant* by it? Is literal physical presence and absence relevant at all?

All post-Freudian psychoanalytic theories have necessarily dealt, in some way, with these questions, and in trying to grasp the debates in a vast literature, I've relied on the synthetic discussion by Greenberg and Mitchell (1983).[7] As they note, the contrast between 'drive theory' and 'object-relations theory' helps to clarify the history of psychoanalytic enquiry. Briefly, within classic Freudian drive theory, which suggests that human behaviour is fundamentally motivated by *internal* drives, an 'external object' (which might or might not be a real person, such as a mother) is primarily the target of a drive, and either helps or hinders its discharge. In this distinctly internalist model, developed primarily from the psychoanalytic treatment of adults, 'social ties are secondary' (Greenberg and Mitchell 1983: 45). Whereas in what is now conventionally known as object-relations theory, priority is given to *external* social ties. An attempt is made to 'confront the potentially confounding observation that people live simultaneously in an external and an internal world, and that the relationship between the two ranges from the most fluid intermingling to the most rigid separation' (Greenberg and Mitchell 1983: 12). Although Freudian drive theory is obviously concerned as well with this intermingling (as seen in the *fort/da* anecdote), the theoretical shift is fundamental. For in object-relations theory 'the creation, or re-creation of specific modes of relatedness with others replaces drive discharge as the force motivating human behaviour' (Greenberg and Mitchell 1983: 3).

This paradigm shift – which may be seen as a move towards empiricism or 'realism' – occurred in part for one rather straightforward methodological reason. Early attempts to extend psychoanalytic theories and therapies, which relied significantly on adult reconstructions of childhood, to the actual treatment of children proved highly problematic. This, in turn, compelled a move away from conventional Freudian psychoanalysis, and towards *naturalistic* observation (e.g. of child's play). This reorientation, which ultimately leads towards development psychology, has been productive, but of course controversial within the psychoanalytic movement itself.[8] Some theorists, e.g. Margaret Mahler, have tried to bridge the divide by holding onto (internalist) Freudian drive theory, while combining it with (externalist) observation-oriented accounts of child development.[9] John Bowlby, however, is one of those who, while remaining loyal to basic Freudian paradigms, moved sharply in the direction of a realist orientation: he and his colleagues closely studied, among other things, the reactions of infants when their mothers literally walked out of the room. (It might even be suggested that their naturalistic orientation made a research focus on easily observable separation anxiety almost inevitable.)

A realist view of separation

Bowlby is the central figure in what has come to be known as 'attachment theory', and I will discuss his work in some detail here because of the issues it raises (for an overview see Holmes 1993 and Parkes et al. 1991).[10] For Bowlby, as for Freud, the nature of adult emotional life is importantly shaped by the quality of early emotional attachments: through the resolution of separation dilemmas (broadly defined) in childhood, we develop 'internal working models' of our own likely position in key relationships. For this reason, Bowlby did *not* see his research as merely addressing narrow questions of infant psychology. On the contrary, an understanding of attachment and separation in childhood should directly illuminate adult emotional life, crucially including the emotions associated with romantic attachment (cf. Hazan and Shaver 1987), and patterns of mourning following death and loss (see below). Bowlby's most famous, and much-debated, contention was that a direct correlation existed between the temporary or permanent loss of a mother-figure and of maternal care during childhood, and the onset of psychiatric problems later in life. But this is not to say that in Bowlby's model processes of attachment and separation, as such, are seen to be pathological. On the contrary, in attachment theory the *normal* course of child development includes not only the building up of strong attachments, but also the healthy expression of *instinctive* separation anxiety when these attachments are threatened.

Rather than addressing the many criticisms of Bowlby's work,[11] here I simply want to draw attention to three features of it which are relevant to my themes. The first is the link he draws between *reactions to separation and reactions to death*. Bowlby and his colleagues[12] investigated, over a period of years, children separated from their mothers (e.g. in residential nurseries), and found highly consistent patterns of response. These Bowlby characterised as being typical of 'mourning' or 'grieving' behaviour. That is, he held that the reactions of children to separation – including a general sequence of protest, despair, and detachment – closely followed the pattern of adult reactions to death or loss (1989: 49, 81–102). Note, however, that Bowlby does *not* make this argument in order to suggest that separation is thought *by children* to be death-like, or to suggest that separation anxiety is a manifestation of an unconscious fear of death (cf. Bowlby 1978: 433–6). On the contrary, in discussing clinical investigations into a range of childhood anxieties, he stresses that:

Fear of becoming ill or dying was conspicuous by its infrequency. It was mentioned by none of the 200 children under nine years of age [in one survey] and by only six of the 200 from nine to twelve. About 3 per cent of young adults recalled fear of illness or death as their most intense or their most persistent fear. Absence of fear of death among children under ten is in keeping with Anthony's study reported in *The Child's Discovery of Death* (1940 [1971]).[13] After examining the steps by which a child gradually acquires the concept of death as an irreversible departure, Anthony concludes that *death acquires its emotional significance through its equation with separation.* (1978: 145, emphasis added)

For Bowlby, then, the point is not that children consider separation to be 'death-like' (here recall the evidence cited above which suggests that young children have a limited grasp of the concept of death). If anything, through the reactions of adults to death we can hypothesize that adults consider death to be 'separation-like', and react to it accordingly. And this is Bowlby's conclusion; he takes 'the grief reaction as a special case of separation anxiety, *bereavement being an irreversible form of separation*' (Holmes 1993: 89, emphasis added). Interestingly, Bowlby also follows Darwin in seeing facial and auditory expressions of grief in human adults as reenactments of childhood expressions of separation anxiety (Holmes 1993: 91). (I would stress that these positions are consistent with the hypothesis that the separation constraint has a developmental priority over the death constraint.)

A second important feature of Bowlby's work is the conclusion that *separation leads to an intensification of attachment behaviour* (indeed, in some cases to pathological levels). Bowlby found, in fact, that following an initial reaction of protest and despair, children often respond to separation with marked detachment. However:

After a child has been back with his mother a few hours or a few days, the detached behaviour is replaced not only by all the old attachment but by *attachment of a greatly heightened intensity* . . . [D]uring detachment the ties binding him to his mother have not quietly faded . . . nor has there been a simple forgetting. On the contrary, the data show that during the phase of detachment the responses that bind the child to his mother and lead him to strive to recover her are subject to a defensive process. In some way they are removed from consciousness, but remain latent and ready to become active again, at high intensity, when circumstances change. (1989: 55, emphasis added)

Note that in Bowlby's analysis, however, part of what is intensified by the experience of separation is what he calls, following Freud, the 'conflict of ambivalence'.[14] This is the ambivalence between on the one hand loving the attachment figure too strongly (having a 'strong libidinal need' for them, or more simply a strong need for attachment),[15] and on the other hand expressing a hatred for them. Bowlby argues that separation experiences such as maternal deprivation lead to *both* 'libidinal craving and hatred running at specially high levels' (1989: 12). (This underlines the potential role of separation experiences in generating *recognition* – if sometimes highly ambivalent recognition – of social attachments and identifications. They arguably intensify relatedness, a fact which may, in my view, have significant sociological implications.)

Third, and finally, I want to note Bowlby's interest in ethological and evolutionary explanations.[16] Not surprisingly, Bowlby was especially fascinated by research on separation anxiety among young primates which showed strong similarities to his own research on children (e.g. Hinde and Spencer-Booth 1971). He notes that:

In most species of monkey studied, protest at separation and depression during it are very pronounced, and, after reunion, clinging to mother is much increased. During the subsequent months, though individuals vary, the separated infants tend on average to explore less and to cling more; and they remain detectably more timid than young monkeys that have not had a separation. (Bowlby 1989: 119)

Based on this and other evidence, Bowlby argued that *attachment behaviour in humans and other animals is instinctive*, i.e. that evolutionary pressures have selected this psychological trait. As Bowlby notes: 'This picture of attachment behaviour as a normal and healthy component of man's instinctive equipment leads us also to regard separation anxiety as the natural and inevitable response whenever an attachment figure is unaccountably missing' (1989: 87).

Now: might Bowlby's realist approach – which defines these behaviours as universal and instinctive, which examines their consequences through naturalistic observation, and which stresses their central role in intensifying human relatedness – be a useful starting point for anthropologists?

Bowlby was criticized for being much too literal and superficial, i.e. for examining surface manifestations (e.g. anxiety about physical separation), and thus misconstruing the underlying, and much more complex, psychological issues of autonomy and dependency (see my discussion below). But surely literal physical separation *does* often provoke – for adults, as it does for infants – important crises of relatedness. The problem, I should stress, cuts in two directions: viz. we are often obliged to part from those with whom we wish to remain, and often obliged to stay with those from whom we would wish to part. Bowlby's orientation, I would suggest, at least has the advantage of *grasping* this obvious feature of human existence: i.e. he gives separation the intellectual consideration it deserves as a fundamental human constraint in its own right. And even if one completely rejects Bowlby's universalism and empiricism, it remains the case that psychologists of completely different persuasions have of course repeatedly turned to separation, in all its complex forms, in their accounts of human emotional development. The difficulty, however, is in making this seemingly 'psychological' issue or constraint a *social* one.

Anthropological approaches to separation

> A Tikopia, on greeting someone who has returned after a long absence, may say the equivalent of 'It is good that you have come.' But it is much more likely that he will open his greeting by '*E aue toku soa!*' (Oh, alas my friend!)
> Raymond Firth[17]

Now back to anthropology. At the outset I suggested that while anthropologists *have* discussed separation, they've tended to do so without grasping its centrality as a human dilemma. Why should this be the case? Why should they have said more, to return to the previous discussion, about death? One possible explanation (perhaps *contra* Rosaldo), is that most anthropologists are in fact writing during the time of life when they begin to experience and comprehend human mortality. For them death is therefore one of the most compelling topics imaginable, whereas separation is arguably so familiar and obvious as to be invisible.

A more straightforward explanation, however, is that during fieldwork anthropologists regularly encounter very explicit ideas and prominent public rituals related to death. Death is a singular, delineated and dramatic event which lends itself to elaboration and ritualisation.[18] Taking their guide from cultural artefacts, anthropologists have assumed that all human societies must deal with the socio-political consequences of death, whatever the psychological consequences of it. By contrast, they only rarely encounter comparably prominent rituals which appear to take separation, *as such*, as their principle theme. This may follow from the fact that unlike death, human separation is often diffuse and sometimes even quite ordinary. Routine greetings and partings may, as in the examples provided by Firth, be wonderfully low-key:

> An ordinary Maori greeting of welcome is *haere mai*, 'walk hither'; while two people who have met in the street greet each other with *tena koe*, 'there you are'. They may clasp hands and press noses, but the verbal greeting is laconic. Saying goodbye is of the same order; the person who is going says 'stay there' to the other, who replies 'go there'. In Tikopia a common greeting to a person who has just entered a house is 'so you've come'. A person about to leave says 'I am about to go', to which the conventional reply is 'go then' or simply 'go'. This seems a very curt comment, almost explosive in the way it is uttered, but it is meant as a simple acquiescence in the decision announced. Diamond Jenness has recorded in parallel fashion 'The Eskimos had no word for farewell in their language, but came and went without ceremony . . . "I am going" I said again, using their only greeting of farewell; and they answered together "You are going"' [Jenness 1964: 61, 245]. In neither instance do the ordinary verbal forms of greeting and parting embody any overt expressions of pleasure or sadness. (Firth 1972: 8–9)

Compared to most funerary ritual, this is very laconic indeed! But Firth stresses that even everyday 'verbal and bodily rituals of greeting and parting' may serve as means of directing attention to particular relationships, reducing uncertainty in social encounters, demonstrating status, and showing more generally the 'incorporation or continuation of persons in a social scheme' (Firth 1972: 1). He points out that 'neither the Tikopia nor the Eskimo *say nothing at all* on such occasions' (1972: 9), and I would stress that in some places – as in China and Taiwan – such rituals can reach considerable complexity.

Of course, as I'll discuss more fully in a moment, separation – far from being restricted to rituals of greeting and parting – is well-known to be a near-universal feature of ritual sequences. It is striking, however, that the ritualised process of temporary physical isolation from a family or community (e.g. during initiations) is very often seen by anthropologists and by their informants to approximate, precisely, the separation-process of death.[19] Interpretations of this kind, and much folk wisdom on the subject, seem to imply that the problem with separation, and the reason for its ritual efficacy, is its similarity to death. Whereas I would argue, following Bowlby, that *the problem with death is its similarity to separation*, of which it is an extreme form. In other words, what we slowly come to encounter and understand in mid-life (death), is an extreme and intractable form of the problem we encounter in earliest childhood (separation) – and arguably then go on to lose track of amidst the complexity of adult experience.

Perhaps more to the point, and regardless of level of ritualisation, this 'childhood' dilemma has *socio-political* consequences which are as profound as those implied by death, and which deserve anthropological scrutiny. With this in mind, in the remainder of this chapter I'll set out – albeit schematically – the existing anthropological literature which relates to separation, placing it in four categories. My point in this survey is certainly *not* to be exhaustive, but rather to trace a connection between, on the one hand, the psychological issues of attachment and separation and, on the other hand, the kinds of sociological and anthropological issues which will be addressed in the remainder of this book. For this reason, I start with cultural psychology and with children. But I hope it will become clear that the seemingly 'narrow' and 'psychological' problem of separation lies at the very heart of anthropological concerns.

1   *Studies of attachment and separation in cultural psychology*

Anthropologists reading about attachment theory will undoubtedly ask how the impact of attachment and separation on infants is shaped by different (i.e. culturally varied) ways of achieving these states. A number of scholars working within the 'cultural psychology' framework have taken this question up. John Whiting, for instance, has conducted comparative research on the 'mother-infant closeness variable', i.e. on variations in the extent to which infants spend time in direct body contact with, or immediately adjacent to, their mothers (e.g. Whiting 1990: 357–65, Whiting 1981). Not surprisingly, the variation is significant, but Whiting delineates two basic styles: in 'close-contact' cultures infants are literally joined to their mothers on back and hip, whereas in 'crib and cradleboard' cultures the relationship of infants to their mothers is less immediate and symbiotic. Whiting suggests this variation has important psychological implications – e.g. in relation to the question of how quickly, and in what ways, children are comforted when distressed, and in relation to the impact of separation. A crib and cradleboard infant is effectively 'separated from his mother at birth', and must actively seek out help from her or from others (1990: 362), whereas:

In the close-contact cultures it is as though the infant is not born until he is weaned from his mother's back. He is to all intents and purposes still a part of her . . . Most of his needs are immediately and directly satisfied . . . When he is weaned from her back and lap, however, the situation changes. The resource-mediator that he has previously depended on has gone back on him. His first reaction to this is one of rage. (Whiting 1990: 360–1)

As this passage implies, cross-cultural variations in mother-infant closeness of the kinds discussed by Whiting have a direct relevance for any theory of attachment; more specifically, ethnographic studies show considerable variation in the extent to which separation is experienced as a traumatic event.

Robert A. LeVine has also studied mother-child interactions, focussing on the infant's first year, and draws one comparison between the Gusii of Kenya and middle-class Bostonians (1990: 464–8). One particularly striking conclusion is that 'the American mothers devoted about twice as much of their observed behaviour to talking to, and more than three times as much to looking at, their infants as the Gusii mothers at the age of both 3–4 months and 9–10 months, while the Gusii mothers held their babies almost twice as much at 3–4 months and more than three times as much at 9–10 months' (1990: 458). LeVine discusses, among other things, the possibility that the 'socially exciting infant experience of American children [by comparison with Gusii children] . . . leaves them more emotionally dependent on a rewarding and motivating attachment to particular adults and thus more vulnerable to emotional upset than Gusii when stable relationships are disrupted by parental death or depression, family conflict or breakup, or discontinuities in caregiving' (1990: 466). In short, they may be more dependent, and therefore more vulnerable to separation trauma.[20]

Barry S. Hewlett, in his work with hunter-gatherer Aka Pygmies, has addressed similar questions (1992). Here infants are raised among small groups of closely related individuals, and living spaces are very densely populated. This has the effect of making the home-base an intensely 'public' space, one in which cooperation and sharing are stressed, whereas time outside of the camp is more likely to be 'private'. The Aka walk a great deal, and mothers therefore spend a considerable amount of time carrying their infants (siblings aren't asked to do this because the distances are great). For this and other reasons, Hewlett suggests that Aka infants and children do become very closely 'attached' to their mothers, and also to their fathers, but in particular ways. First, as Bowlby's model would predict, Aka modes of attachment are so secure that they actually enable and encourage considerable autonomy in the young (that is, they do not generally produce extreme anxiety about separation). Second, Hewlett reports very close husband-wife relations among the Aka, with fathers heavily involved in most aspects of childcare. He suggests that ethnographic data of this kind helps challenge the over-valuation of mothering, as such, in attachment theory.

The studies by Whiting, LeVine and Hewlett – directly influenced by psychology – present challenges for attachment theory by showing significant cross-cultural variation in the treatment of infants and in the roles of their primary care-givers. But none of these authors suggests that the general issue of infantile attachment and separation simply vanishes in the face of this variation. On the contrary, the questions they pose are precisely those implied by a universalist psychology. But how can this discussion go beyond child psychology?

As I've noted, Freud raised the issue of separation because for him it was part of a wider problem of libidinal rejection, i.e. part of the background to the Oedipus Complex. Not surprisingly then, Melford Spiro, in his famous defence of the universality of the Oedipus Complex (i.e. in his critique of Malinowski's claim that it did *not* exist in the Trobriands), also turns to the question of separation in this extended sense. Spiro argues that child-care practices among the Trobrianders, including a long postpartum sex taboo and a pattern in which children sleep with their mothers, lead to exceptionally strong, indeed 'passionate', mother-child attachments (1982: 85–95). Spiro suggests, *contra* Malinowksi, that this in turn helps produce an especially intense Oedipus Complex among Trobriand boys when they are banished from the maternal bed upon the return of the father.

He goes on to argue that incestuous desires for the mother are thereafter 'incompletely repressed'. According to Spiro, this helps explain why in the Trobriands we find 'son extrusion' from the maternal home at puberty – as a way of *enforcing*, through separation, the maternal incest taboo, as well as enforcing the taboo against aggression towards the father. Spiro hypothesizes that societies where the Oedipus Complex is 'incompletely repressed' (as in the Trobriands) are more likely to practice either son extrusion or traumatic initiation rituals (1982: 144–80). Whereas son extrusion helps enforce taboos against maternal incest by literally removing the son from the scene of the potential crime, initiation rituals effectively 'remove' the potential crime from the realm of the son's desires – by brutally breaking (even if incompletely) his attachment to his mother (1982: 168–9). Here I should stress that Spiro's work is not trying to show that separation, as such, is a universal problem. He is rather trying to do something much more complex: to show the universality of the Oedipus Complex. In this sense, his work is primarily psychological (more specifically, Freudian), but Spiro's discussion of ritualised separations does take him firmly onto sociological ground.

2   *Studies of ritual separations*

In support of his thesis about social enforcement of the incest taboo, Spiro draws attention to ethnographic accounts of unusually severe initiation rituals in Australia and New Guinea, and cites the early work of Gilbert Herdt on rituals for boys among the Sambia.[21] In a more recent article on the Sambia, Herdt relates his discussion of ritual directly to psychological theories of attachment and separation, including those of Bowlby:

The great impetus of Sambia initiation concerns the physical separation of boys from women and children, followed by their irreversible insertion into exclusive male association. This dual process is well-known from the literature . . . But with few exceptions writers have tended not to view the behavioural experience of initiation in the context of the nature of the boy's tie to his mother . . . In New Guinea societies like that of the Sambia this tie amounts to an 'exclusive attachment' to mother and the female domain. Initiation is the most radical means of breaking that bond in order to subjectively create a new identity in the boy. This conclusion – which is no news to New Guineasts – is novel only in its psychosocial stress: boys must be traumatically detached from their mothers and kept away from them at all costs, otherwise the desired identity transformation cannot take place. (1990: 383)

The point for Herdt is not simply that this separation happens, and that it has psychological implications, but that for the Sambia it *must* happen in an especially traumatic and anxiety-provoking way in order to *produce* what this ritual system aims to produce: fierce Sambia warriors.

Initiation begins with boys being taken from their mothers in a way that guarantees anxiety in the novice. They are kept in the dark about whether or not they will be initiated. It is true that most boys 'know' (at some level of awareness) that they will be initiated eventually. It is also true that initiation is associated with male pride and glory . . . But remember that Sambia boys are only 7–10 years old, that initiation is designed as a surprise, and that its symbolic messages are coded to create anxiety in the boy's wrenching from hearth and family: feelings of loss arising from the irreversible awareness that the initiate may never again "be with" – touch, hold, talk to, eat with, or look at – his mother. (1990: 385)

This initiation complex, Herdt argues, provokes in its early stages what Bowlby calls 'anxious attachment', but also, as Bowlby would again predict, '*De*tachment: despair, crying, searching behaviour, including depression or its suppressed counterpart, anger' (1990: 385). Herdt implies that all of this is hard psychological *and* cultural work – that ripping boys away from their mothers is a way of producing the men who are the 'glory' of the Sambia. This argument is of interest because of the direct link Herdt makes between the emotions of separation, and the socio-political attachments thus produced (here recall Freud on the 'great cultural achievement' of mastering separation).

Although Herdt is unusual in considering ritual separations so directly in light of attachment theory, within anthropology there is of course already an enormous literature on separations in ritual sequences. Undoubtedly the most influential work in this regard is Van Gennep's study of rites of passage. (Note that his work is *not* restricted to initiations, i.e. to the rites of passage in which the 'psychological' element of separation is arguably most dramatic and obvious.) Van Gennep famously observes that transitions between social statuses are consistently marked by rituals which first separate people (often literally) from their normal contexts and communities; then place them in a transformative state of liminality; and finally reincorporate them into the flow of life – but with newly transformed statuses. The link between 'passages' which are both *physical* and *social* is obviously at the heart of Van Gennep's concerns, and in respect of this link he adopts what is arguably a realist perspective: namely, the framework of separation, liminality and reintegration for the explication of ritual. His discussion notably begins with the most literal of examples, the 'territorial passages' which involve crossing doorways and thresholds:

> In order to understand rites pertaining to the threshold, one should always remember that the threshold is only a part of the door and that most of these rites should be understood as *direct and physical rites of entrance, of waiting, and of departure –* that is, as rites of passage. (Van Gennep 1960: 25, emphasis added)

From this 'direct and physical' beginning, Van Gennep goes on to build a very ambitious theory of all rites of passage – for him a truly vast category which includes rituals of the human life-cycle (such as initiations, weddings and funerals), as well as calendrical rites and procedures for greeting and parting. But for all that Van Gennep focuses on rites of separation, and the near-universal existence of them within rites of passage, I want to stress that for him separation is primarily part of a ritual *solution*, not a problem in its own right. That is, rituals of separation are for Van Gennep a way of dealing with the problem of social transitions, i.e. a means for moving people between social categories, and not a reflection of (or reflection on) the psychological or sociological dilemma of separation, as such. It is also true, as Terence Turner has pointed out, that Van Gennep completely failed to account, in theoretical terms, for the ritualised pattern which he so admirably described.[22] Why so many separations?

A number of anthropologists have subsequently taken up Van Gennep's work, including Victor Turner, who made Van Gennep's notion of liminality central to his discussion of pilgrimage (and of ritual in general). Briefly, Turner argued that during pilgrimages the condition of liminality – i.e. the condition of being separated from the normal flow of daily life and of human relatedness – helps to produce a sentiment of belonging or 'communitas' among fellow-pilgrims (V. Turner 1977a: 94–130). Although his notion of communitas has been challenged, Turner's work on pilgrimage and liminality undoubtedly produced some important insights. As with Van Gennep, both the process of separation and the state of liminality are taken by Turner to be ritual means, effective ritual solutions to the problem of lack of 'communitas', rather than as existential *givens* which are themselves problematic. But Turner's work arguably underlines, as does the work of Van Gennep, the sociological significance of two important matters: on the one hand, the apparent potential of (literal) separation experiences to evoke or generate transformative emotional states and social attachments, and, on the other hand, the near-universal distribution of rituals which draw on this potential. Interestingly, however (at least from my point of view), Turner seems much more intrigued by the *state* of liminality, than by the *process* of separation and reintegration itself:

These rites of transition . . . are marked by three phases: separation; margin (or *limen*); and re-aggregation. The first and last *speak for themselves*; they detach ritual subjects from their old places in society and return them, inwardly transformed and outwardly changed, to new places. A more interesting problem is provided by the middle, (marginal) or liminal phase. (V. Turner 1977b: 36, emphasis added)

In his recent attempt to develop a general theory of the politics of religion, Maurice Bloch has introduced several significant alterations to these classic accounts by Van Gennep and Turner (Bloch 1992: 6). One is that for Bloch the separation subphase of initiation rituals in particular should be seen to involve a splitting which occurs *within* the initiates. That is, during traumatic separation rituals, which are often represented as a kind of 'death', a splitting takes place between the initiate's own vital and transcendent elements (Bloch 1992: 8–23). In Bloch's analysis, such death-like separations – which have undoubted psychological effects – are the necessary prelude to the ritualised conquering in later ritual stages of human vitality by human transcendence. Here separation is, again, seen as a (temporary) *solution* to an underlying problem. But in this regard Bloch introduces a crucial insight. Whereas for Van Gennep the problem is the need to mark social transitions, for Bloch the problem is much more general: the need to 'represent human life as occurring within a permanent framework which transcends the *natural transformative process* of birth, growth, reproduction, ageing and death' (Bloch 1992: 3, emphasis added). These underlying facts of human life, these 'universal human constraints', help explain the constancy of ritual patterns in different times and places.

   And here we might ask: how would anthropological models of ritual be modified if separation were itself taken as a universal human constraint? What if separation were seen to be, in some senses, even *more* problematic – especially for the young, i.e. for the mass of participants in most 'rites of passage' – than ageing or death? As has often been noted, rituals which follow dramatic narratives of parting and return clearly derive much of their emotional force through focussing attention on separation itself – i.e. on an inevitable, and sometimes highly problematic, feature of human existence. The participants in initiations, marriages, and funeral rites, as well as in calendrical festivities and pilgrimages, will all, by virtue of their common humanity, have sustained personal experience of the problematics of separation. Following Bowlby, we might suggest that they *instinctively* have (ambivalent) anxieties about it, and will inevitably see the ritualised breaking of attachments as a powerful, and attention-focussing, threat. But my point isn't to emphasise, much less over-emphasise, the 'psychological' aspects of ritual – something already fully discussed by others. Instead I want to suggest that rituals of separation make manifest the collective, i.e. *social*, need to transcend the dilemmas imposed on collectivities themselves by the separation constraint. For as I'll discuss below, this constraint, a given feature of our natural history, is intimately linked to basic issues of human relatedness (in both individual and collective senses). It therefore often provokes key crises of relatedness which must, in some way, be 'socially' resolved.

3   *Studies of separation through social displacement*

If studies of ritual have suggested ways in which separation is socially productive or useful, a third category of studies – the anthropology of social displacement – examines, among other things, its disruptive potential. This research is of two different, and yet strongly interconnected kinds. The first is exemplified by studies of migrants and refugees, and focuses on the sometimes *exceptional* historical circumstances (e.g. war, famine, economic change) which provoke movements of human populations (for two especially thought-provoking accounts, see Turton 1996 and Parkin 1997). Here separation is often taken to be problematic, even when some of the underlying motivations for it are positive. An illustrative example is found in Peter Loizos's account of Cypriot war refugees, who eventually grasped that because of an ongoing conflict they would be unable to return to their homes and villages. Loizos observes:

Nothing prepared me for the strength of the villagers' preoccupation with their losses . . . [which] showed up in several ways: people would recite long lists of the things they had in their homes; they would talk with great feeling about the superiority of the village and their way of life in it; women from Argaki, if meeting for the first time since the war, would fall weeping into each other's arms, weeping for the unnatural separation they had suffered, and because meeting reminded them forcefully of a rich social life now in tatters. (1981: 128–9)

These informants expressed understandable shock at their seemingly arbitrary and suspended liminality, i.e. their unexpected separation from the normal setting and flow of life. Reunion, and its impossibility, became obsessions. Loizos therefore makes a direct connection between this case and the more general human problem of separation and loss. Citing attachment theory research on grief and mourning in adult life (1981: 196–200), Loizos uses it to reconsider some of the themes of his own research. He implies that while the condition of Cypriot (and other) refugees is in some respects exceptional, they also face characteristically human dilemmas, which they deal with in characteristic ways. But in the context of specific political histories – and I will hope to show this in the case of China – these dilemmas come into particularly sharp focus, and may also become a source of powerful political rhetoric.

The second kind of literature on social displacement – if that is the correct term for a large and growing body of work – focusses on displacement in the 'global' era (e.g. Appadurai 1996, Basch et al. 1994). Here it is accepted that new technologies, e.g. of transportation, make long-distance travel both possible and affordable for many, simultaneously bringing increased dislocation to the world *and* helping it to be overcome. Meanwhile, other technologies, e.g. of communication, make it theoretically possible for distance not to matter (i.e. they help to 'collapse space'). Reunions are achieved electronically, and separation is as likely to be caused by systems failure as anything else. Such developments, linked to issues of political-economy in general and of so-called globalisation in particular, are of interest to anthropologists because they raise new questions about cultural identity. For example, the Chinese diaspora has produced, over a long historical period, a large and diverse international community of 'Overseas Chinese'. But in the modern era – because of changes in travel, in ways of doing business, and in communications and mass media – the relationship of this community to its 'homeland' is arguably transformed (cf. Ong and Nonini 1997). As I will later discuss, it has even been suggested that these displaced or 'separated' communities, located on the Chinese 'periphery', have become more *central* to Chinese cultural identity than the centre itself (cf. Tu 1994).

4   Studies of human relatedness

In the previous three sections, I've briefly noted some of the ways in which anthropologists have dealt with the issue of separation. Cultural psychology has considered attachment theory in light of cross-cultural ethnography, and examined separation as an aspect of the Oedipus Complex. Anthropological analyses of ritual, following Van Gennep, have examined, and generally given considerable significance to, rites of separation as a way of marking and helping to produce changes in social status. Studies of human displacement due to migration, war, etc., have drawn attention to the forceful impact of separation under exceptional historical circumstances; while other studies have stressed the uniquely 'modern' configurations of displacement, and thus separation, in the contemporary world. To some extent, all of these studies return to the general problem of human relatedness – i.e. to what is arguably the central concern of all social anthropology.

In this section, instead of summarising the vast anthropological literature on relatedness, I want to draw particular attention to the work of Fred Myers. His writings on Pintupi aborigines deal directly with psychological issues of attachment and separation, but do so in a way which places them firmly within the anthropological tradition. While the general theme of relatedness is addressed in his monograph on the Pintupi (Myers 1986), here I will cite an important article in which he draws explicitly on Bowlby's attachment theory, and in which he sets out to synthesize universalist and interpretivist accounts of human emotional life (Myers 1988). Briefly, Myers argues that while 'social structure and cultural context determine the [variable] meaning and content of the emotions', the 'underlying *logic* of emotions is universal' (1988: 591). This universal underlying logic is largely derived from conflicting human needs for autonomy and dependency. The relationship of these basic needs to the issues surrounding attachment and separation should hopefully, by this stage, be clear enough. If separation is indeed a universal human dilemma or constraint, it is because humans are dependent – e.g. emotionally or economically – on others. But given our potential ambivalence about such dependency, we may have strongly conflicting desires for autonomy, i.e. for separation from those on whom we depend (cf. Freud's 'conflict of ambivalence').

Myers describes the tension in Pintupi thought between the two social states of autonomy and dependency (both of which are highly valued), and the relationship of these contrasting states to the Pintupi emotions 'anger' and 'compassion':

Compassion, an expression of relatedness or identity with others, reflects Pintupi judgements that autonomy (the capacity and respect for self-direction such that no one is prepared to be told by others what to do) depends on sustaining relationships with others. Conversely, anger – understood by Pintupi as a negation of compassion (one who is angry typically has no compassion for the object of one's anger) – derives from perceived rejection of relatedness, asserting autonomy in the face of loss. (Myers 1988: 596)

Myers illustrates this logic with one (seemingly) unusual case of 'anger' involving a small group of Pintupi who, after twenty years of isolation in the bush, emerged to regain contact with their kin. At one point this 'new group' were reunited with a woman who had left them twenty years before, a reunion which at first provoked extraordinary scenes: her brothers, furious, tried to strike the returning woman with fighting sticks, and had to be restrained and then calmed down by standers-by. Her decision to *go away* was explicitly interpreted by her brothers as a rejection of relatedness, and her *return* therefore provoked an angry welcome. Myers observes that this case, while unusual, illuminates both the 'ordinary qualities of daily life', and the meanings of emotions, among the Pintupi. He points out that even ordinary leave-taking is 'managed carefully in order to avoid giving the impression that departure represents a rejection of relations with those who remain behind' (1988: 596).

Myers goes on to suggest that Pintupi emotions, for all their interpretive peculiarities, are 'logically' not really exceptional at all. Drawing on universalist explanations from Bowlby and others, he suggests that the 'underlying logics of attachment and autonomy are . . . absolutely fundamental issues for the understanding of emotion in human society', i.e. in *all* human societies (1988: 601). In short, the dependency of humans on relations with others, matched with the need to establish and assert autonomy from others, produces some of the most challenging dilemmas faced by human beings. Myers suggests that for the Pintupi 'the ultimate cultural resolution of this existential dilemma', i.e. the overcoming of the problematics of attachment and separation, 'lies in the identification of people with places, representing an unalienable shared identity with others' (1988: 602). This 'cultural resolution' of a central problem of relatedness, this way of overcoming separation, must however be seen in the context of a world in which separation does nevertheless constantly take place.

Grasping the separation constraint

Extrapolating from the work of Myers, one could make the case that *all* anthropological discussions of relatedness – e.g. the accounts by Malinowski, Mauss, and a great many others of the ways in which gift exchange and reciprocity, or commensality and the sharing of 'substance', help to constitute human relatedness – are also, by definition, dealing with intractable problems of attachment and separation in social life. In which case, my opening charge, that anthropologists have largely not grasped the separation constraint, would be entirely groundless! I would suggest, however, that much of the most influential anthropological work on these themes is primarily idealist or culturalist in orientation, and therefore actually serves to *obscure* the concrete problem of separation. In other words, by starting with, and remaining with, the culturally specific or idealist solution (for instance, the gift-exchange system which produces connections), these approaches arguably lose track of one of the 'obvious' problems which needed solving in the first place.

Now it goes without saying that the possible alternatives to this idealism – namely, realist approaches to separation and to human relatedness – whether in psychology (as represented by Bowlby), or in anthropology, have been challenged on many fronts. These challenges to realism derive, in a general sense, from three interrelated positions in twentieth-century social theory. The first stresses the constitutive nature of language and of symbolic representation, i.e. it holds that representations produce realities, and more specifically that they produce human subjectivities. This means, for example, that separation in a realist sense (e.g. a child's mother literally walking out of the room) is in fact heavily mediated by, and even produced by, language, images and representations of separation – and as such it is to be seen primarily as a linguistic and/or conceptual problem. The second position has to do with the nature of the subjectivities produced through such language and symbols. Here it is stressed that these subjectivities are not neatly defined and unitary; and that they are instead often fluid and unbounded (so Lacan, for example, describes the fundamentally conflictual and fragmentary nature of human subjectivity). From this perspective, the notion of clear-cut separation becomes distinctly problematic. The third position may be characterised as relativist: it stresses the variability in the realities and subjectivities produced by cultural representations. This means, from the standpoint of separation experiences, that we should expect them to be dramatically different (and perhaps even totally incommensurable) in different cultures.

Once separation is defined as an ideal or *conceptual* problem faced by *fragmentary* subjects, themselves produced by *incommensurable* cultures, then one has to agree that there are hardly any constraints to its conceptualisation. Many anthropological accounts of the person and of human subjectivity (some influenced directly by psychoanalysis) have effectively moved in this direction, by rejecting the notion that physically bounded individuals should be taken as the agents of social action. Through stressing the apparent fluidity of human relationships, or the permeability and divisibility of the self, these theories directly undermine the notion that social persons are located in one physical space. By extension, terms such as 'separation', 'absence', and 'reunion' – which imply states of physically bounded individuals – become problematic. Persons who share food or exchange gifts, for example, may be said to establish through these processes a form of relatedness which transcends their individuality as distinct organisms. In this way the apparently inevitable natural boundedness of humans is challenged, and arguably overcome, by cultural practices. In which case, does it remain meaningful to speak of separation? Anthropological and psychoanalytic questions of these kinds arguably serve, by pulling apart the notion of individual personhood, to diffuse or obscure the problem of separation (because they imply a cultural solution to it), or at least to reinvent it in different terms. Against the background of these questions, which are certainly fundamental ones, I am aware that my insistence on separation as a universal may seem a kind of crude materialism – a reassertion of biological individuality, and a denial of the ability of humans to imagine things to be other than what they ('materially') are.

But I am nevertheless drawn, for two basic reasons, to the realistic study of separation as a universal experience of humans in their natural environments. The first is precisely that as a *material* event, physical separations may call the bluff of cultural conceptualisations which deny human individuality, autonomy, and corporeality. For this very reason, literal separation (and reunion) experiences often provoke crises of relatedness (i.e. crises in relation to our underlying patterns of autonomy/dependency). The second, however, is that separation (and reunion) experiences may simultaneously help to constitute – precisely – our sense of relatedness, i.e. our awareness (however ambivalent) of 'non-individuality' and dependency. In other words, the reality of our autonomy and the reality of dependency may *both* be dramatically brought home by contexts of literal separation and reunion (just as they are by death). Although sometimes quite everyday, moments of parting and return may at other times provoke complex learning processes by *drawing attention* to features of our social existence, thereby helping to produce and intensify our sense of relatedness with others. This may be especially true in the many cases where separation (or non-separation) is experienced as a kind of 'obstruction', i.e. as a frustrating impediment to a desired end.

Psychological attachment theory (as exemplified in the work of Bowlby) is important because it seeks to explain, under the heading of one 'constraint', a range of key emotional issues which all human beings must confront – not only infantile separation anxiety, but also the ongoing problematics of romantic attachment, emotional dependency, death and loss. Taking our lead from highly emotive separation-rituals (brought together in the work of Van Gennep and others), a realist approach to separation enables anthropologists to connect these 'individual' emotional matters to universal social ones – i.e. to grasp that separation everywhere provokes important collective dilemmas as well.

Conclusion

In the next chapter I'll begin to explore the separation constraint in China and Taiwan, basing myself, as I should stress, on ethnographic rather than psychological research. No one will be surprised to learn that Chinese infants sometimes become upset and anxious when those to whom they are 'attached' try to leave the room, or that Chinese friends sometimes become sentimental when parting from one another. Not surprisingly, Chinese lovers often find separation difficult, in a bittersweet kind of way, while the death of loved ones regularly provokes, in China and Taiwan, weeping and other characteristic symptoms of grief. All of this seems simply human. But what happens when these human tendencies encounter a cultural tradition which consistently emphasises and elaborates, across a whole range of social contexts, the themes of separation and reunion? In this book, I'll suggest that rethinking Chinese society and culture through the filter of the separation constraint enables us to see some old issues – related to kinship, gender, religion, history, and politics – in new and interesting ways.

Take gender for example. It is striking that the rituals of separation and reunion imply very different trajectories in the lives of Chinese men and women. On the surface, men are the primary agents of separation and reunion: they are the ones who publicly greet gods and others visitors; they are the ones who make speeches during 'reunion' banquets; and they are the ones who have written most of the poetry, and the political rhetoric, of parting and return. But beyond this, one sees that women's lives are at least equally shaped, and perhaps more fully determined, by patterns of separation and reunion. Women leave their natal homes via the dramatic separation rituals of weddings, but they nevertheless repeatedly return to reassert kinship there. And having then *produced* relatedness – including the patrilineal kind – through cycles of reciprocity and nurturance (what I call 'cycles of *yang*'), it is arguably women as mothers who embody most acutely, for their own children, the ongoing emotional problematics of separation (see chapters five and six). By examining these issues, I'll suggest, we can significantly reformulate our understanding of women's roles in Chinese kinship.

But this material – related to kinship and the emotions of maternal care – leads me to an obviously important question. If, as I am asserting, separation is a universal constraint, then why should it be any *more* significant in China than elsewhere? The brief answer, to be taken up again in the conclusion, is that it is probably not. (Bear in mind that rituals of separation may be a means of actually ameliorating the separation constraint, rather than making it worse.) But this still leaves us with many complex issues, including why it is that the separation constraint should be so *explicitly* focussed-upon in so many different spheres of Chinese social life. One possible answer (suggested to me in part by Sangren's intriguing analysis (1999) of 'autonomy and recognition' in Chinese mythology) lies within Chinese kinship itself. Briefly, Chinese patrilineal ideology repeatedly and very strongly celebrates the notions, or fantasies, of reunion and unity (see chapter one). This attempt to deny, in certain cases, even the possibility of separation can be intensely frustrating and provocative: because in real life autonomy (e.g. from one's own parents) is sometimes highly desirable, while the ideal state of 'perpetual union' (even when desirable) is clearly impossible to achieve in reality. Perhaps more to the point, as Sangren suggests, Chinese kinship ideals – inculcated through narratives which are almost universally known – imply very different 'obstacles' for sons (who are, at least in theory, not allowed to leave), and for daughters (who are, at least in theory, not allowed to stay). The frustrations these classical kinship obstacles imply find echoes throughout Chinese culture, where they are explicitly commented on and elaborated. As a result the separation constraint is perhaps here made especially frustrating and problematic, at least at the level of *consciousness*, by the Chinese cultural context in which it is played out.

I'll come back to this later on, but it leads me to a second question. Assuming it is true that Chinese patrilineal kinship serves to intensify, within families, emotions related to universal issues of autonomy and dependency, how can these 'private' emotions be linked to large-scale political effects? To put this differently: is it possible to trace, through practices of separation and reunion, linkages between family-based attachments and sentiments, and those focussed on much larger communities such as the nation? It is certainly the case that in China idioms of separation and reunion (often kinship-derived) have become objects of state control and political contestation (e.g. when the Cultural Revolution effectively halted many ancestral 'reunions'). Given the salience of these idioms, this is hardly surprising, and I will discuss this matter more fully in chapter nine.

But here I should at least draw attention to one political matter in relation to my own ethnography. As I've said, most of my evidence about separation and reunion comes from material gathered in northeastern mainland China and southeastern Taiwan. An emphasis on separation and reunion is one of the things which seems, from my perspective, to 'unite', at least somewhat, the people who live in these two places. It even seems, again from my perspective, to 'unite' – at least somewhat – those who live in the Chinese present with those who lived in the past; i.e. it is an important source of cultural continuity. When trying to conceptualise China in a coherent way, for whatever reason, reconstructions of this kind, which stress linkages across time and space, are of course quite compelling – and not only for anthropologists. For similar efforts to conceptually 'unify China' have also often been made by Chinese people themselves, and sometimes in the service of political goals. As I said: dangerous territory! Thus it is that the apparent cultural unity of China has been, for some decades, one of the central arguments used both in the PRC and in Taiwan in support of reunification. The emotional force of Chinese separation and reunion idioms – used repeatedly in these arguments – is perhaps such that it makes political reunification *seem* inevitable, and this conclusion has, until recently, been scarcely debatable in Taiwan, much less in mainland China. By the end of the book it will perhaps be clearer why this might have been the case.

1   Two festivals of reunion

I'll begin my discussion of the separation constraint in China and Taiwan by relating what happens at an 'obviously' important moment: namely midnight on new year's eve. For although the Chinese lunar calendar (*yueli, nongli*) has no shortage of significant and celebrated occasions, by far the most elaborate and extended celebrations are prompted by the 'turning of the year' (*guonian*) – i.e. the passage into the next annual cycle. And as I'll show in this chapter, the new year festival, with its solemn rituals and raucous banqueting, explicitly and repeatedly celebrates the ideals of 'unity' and 'reunion'. It elaborates, on some levels, a fantasy of perpetual 'non-separation', and its key moment entails reunification with the dead. This is also true of the important festival marking the arrival of 'mid-autumn' (*zhongqiu*), which I will also discuss. But I should stress that the emphasis of these two festivals on reunion is far from unique. For as Göran Aijmer has pointed out, the *entire* Chinese ceremonial calendar is built around reciprocal visits, especially those between ancestors and descendants (Aijmer 1991). Such visits – marked off by rituals of arrival and departure – inevitably highlight ongoing reciprocity and 'unity' in the face of death and spatial separation.[1]

Calendrical festivals are thus my first, perhaps rather obvious and public, evidence that processes of separation and reunion are a matter of concern in China. In this chapter, I will describe at some length new year celebrations in the rural northeast (primarily as seen from the household of one local cadre in the village of Dragon-head), and also in the Taiwanese community of Angang. In both places the new year *compels*, or at least appears to compel, reunions of many kinds. Then I will turn, albeit more briefly, to the mid-autumn festival as celebrated, also in northeastern China, at a teacher's training college (*shizhuan*). The students of this college – village-born migrants through an educational system which has often been strongly anti-traditional – do *not* go home for the 'mid-autumn' celebrations, and instead are compelled to reunite in new configurations. This is of interest, because when people in China and Taiwan discuss the new year and mid-autumn festivals, they often say the traditions associated with them are 'unchangeable' (*gaibuliao*). But the fact is that they are very changeable indeed, and the reunions which are meant to accompany them are far from inevitable. In other words, and to put the conclusion of this chapter simply: reunions may be highly desirable in China, but history has a way of interfering with them.

The turning of the year

First, the new year. There are, of course, highly coherent cosmological and theological explanations for what transpires during the lunar new year festival. According to official (imperial) logic, its rituals are meant to reaffirm a uniquely Chinese cosmic hierarchy. Stephan Feuchtwang has convincingly argued, however, that this orthodox view – while in some respects still widely-held – has long been subject to popular reinterpretation: 'Under the sweet talk of a benign imperial cosmos', he suggests, 'is another demonic cosmos of great destructive powers and the capacity to withhold or command them' (Feuchtwang 1992: 55). From the perspective of this popular heterodoxy, what is celebrated on new year's day is not 'cosmic order', as such, but rather the remarkable survival by families and communities of an 'annual apocalypse' in which everyone might just as well have been killed (Feuchtwang 1992: 25–60).

Simultaneously, and perhaps at a more obvious level, the entire festival – during which one 'welcomes the year' (*yingnian*), or 'welcomes the spring' (*yingchun*) – is a powerful manifestation of something else. For as Feuchtwang notes, each new year implies, by definition, a highly desired familial reunion or 'completion' (which survival of the annual apocalypse makes possible):

The eve is a return home and a completion of the family household. At the very least a member of a Chinese family would feel absence from it. Many would regret their absence poignantly. Most would be home, celebrating the continuing narrative of a complete household, renewed by their homecoming. (1992: 25)

As I've already suggested in the introduction, such 'household narratives', along with the narratives of friendship and community, are based in China on the premise that human and spiritual relationships are always in spatial flux, and that separation is therefore inevitable. But at this crucial calendrical juncture, one encounters a fleeting solution to the separation constraint: a suspended moment during which work is halted, divisions and death overcome, the pace of visits intensified, and meals and games prolonged as if people could produce, through sheer collective will, a state of permanent, celebratory reunion.

This, I want to suggest, is what most people find most interesting and important about the festival. In speaking to friends and acquaintances in mainland China about the new year celebrations I found – to my surprise – that they tended to stress, endlessly, what takes place in the period *following* the first day of the first lunar month, and what in many cases takes place completely *after* the official three-day holiday period has come to an end. That is, instead of stressing the activities which, at least from my perspective, form the true cosmological, theological, and moral 'core' of the new year, and about which they said little in spite of my prompting, they stressed the subsequent period. This is the time when relatives and friends come together for reunion visits and meals in the process known as *bainian*, 'giving new year's greetings', or *chuanmenr*, literally 'stringing together doors', a process which only ends with the 'lantern festival' (*yuanxiaojie*) on the fifteenth day of the first month.[2] While these get-togethers are not explicitly 'ritualised', and are not obviously 'religious', they do certainly follow predictable patterns, and during them people have very clear ideas about how one is meant to behave.

But what I want to stress here is neither the ritual-like nature of these gatherings, nor the indifference of people to the 'proper' new year celebrations which precede them, but rather the striking *continuity* of post-new year reunion activities with the obviously 'ritualised' events which take place earlier in the festival – a continuity which is explicable in terms of the Chinese concern with separation and reunion. Let me explain. At the simplest level, two fundamental things can be said to happen during *guonian*, the 'turning of the year'. First, a complicated series of rituals are held for the purpose of dealing with the seasonal movements of spirits, namely: (1) the 'sending-off' of gods; (2) the 'greeting' of ancestors; (3) the 'sending-off' of ancestors; and (4) the 'greeting' of gods. These rites, and especially those involving the ancestors, frame the central days of the festival. Second, at the exact moment of the turning of the year – precisely in conjunction with the ancestral 'greeting' – and then for many days following, a series of reunions (usually 'reunion meals') are held between various categories of (living) persons. These involve, first of all, immediate patrilineal and affinal kin, but then also extend outwards to encompass, in most cases, large (extended) networks of relatives, neighbours, friends, and colleagues. In short, at this time of year almost all Chinese beings (living and dead) *move*, and at particular moments these moving beings *reunite* in different – and differently celebrated – configurations, before dispersing yet again.

Old Yang's new year

In this section, I'll provide a narrative sketch of part of the festival from the perspective of one family in Dragon-head, so that readers will get at least a general sense of the flow of the festival, and of what takes place in one Chinese community at this important time of year. In Dragon- head, the celebration of the new year (officially known as *chunjie*, the Spring Festival), falls during the dead of winter when it is bitterly cold. The apple and pear orchards which surround the community, and the fields where maize will be planted several months later, are still silent, barren and icy. For those who rely on agriculture, i.e. for almost everyone in Dragon-head, not much work can happen at this time of year. But the external quietness and frozenness of the surrounding countryside belie a great deal of activity and expenditure, as villagers prepare for the 'turning of the year', and make efforts to ensure that its celebration, whatever the weather, will be 'hot and noisy' (*renao*), i.e. boisterous and intense.

Here, on the late afternoon of *chuxi*, the final day of the final lunar month, i.e. on new year's eve, I sat in the home of Old Yang, a successful farmer and a village-level cadre (*ganbu*), keeping myself comfortably warm on his *kang* (fire-heated platform bed), while half-watching one of his infant grandsons, also on the *kang*, demolish a cigarette-carton. Old Yang himself was out in the cold gathering fire-wood, great quantities of which would be needed for the stove in the coming days, while his wife was in the kitchen, preparing various special foods for the festival, including sweet *baozi* (steamed rice-filled buns), the favourite of her youngest son. Earlier in the day I had watched Yang decorate his home in standard (if somewhat modest) fashion for the new year. A red lantern had been installed on a pole in front of the house, and *duilian*, auspicious poetic couplets, had been hung in matching pairs around various doors and gates (even around the gates to the enclosures for pigs). Over the main doorway, Yang posted a red paper banner which proclaimed in gold letters: 'The Family United in Joy!' (*quan jia huan le*). The doorway below was framed by a matching couplet:

> Prosperity increasing on all fronts,
> abundance year after year!
> Every blessing achieved to the full,
> glorious step after step![3]

A similar verse was posted by his sons on the main outside gate (*waimenr*) of the family's compound, later supplemented with a string of brightly coloured electric lights.

In spite of these conventional preparations, Old Yang more than once told me, apologetically, that he and his family were mostly 'indifferent' (*wusuowei*) to the question of the new year and its traditions (*chuantong*). By this he seemed primarily to mean the various folk-beliefs (of which there are a great many) about what should and should not be done, or said, or eaten, etc., during the new year festival, and ideas concerning the worship of ancestors and deities. These, he said, were 'superstitions' or 'misguided beliefs' (*mixin*), and things of the past – although of course, as he noted, many local families still observed them. I was repeatedly told, by Yang and others, that many 'customary practices' (*fengsu xiguan*) had 'gone cold' (*leng*) since 1949, and particularly during and after the Great Proletarian Cultural Revolution (*wenhua da geming*). But I was also repeatedly told, and in some cases by the very same people, that Chinese traditions had proved themselves 'unchangeable' (*gaibuliao*), and 'unprohibitable' (*jinzhibuliao*) – in spite of considerable efforts to change and prohibit them – and that the celebration of the new year festival had therefore 'not changed in the least' (*shenme gaibian dou meiyou*). Be that as it may, cadres such as Yang, along with many non-cadres (and even in the post-Mao era with its apparent tolerance of tradition and of popular religion), generally avoid statements and actions which might be construed as products of 'feudal thinking' (*fengjian sixiang*). In this and other ways, Yang struck me, in the entrepreneurial mood of early-1990s China, as a rather old-fashioned cadre, with very clear and genuinely-held ideas about 'serving the people', and serious misgivings about displays of frivolity, wasteful consumption, or feudal thinking. So in spite of his preparations, and the mood of cheerful anticipation among his wife and children, I was expecting the festival, in Yang's home at least, to be a low-key, and perhaps even austerely anti-traditional, affair.

Then, as I sat on his *kang* at sunset on new year's eve, Old Yang's youngest son (an unmarried nineteen-year-old who lived with his parents, and who, as the youngest son, would continue to do so after marriage) came in and asked if I wanted to join him in 'shooting off firecrackers'. This invitation was so off-hand that I very nearly declined in favour of playing with the grandchildren in the warm house. But I did decide to go, and as we left the farmhouse we were joined at the outside gate of the compound, in what obviously was an organised affair, by Yang's eldest son, and by several male cousins (the sons of Yang's brothers). Old Yang himself was nowhere in sight. In the gathering darkness, our small group walked, in silence, the short distance up a frozen hill directly behind the farmhouse to a clump of trees, where we stopped.

We were standing in front of three graves. These simple burial mounds – so inconspicuous among the trees that I had not even noticed them before that moment – were rounded piles of dirt, covered with branches, and fronted by a small brick archway or gate (*men*). Things then proceeded quickly and without much fuss. First, one of the young men tied a long string of firecrackers to a nearby tree, lit the string, and stood back. The blasts echoed around the surrounding hills. At the same time, another young man knelt to place a small pile of unmarked yellowish-gold paper in front of each of the three graves, adjacent to the openings of the small gates. They called this 'earth paper', *tuzhi*, and later confirmed that it 'represents money' (*daibiao qian*) which can be used by spirits to buy necessities and bribe officials in the other world. The three stacks of 'earth paper' were then burnt. One stack, however, did not burn very completely, in spite of several attempts to ignite it. The men *looked* at each other as if to say (or so I thought) that this might be a bad omen. But one of them *said*: 'it's nothing' (*meiyou shi*). (Note that for the entire period of the festival it is considered unlucky to say unlucky things.) The young men then formed a group in front of the mounds, knelt down, and bowed (*ketou*), foreheads to the ground, three times in unison. The whole procedure took only a few minutes: setting off firecrackers, burning 'earth paper', bowing three times. Then Yang's sons and I walked back down the hill to their father's farmhouse, while their cousins set off through an adjacent field, on their way to make offerings in front of other graves.

Back at Old Yang's, the two brothers exploded more strings of fire-crackers, after which we went inside and warmed our hands on the *kang*. Now it was dark outside. In our absence someone had placed a colourful 'God of Wealth' (*caishen*) poster on the wall, which for the moment was being ignored. Old Yang had meanwhile returned from his wood-gathering expedition, and his daughter and son-in-law (who lived nearby in Dragon-head) had also arrived at the farmhouse for the celebrations. Soon after our return all of the adult men (i.e. Yang, his two sons, his son-in-law, and I) sat down to eat a meal which centred on dumplings (*jiaozi*). We were then shortly joined at the table by Yang's wife, his daughter, his daughter-in-law, and two infant grandsons. Small coins had been hidden in two of the dumplings, and I was told that those who found the lucky dumplings would have 'blessings' in the coming year (*shei chi shei fu*).

When the food from this brief and relatively modest new year's eve meal had been cleared away, the family immediately sat together on the *kang* and started playing cards, gambling for small change. Virtually the entire evening was taken up with this card-game, which lasted for about five hours, almost until midnight, and it was the occasion for much affectionate joking and teasing. At one point (and, as far as I could tell, completely spontaneously), the infant grandsons were waved up and down in front of their grandmother, Yang's wife, in the semblance of a respectful bow. In return for this, and as everyone laughed, Mrs Yang gave money to the infants, twenty *kuai* each (pocketed for safe-keeping by their mothers). Later, the poster of the God of Wealth came unstuck from the wall, fell, and landed on Old Yang's youngest son, literally sticking to his shoulder. At first he seemed startled, then he broke into a broad grin and shouted with delight: 'Now that means something good!' (*hao de yisi!*).

As it neared midnight – and the start of a new year – the game drew to a close. The sons went outside and set off more long strings of firecrackers in front of the house, something which was simultaneously being done at neighbouring farmhouses throughout the countryside. Mrs Yang stood at the door, holding one of her rather terrified-looking grandsons, admiring the noise, and commenting on the expense of it all. When this very impressive barrage had died down, everyone came back inside and a table was once more set up next to the *kang*. A relatively sombre midnight meal of dumplings was eaten, this time by the men only, and almost in silence. Yang's youngest son – the unmarried one – did not eat at all. Then, as the new year began, the two sons and the son-in-law hurried off into the darkness – but they were not allowed to leave before midnight. And I was not, on this occasion, invited to join them. I was later told that they were playing all-night *majiang*, the result of which – whether a 'win' (*ying*) or a 'loss' (*shu*) – would indicate the kind of luck they could expect for the coming year. After their departure, Yang, his wife, his daughter, and his grandson settled in to sleep on the main *kang*, while I stretched out on the warm *kang* in the room opposite.

It was (for everyone, I think) a bad night's sleep, one which started later than usual and was interrupted by periodic bursts of early-morning firecrackers which sent the dogs and chickens into a frenzy. At sunrise (i.e. the first sunrise of the lunar new year), the three young men noisily returned to the house from their all-night round of *majiang*. Almost immediately, they sat down at the table with Old Yang for another hasty meal: a breakfast of yet more *jiaozi* (dumplings). Mrs Yang proudly informed me that the omens were good: all three of 'her sons' (i.e. her two sons and her son-in-law) had won something during the night, even if not very much, only about twenty kuai. The important thing, as she stressed, was to win and not lose. Once the breakfast table had been cleared, the young men sprawled out on the *kang* and tried to sleep, for which they were roundly criticised by Yang's daughter. But before long guests began to arrive at the house, and everyone had to wake up. The first visit, a very brief one, was from Old Yang's sister's son-in-law, a man who lived only about one minute away in an adjacent farmhouse. He was accompanied by his young daughter, to whom Mrs Yang tried to give ten kuai as a new year's gift. At first the offer was politely refused, as is expected on these occasions, but when pressed the girl accepted the money before departing with her father. Soon afterwards, Yang's son-in-law left the house to return to his own parent's home, accompanied by his wife (Yang's daughter) and their son.

Then, at around ten o'clock, a large group of visitors arrived. These were Yang's closest patrilineal relatives, i.e. the families of the young men who had joined Yang's sons in making offerings at the nearby graves on the previous evening. Almost immediately, the men in this group set up a table on the floor and started playing cards, while the women started playing *majiang* next to them on the *kang*. While playing, they ate seeds and fruit, and the men smoked, always sharing cigarettes back and forth. The children meanwhile played outside, shooting off spare firecrackers. Most of the visitors arrived carrying bags and baskets of gifts – usually rice wine, cakes, and tinned foods, in lucky combinations of four or eight – which were left lying about the house, often without comment. During the course of the day, Mrs Yang emptied these out, again often without comment, and returned the bags and baskets to the owners. Old Yang himself had meanwhile quietly gone outside to work, gathering more firewood; when he later returned to the house he did not join in the games, but instead played with his grandson in the second *kang*-room. Occasionally a visitor would come and speak with him for a few moments. During all of this activity, Mrs Yang, assisted primarily by her daughter-in-law, was preparing large quantities of food in the kitchen; and eventually the games were stopped so that this could be set out on the tables. Married men (including Yang) sat in chairs at the main table on the floor, while women squatted around low tables placed on the *kangs*. Children either joined their mothers, or simply walked around with bowls in hand, grabbing the occasional piece of food. This meal was a noisy and familiar affair, and in the middle of it arrangements were made for meals to be held in coming days at *other* houses.

There was a kind of shambolic intensity to the whole first day of the new year at Yang's house. Many of the guests were slightly drunk, and complained that they had really eaten too much. The friendly and boisterous games of cards and *majiang* – which were started up again as soon as the food was cleared away – went on for many hours. Through it all, the children raced in and out of the house, and the whole noisy place was soon littered with seeds, fag-ends, wrappers, bottle-caps, and spent firecrackers. Eventually, late in the afternoon, and although everyone was encouraged *not* to leave, these relatives began to slip away, departing by foot or bicycle or motorcycle. In the afternoon and early evening of the first day of the first month, the north China countryside around Dragon-head was filled with those similarly, i.e. somewhat drunkenly, weaving their way towards home.

In the coming days, the same scenes were repeated many times at Old Yang's: the arrival of guests, the seemingly nonchalant gift-giving, the playing of card-games and *majiang*, the sharing of food and drink, negotiations over future reunions (which were always either explicitly arranged or vaguely promised), and so on. I did eventually see how relatively protracted and 'hot and noisy' the celebrations at Yang's home were, in part because I also spent time in another household where things passed much more quietly. This second family had fewer relatives in the immediate vicinity, and their celebrations of *kinship* were thus dispensed with fairly quickly. They also had considerably fewer non-kin visitors, I suspect largely because they lacked the local political or economic influence which, during this festival, is a kind of magnet. That is, many people in and around Dragon-head seemed to *want* to express their connection to Old Yang, who has power and prestige in the local community, by visiting him during the festival. But the members of this second family were nevertheless also very busy during the new year. As local people say, they were 'busy playing' (*mangzhewanr*), i.e. actively engaged in visiting relatives, neighbours and friends.

Old Yang's family, meanwhile, and in spite of his comments about 'superstition', had surely observed almost all of the basic things which people say 'should be done' (*yinggai zuode*) during the festival, including the basic religious (ancestral) rites. In this respect, the Yang family's new year strikes me as typical, and much of it will undoubtedly seem very familiar to readers already acquainted with the Chinese lunar new year festival. But what exactly makes it seem familiar? First, because their house was specifically decorated for the festival, with careful attention paid to doors, gates, and windows. Second, because they 'gathered together' (*tuanyuan*) as a family, and momentarily stayed together for a meal at a particular moment in time (i.e. at midnight on *chuxi*, the last evening of the last lunar month). Third, because prior to this gathering together they honoured their ancestors in the usual way (with firecrackers, offerings, and *ketou*). Fourth, because at the moment of ancestral return they ate particular foods, including dumplings (*jiaozi*), which 'represent reunion'. Fifth, because they acknowledged, at least minimally, the movements of gods, who both come and go during the festival (the God of Wealth poster which appeared on their wall bore the legend 'The God of Wealth *Arrives!*'). Sixth, because the hierarchy of generations was acknowledged (even if only jokingly) by the waving of grandsons in front of their grandmother, and by her gifts to them (and later to other children) of money. Seventh, because they went on to reunite (usually for meals) with virtually all of their significant relations during the subsequent period of 'stringing together doors', and exchanged new year gifts with them. Eighth, because the family – especially the sons – indulged in card-games and *majiang*, and more generally 'played' (*wanr*) during the festival rather than working (although note the hard work of Old Yang and his wife during the festival). And, finally, because they observed some of the 'good-luck' codes of the festival: i.e. they avoided talking about bad or inauspicious things, and certain occurrences (e.g. the outcome of *majiang* games, the distribution of lucky dumplings) were read by them as omens of the year to come.

Some key aspects of the festival

Having given a brief description of a portion of the lunar new year as seen from one home, I now want to discuss certain aspects of the festival more generally, drawing on material from other families in Dragon-head, and also from Angang in Taiwan (this latter material will be indented). In both places, the central moment of the festival is arguably the *reunion* with the ancestors which takes place on new year's eve (*chuxi*), and which marks the 'turning of the year'. But as I've already noted, the entire lengthy process of celebrating the new year may in fact be seen as an intricate and extended cycle of separations and reunions. As I've also pointed out, this cycle within the lunar calendar effectively never comes to a stop (again cf. Aijmer 1991). That is, families are always building up – in part via separations – to the culminating ancestral reunion on new year's eve, which in turn sets in train a new sequence of partings and returns. But the festival period could be said to properly 'begin' with a separation which takes place on *xiaonian*, the 'little new year', which falls on the twenty-third or twenty-fourth day of the last lunar month. At around this time, people begin in earnest to make their final new year preparations.

1   *'Attending the new year market'* (gan nianji) *and conventional preparations*

In Dragon-head, the purchase of most *nianhuo* ('new year goods') is made in the nearest market- town (which is a brief bicycle ride away). In light of my argument, it may be of interest to note that these periodic rural markets are called *ji*, literally 'to gather together', and I would suggest that they do represent a remarkable moment of unity and 'gathering together' for the residents of the local marketing community. This is true of the 'big markets' (*daji*) held twice a week throughout the year, for which people arrive from villages scattered throughout the countryside. But it is especially true of the last market of the old year – called the 'new year market', *nianji* – which is an extraordinarily intense occasion. On this day many thousands of villagers descend on the market town to buy their new year goods, and on the occasion I attended it became literally impossible to move on the streets and alleyways because of the crush of human bodies. If nothing else, the *nianji* is a striking manifestation of the mass preparations, following conventional patterns, for the new year celebration, and even possibly – by extension – a manifestation of the fact that this festival of reunion 'unites China'. (This is not a trivial observation. The integration of local and regional systems in China via marketing centres – a notion associated with the important work of G William Skinner – has been widely discussed in the literature; for perspectives on this issue in relation to Taiwan, for example, see Crissman (1981) and Sangren (1985).)

If they have not already done so, many people attending the market will buy new clothes, especially for their children, because new clothes, it is said, should be worn by children at the beginning of a new year. Almost everyone will buy decorations for their homes, including matching couplets (*duilian*) which are often written on the spot for them by local calligraphers, and mass-produced posters celebrating 'wealth' and 'fertility'. Almost everyone will buy food to be eaten by guests during the process of 'stringing together doors', because these guests, as everyone agrees, must be well-fed. Almost everyone will also buy gifts, including bottles of rice-wine and tinned fruits, which will be given away when they visit the homes of others, because gifts always circulate during the festival. And almost everyone will buy 'earth paper' and incense and firecrackers, so that the movements of the ancestors and gods may be properly acknowledged. (Note the direct or indirect relationship of many of these *nianhuo*, new year goods, to processes of separation and reunion.)

On returning to their homes from the market, people in Dragon-head continue with preparations. Houses, as I have mentioned, are at least modestly decorated, for instance with brightly coloured posters comprising single auspicious characters such as *fu* ('blessings'). (*Fu* posters are often turned 'upside down', *dao*, because the characters *fu* and *dao* spoken together sound the same as 'blessings *arrive*'.) Careful attention is given to doors, gates, and other openings, including the 'outside gates' (*waimen*) which lead into farmhouse compounds, the front doors of houses, inside bedroom and kitchen doors, windows, and even gates to animal enclosures. As at Old Yang's home, virtually all the main doorways and gates in the village are framed with *duilian*, matching auspicious couplets written in dramatic language. Most of those displayed in Dragon-head were written in gold or black ink on red paper, and the flourishing style of the *duilian* calligraphy is felt to be as important as the poetic content itself – which almost always refers in some way to increased fertility, prosperity, and happiness.

Later, I'll be discussing both doorways and poetry, but here I want briefly to make one observation on their significance in relation to separation and reunion. It seems plausible that these decorations might focus attention on the door or gate itself and on what passes through it *as part of*

arriving and departing. This most obviously includes relatives, guests, ancestors, and gods. But it also includes – and this is the explicit reason for the
decorations – two further things. The first is good fortune, *haoyun*, (and
more abstractly good 'cosmic energies', *qi*), which may 'arrive' through the
front door or gate of a house, and which is said to be enticed by auspicious
words of greeting. The second is *bad* fortune (often in the form of evil
spirits) which may need to be kept away, or made to 'depart', at times
through the use of charms and door gods which 'prevent evil' (*bixie*) from
entering, but also through the deflecting power of auspicious *duilian* poetry
and calligraphy.

For related reasons, houses are thoroughly cleaned and 'swept out'
before the end of the year (*saodi*). This is done in order to rid the house of
the old year's dust (*jiunian de huichen*) and, by extension, of any lingering
bad luck, which is literally pushed out of the front door. But note that
during the festival period itself, by contrast, people generally do *not* sweep
out rubbish, especially firecracker debris, which is said to represent wealth.
On the contrary, this is swept *in* through the door, and kept in a corner
until the festival is over, welcomed as an omen of prosperity. People
sometimes also specifically go out of the house (usually on new year's eve)
in order to carry back in a bundle of wood; this is because the expression
'carrying much firewood' (*bao dachai*), is similar to the expression 'carrying
great wealth' (*bao dacai*), something which is very welcome *inside* the home.

Another key activity in the build-up to the festival (and something
frequently mentioned by informants in general discussions of the new year)
is the slaughtering of animals, especially pigs, which will be consumed
during the festival itself. In Dragon-head as elsewhere, 'killing the new year
pig' (*sha nianzhu*) is taken as a clear signal that the old year is coming to an
end. People explain that in the past it was often *only* possible to eat meat
during this one festival, and so *sha nianzhu* had a special significance.
People often comment on the 'boisterousness' of their family celebrations
by saying that the meat from the new year pig has been 'completely eaten
up' (*chiguang*) due to the flood of visitors. It should be noted that these
animals – a key symbol of new year commensality – are generally the
property of women, and are normally taken care of by them throughout the
year in preparation for slaughtering at the end of it.[4]

In Angang, Taiwan, people similarly engage in intense marketing in
preparation for the new year, although they are more likely to travel
to the city in order to do so. They buy new clothes (especially for their
children to wear). They buy great quantities of incense and spirit
money for use in new year offerings to spirits, including the especially
large spirit money which is offered only to Tiangong (the Emperor of

Heaven). They buy food, drink, and gifts for the process of *bainian*, and they purchase *duilian* poetry and posters with which to decorate their homes. These homes are duly decorated, and the old dirt is swept out of them in preparation for the arrival of a new year. (In Angang, as it happens, I found myself caught up in the rather arduous new year task of cleaning the walls surrounding spirit medium altars – arduous because these walls had been almost completely blackened by the accumulated incense smoke of the old year.) As in Dragon-head, during the festival itself rubbish is swept into rather than out of the home. Pigs and other animals are slaughtered in anticipation of the coming moments of reunion commensality. 'Eating up' (*chiguang*) such food, including the 'new year pig' (*nianzhu*), along with the food bought in new year markets (*nianji*), is an important sign – in Angang as in Dragon-head – of having had a good celebration.

2   *The 'sending-off' and 'greeting' of the Stove God, and other deities*

On the 'little new year', *xiaonian*, which as I've noted for many Chinese marks the proper beginning of the festive season, the Stove God (*zao wang ye*, or *zaoshen*) is ritually 'sent off' (*song zao*). According to legend, this deity observes, from his position at the family stove, the daily activities of his hosts. At the end of each year he then travels, along with his wife, to Heaven (Tian) in order to present an account of the host family's behaviour (cf. Chard 1990, Feuchtwang 1992: 58–60, Bray 1997: 107–14). In spite of the usual modesty of his icons, this god is referred to as the 'Master of the Entire Family' (*yi jia zhi zhu*) in the calligraphy over most stoves in Dragon-head. A celebratory couplet is also often posted there: 'Ascending to Heaven Convey Good News, Descending to Earth Protect the Peace' (*shangtian yan haoshi, xiajie bao pingan*). It is said that the Stove God's new year report will influence the fortunes of his host family in the coming year, and for this reason special offerings are made in his honour during his 'sending-off'; firecrackers are exploded, and he is made offerings of food, incense, and spirit money. He is also offered a sweet 'stove candy' (*zaotang*), which is said to stick his lips or teeth together, thus making it more difficult for him to make an unflattering report (*buneng shuo huai hua*). This candy is eaten by people as well, so that they will be less likely to say inauspicious things, *bu jili de hua*, during the festival period.

Here I want to stress the significance which attaches specifically to the way in which the Stove God is sent off – and to note that this particular activity (*song zao*) effectively marks the beginning of the festive season. It is important for the household that this should be done properly, as a show of respect to the God in advance of his annual report to Heaven. The connection between the respectful sending-off and the hoped-for result (a good report) is quite explicit. For this reason, as Chard has noted, the offerings made to the Stove God during the new year festival are much more elaborate than at any other time of the year (Chard 1990: 151). But one should reflect, as well, on the message of the sticky candy which is given to him. Here a departure offering literally produces a bind on the divine recipient, and devotees thus try to exert some control over events. Having departed from the home on the 'little new year', the Stove God does, of course, later return to resume his residence, at which point he will be 'greeted', *jie*, with offerings.

But in taking a new year 'journey' of this kind the Stove God is not exceptional and, on the contrary, divine movements are a central feature of the festival. (More generally, as I will later discuss, the movements of gods are central to Chinese popular religion, and are among the most common immediate justifications for the mounting of rituals.) In describing Old Yang's new year, I noted that a poster for the God of Wealth (*caishen*) made a sudden appearance in his home on new year's eve. This poster – a colourful tribute to prosperity complete with images of American dollars and Chinese *renminbi* – reads 'The God of Wealth Arrives!' (*caishendao*); and the explicitly stated hope is precisely that this God will now, at the 'turning of the year', 'arrive' or 'descend' (*dao*) to bless this household with prosperity in the coming months. For the Yang household, displaying this poster was a simple way of 'greeting the God of Wealth' (*jie caishen*) upon his arrival. Similar, and often much more elaborate, greetings of this deity are conducted across China.

In Angang (where worship of the Stove God is not taken very serious-ly, but where worship in general is taken very seriously indeed) many people engage in a much more complex and elaborate process of 'sending-off' deities in the days leading up to the end of the last lunar month. Here I was told that before the new year begins, *all* of the many Buddhist and Daoist spirits worshipped by local people (both in temples and at their own domestic altars) 'go to heaven' (*shangtian*) in order to 'hold a meeting' (*kaihui*) during which they report to the highest god, i.e. to the Emperor of Heaven, Tiangong, on the activities of the mortals below. Each one must be 'sent-off' (*song*). To cite one example: on 'the little new year' in Angang I attended a rather grand sending-off celebration at the home of a local woman who was a spirit medium. Her house was crowded with devotees who provided offer-ings 'freely given from the heart'. Each of the female deities for whom she spoke was given food and spirit money as a sending-off tribute, and their carved images were draped in newly-acquired imperial-style robes prior to departure.[5] This divine exodus is said to explain two features of the new year period in Angang. First, because the gods are 'gone' (*buzai*), it is impossible for spirit mediums to become possessed, with the result that the normally lively spirit-possession business comes to a halt. Second, because the gods are not present during the festival, it is possible for locals (including spirit mediums) to indulge without fear in activities which might normally meet with divine disapproval – such as gambling and drinking. However, on one occasion in Angang I was told that some of the gods had unexpectedly returned on the day following the 'little new year', in order to see what mischief people might be getting up to in their absence!

3   The 'greeting' and 'sending off' of the ancestors

I've described the offerings made in front of the Yang family burial mounds in Dragon-head. These coincide with the emergence of the ancestors (*zugong*), who on new year's eve are 'invited to return' to their homes (*qinghuilai*). In response to this invitation, they are said to temporarily emerge from their graves – literally exiting through the gate (*men*) at the front of each burial mound – and subsequently to enter farmhouses in Dragon-head through their (newly decorated) gates and front doors. This is in order to be reunited (*tuanyuan*) with their descendants for 'the turning of the year'. A new year's eve meal of dumplings (*jiaozi*), which is eaten *after* the grave-side offerings have been made, is said to be shared with the newly-arrived ancestors, i.e. as a way of 'greeting the spirits of the dead', *jieying guihun*. In many homes – although not in Old Yang's – a brightly decorated lineage chart (*jiapu* or *zongpu*), a listing of the names of the dead which is usually kept discretely rolled up and placed out of the way, will be unrolled at this point and placed upon the wall as a physical manifestation of the fact that the ancestors have arrived. In front of this chart – an object which is said to be 'invited' (*qing*) into a home rather than 'bought' (*mai*) – offerings are made and the ancestors worshipped (*gong lao zu gong*) for the duration of their stay.

But why, one might ask, must these Chinese ancestors *arrive*? Why not simply say that they exist, that they are always there? As I have already suggested, this derives in part from a certain way of conceptualising relationships. Relationships with ancestors, as with other spirits and also with the living, are importantly *realised* through the process of greeting and sending off, in spite of the fact that in some ways the continuous presence of the ancestors is *also* acknowledged. To not have separations and reunions, from this perspective, is to not have a relationship. By this, however, I do not mean that the point of these practices is necessarily to build a closer relationship with the ancestors. In fact, as I will later discuss, Chinese ancestral cults seem at times to simultaneously embrace *and* push away the dead. During traditional Chinese funerals, for example, steps are taken which clearly represent a cutting off, an ending of relationships with the deceased. This may be seen as necessary because of the dangers which ancestors potentially represent to their own families (cf. Thompson 1988). But the ancestors do nevertheless return, and they continue (in Dragonhead at least) to eat dumplings together with their descendants at midnight on each lunar new year's eve.

This reunion, in turn, ends with another separation in which the ancestors are noisily sent off – they are 'seen on their way' (*songhuiqu*) on the evening of the second day of the new year – again with firecrackers and dumplings. This is called *songnian*, literally 'sending off the year', here meaning the send-off which closes the beginning of a new year. On this occasion, offerings (of incense, food, wine, and spirit money) are generally made outside of the home in the courtyard. Members of the family bow to the ancestors (in generational order), after which the household head drops some of the food offerings onto the ground, and also pours out some wine. Each separation of this kind creates the possibility of a reunion, and each reunion creates the possibility of a separation – one which is, in some ways, desirable, because one would not want to live, throughout the year, with the immediate presence of the ancestors. The three pivotal days of the 'turning of the year' are framed by the ancestral greeting (*jie*) on new year's eve, and their subsequent sending off (*song*) on the second day of the first lunar month. But soon afterwards, on the fifteenth day of the first month, the ancestors return once again (for the 'lantern festival'), and share another meal of dumplings with their descendants.

In Angang, the simultaneous presence and absence of the ancestors is more clearly seen. There, they are physically represented throughout the year on almost every domestic altar by wooden ancestral tablets (at which regular, usually daily, offerings are made). And in most homes the dead of more recent generations are also represented by sombre 'ancestral-style' photographs or drawings which are very prominently displayed in sitting rooms throughout the year. Nevertheless, they do also 'return' for the new year reunion, and they are 'sent off' following its conclusion. Special offerings mark their presence during this time, and these are often 'personalised' with the favourite foods, drinks, or cigarettes of the deceased being placed in front of their tablets.

4   *The reunion of the immediate family* (tuanyuan)

Earlier I cited Feuchtwang's observation that *chuxi*, new year's eve, is a time of home-coming, and a celebration of 'the continuing narrative of a complete household' (1992: 25). Indeed, by the time *chuxi* arrives in Dragon-head, and across China, many of the people who have moved away from home, for example to work or study in other places, will have *already* returned for the holidays. As more or less the entire nation prepares to celebrate, and to come to an effective halt for several weeks, trains and buses, crowded at the best of times, are literally crammed-full of people returning home, and it is nearly impossible for those without some form of useful 'connection' to purchase tickets. Television broadcasts praise the heroism of vacationless railway workers, and focus on the remarkable transportation crush caused by the festival. People are quite simply determined to get home, and in the countryside entire families bearing large parcels of food and gifts go past, perilously balanced on one bicycle or motor-bike, or on the back of a mule-driven cart, on the way to their moments of reunion.

Going home (*huijia*), and being home, for the 'passing of the year' is not simply thought of as a pleasurable or a desirable thing (although it is often both of these things as well). The new year's reunion is something which almost certainly *should* happen, and which only exceptionally does not. As Cohen has put it with reference to Taiwan, 'Everyone is expected to be with his [family] on the lunar new year's first day; eating elsewhere or entertaining a [non-family] member verges on the socially unacceptable' (1976: 113). This helps explain the rush to get home for an annual moment of reunion which, as Cohen's comment makes clear, is as much an exclusion of outsiders as a delineation of insiders. The undivided 'patrilineal family' – variously, and sometimes in fact rather flexibly defined – closes in upon itself, a gathering together in a circle, and those without families to return to may be distinctly isolated.

Note that in addition to the moral obligation to attend the moment of ancestral *reunion* on new year's eve, there is often a specific prohibition against *separation* on that night, just as Yang's sons were prohibited from leaving their home before midnight. In almost all families, children are similarly instructed not to leave the house, and/or are made to stay up late into the night in order to protect their parent's longevity. During the evening, the family must spend their time together, relaxing and playing (*wanr*), and these days often watching special new year's eve television programmes. Of course, many, if not all, of the people in the family which gathers around a particular new year's eve meal may not have been away at all. But the word used to describe such events strongly suggests a 'gathering together', a reunion, of the family. *Tuanyuan* may mean both 'union' or 'reunion', and consists of two different characters which mean 'round' or 'spherical' (*tuan* by itself may be used as a verb meaning 'to roll something into a ball'). The meal on *chuxi* is specifically referred to as a *tuanyuan fan*, i.e. a '[family] reunion meal'. In any case – and regardless of who has and has not been away – this reunion circle also involves the dead (see above), who are certainly thought to have returned (*huilai*) for the event. Those who have moved away, along with those who have died, i.e. the ancestors, must come back to be reunited, and momentarily stay united, with those still living in the family home.

During this reunion, the hierarchy of generations must also be acknowledged, and although this sometimes happens in a rather perfunctory way, the rite of acknowledgement is arguably the high point of the entire festival. Just as the head of the household should bow to the ancestors and make offerings to them, children and grandchildren should respectfully bow to their parents and grandparents. Following this show of respect, elders usually give children and grandchildren gifts of money, known as *yasuiqian* (literally, 'press-the-year money'). (Throughout the new year period, in an echo of this, children receive gifts of *yasuiqian* from other adults in the community and also sometimes from outside visitors.) The familial rites and exchanges make clear, among other things, the *practical* inter-dependence of the ancestors, adults, and children. Just as the ancestors rely on the practical support of living adults, (for offerings which keep them 'comfortable'), children rely on the support and nurturance (*yang*) of adults (from whom they receive housing, food and money). But adults will *also* eventually rely on the practical support of their children. The giving to children of *yasuiqian* – a strange echo of the respectful offerings to ancestors and gods of money in return for future blessings and protection – arguably reflects this fact.

In Angang, and in all of Taiwan, the pre-new year period is also characterised by the rush to return home, and once this is achieved families effectively close in upon themselves (excluding outsiders) for the new year's eve meal. On the night of *chuxi*, children are prohibited from leaving the home and must stay awake in order to protect the longevity of their parents. A meal is eaten which symbolises unity and prosperity; this meal now often includes a 'hot pot' (which involves communal eating out of one bowl). Fish is normally also served because the word *yu*, 'fish', sounds like 'abundance', and to eat this food every year means 'year after year of abundance' (*niannian youyu*). During the evening, the hierarchy of generations is acknowledged, with juniors respectfully bowing in front of seniors in a display of *xiao*, filial obedience, and with seniors bestowing gifts of *yasuiqian* – here more often known simply as *hongbao* (red envelopes) – on children. As I have discussed elsewhere, a *hongbao* is also a 'bribe', and these gifts to children in Angang may partly be seen (as in Dragon-head) as a way of ensuring future support for parents in their old age, something upon which they are often entirely dependent:

> Xiao, filial obedience, is conventionally portrayed as a hierarchical relationship in which the child is controlled by the parents. But at the centre of the lunar new year, representative in many ways of this hierarchy, we find a transfer of money which arguably evokes the opposite: the power children have over their parents (Stafford 1995: 85).

In short, the new year reunion evokes both hierarchy and reciprocity; and just as it reveals the subordination of descendants to ancestors, and children to parents, it also reveals the dependence of ancestors on descendants, and of parents on children.

5   Stringing together doors: new year visits

Then, on the first day of the first lunar month, visits between different combinations of relatives, friends, neighbours, and colleagues begin. The meals on the first and second days of the new year are normally shared with close patrilineal relatives. On the second day, the ancestors are sent off. On the third day, married women normally return, along with their husbands and children, for a reunion with their parents at their natal homes, a visit known as *hui niangjia* ('returning to mother's home'). I mentioned that funerals are not a permanent separation of the dead from their families, in spite of the symbolism of separation found in funerals. Similarly, as I will later discuss, Chinese weddings symbolise the separation of a woman from her natal home; but the separation brought by marriage is, again, only one in a cycle. In fact, a bride returns home almost immediately after marriage, i.e. within a few days, for a reunion which is called *huimenr*, literally 'returning to the door', and every year thereafter she returns home for a meal during the lunar new year festival. Note, however, that these return visits, rather like the return of the ancestors, are arguably somewhat problematic. By stressing the ongoing tie of a woman to her natal home, the visits also highlight her position as an *outsider* in her husband's family. But on these occasions the affinal tie is usually warmly celebrated, as are all of the ties celebrated during the reunion meals of the post-new year period.

As I've said, these visits (during which eating, drinking, and 'playing' [*wanr*] are usually the central preoccupations) are sometimes referred to as *bainian*, meaning to 'give new year's greetings'. The word *bai* also means 'to pay respect' – to worship deities is to *bai* them – and there is an idea that *bainian* visits are made to pay respect to one's superiors. This partly explains the crush of visitors at Old Yang's house during the festival; his status as a cadre made people want to pay their respects. But in Dragon-head the post-new year visits are more typically referred to as *chuanmenr*, literally to 'link up' or 'string together' doors. The word *chuan* means to get things mixed together, for example to cross telephone lines, and the character itself resembles two objects pierced on a skewer. It is also significant, as I will later discuss, that the word *men*, 'door', is one of the terms for 'family' – so the expression *chuanmenr* also means 'to string together families'. (Similarly, a woman's 'return to the door' after marriage, *huimenr*, is a return to her family.)

During the reciprocal new year visits, as I have described, gifts are left behind – always in 'auspicious' (*jixiang*) combinations of four or eight. In Dragon-head (and this differs in some respects from Yan Yunxiang's comprehensive account (1996) of gift-giving in Shandong province) if the guest is a neighbour, little or nothing will be said about the gifts, and they will simply be put away. A few days later the neighbour will receive a return visit, and be given comparable gifts. However, if the visitor is from far away, a return visit may be difficult or impossible. In this case gifts might be given in return immediately, although this is usually handled in a rather indirect way. On departure, the guest might be handed a bag (more often than not containing local produce, e.g. duck's eggs or fruit), and told 'Here's something for your mother back at home', implying that the gift is not *really* intended for the visitor himself. But ideally, and often in practice, each visit will produce more visits, and each banquet will produce more banquets.

Here I will briefly mention one example of banquet and counter-banquet: a series of meals participated in by the families of seven sisters as an elaborate form of *hui niangjia* (i.e. 'returning to the natal home'). The sisters had all married and moved away to live virilocally, i.e. with the families of their husbands, and their parents had also subsequently died. But every new year the sisters reunited to share a series of meals which were held at their marital homes. The head table at these meals was, in fact, reserved for the *husbands* of the sisters, rather than for the sisters themselves, who ate with their children and grand-children at tables set off to the side. The women would usually finish their meals rather quickly and turn to games of cards or *majiang*. Meanwhile, the meal at the men's table would go on for hours, as the brothers-in-law engaged in the complicated behaviour expected of adult men during formal and semi-formal banquets. They drank equal quantities of the same kind of alcohol (rice wine and/or beer), from glasses of the same size, lest the 'meaning' of the drinking be lost – as they would noisily protest if anyone tried to shirk his responsibility. They teased each other roughly, but at times also dispensed stereotypically high-blown praise, and made long-winded (*luosuo*) speeches. Some of the meals were the occasion for serious, and sometimes rather direct, discussion of conflicts and problems from the past.

Meals of this semi-formal kind – a great many of which are held during the 'stringing together of doors' – are often notably prolonged, and there is an explicit recognition of the bittersweet nature of such events, i.e. a recognition that they cannot go on forever. As the saying has it, 'There is no banquet, under Heaven, which does not come to an end.' And when the end does, inevitably, come, the sadness of the moment is tempered by negotiating the next reunion in advance. As the meal draws to a close, someone will usually make a rather sombre statement of the unity of those sharing it (e.g. of the seven brothers-in-law). It will be said that in the future, if one of them encounters difficulties (*kunan*) of any kind, he will surely be able to count on the support of all the others. Then someone will invite the group to come to his house for a meal, apologising in advance for the fact that the food will probably not be very good or very plentiful, and the cycle will resume on another day. But any one cycle – such as that involving the husbands of the seven sisters – will overlap with other cycles, and many people in fact spend the entire new year festival period almost literally racing from one banquet table to another. To repeat, for many people this is the most notable activity of the lunar new year.

In Angang, the post-new year period is also heavily dominated by *bainian*, the cycle of visits between relatives, neighbours and friends. Brothers and patrilineal relatives join together for meals, women return to their natal homes, and the expanding cycles of reunion banquets (and of gambling circles) encompass the entire community, along with many who live outside. I was told that at this time of year people are really *obliged* to accept the invitations they would normally brush off in the course of the year, and as a result the pressure to eat and drink throughout the festival is very intense. In fact, when I became ill, at one point, from over-drinking, I was told not only that I must continue to accept all invitations to eat and drink, but that I must also drink *enough* for it to have a significant 'meaning' (*yisi*).

6   *The conclusion of the festival*

For some families in Dragon-head – as in Angang – things return to relative calm soon after the 'turning of the year', i.e. several days into the new year when many visitors must depart, and many resume working. But the 'stringing together of doors' still carries on in most rural communities for some days, and it is only with the 'lantern festival' (*yuanxiaojie*) on the fifteenth (which coincides with the full moon) that the 'turning of the year' has truly, for most people, come to its end. Note however, that this apparent ending to the festival is marked by reunion: people gather together to eat with their ancestors, guided home by lanterns, before once again sending them on their way. In sum, the new year festival is a period of intense consumption and exchange, an annual reaffirmation of relationships between people, an expanding echo of the family reunion meal held with the ancestors on the pivotal night of *chuxi*, new year's eve. People say this time of year should be hectic, filled with activity and fun. More specifically, as one woman told me: 'It's good to have plenty of people. The more people there are, the better; the 'hotter and noisier' it is, the better!' (*Ren duo hao – yue duo yue hao, yue renao yue hao!*) While the intense togetherness of the lunar new year festival is perhaps not very desirable as a mode of everyday life, it is precisely what is *imagined* during the festival to be the ideal form of existence.

If one were to count the number of separations and reunions taking place in communities like Dragon-head and Angang during the new year festival – and especially if one counted the simple 'greetings' and 'farewells' which take place between people bumping into each other on the street – there would be a great many of them, so many (and often so drunkenly attended to) that they would present themselves as something of a blur. But three points should be made about this. First, the separations and reunions which take place during the new year are for the most part *not* random, but on the contrary are highly structured and central to the ideological concerns of the festival as a whole. Second, this coherent structure of separations and reunions is 'historical', i.e. it situates people in relation to the historical narratives of particular communities (including relatives to whom one *must* return). And, third, although the new year is an occasion during which such separations and reunions take place with special intensity, it should be recognised that they also happen with considerable frequency – indeed non-stop – throughout the rest of the year. In a later chapter, I will discuss more fully the experience of the new year festival in relation to Chinese historical consciousness. There I will suggest that the festival is one part of a complex learning environment in which children (and others) develop a sense of themselves as historical agents, i.e. as persons in the flow of familial/historical time. But I want to conclude this chapter by showing how the flow of such historical narratives – which seem to imply the *inevitability* of reunion – may be disrupted by histories of other kinds.

The mid-autumn festival in a 'civilised work-unit'

The 'mid-autumn festival' (*zhongqiu jie*) on the fifteenth day of the eighth lunar month is another extremely popular occasion – albeit much simpler then the new year – when reunion is an important theme and an expected occurrence in China. In the ideal scenario for this harvest festival, the 'complete' family should gather together in the evening in its own courtyard (i.e. surrounded by the arms of the family home), in order to enjoy, in a moment of unity, and weather permitting, the full autumn moon. Adding to the symbolism of 'completeness', they should eat round 'mooncakes' (*yue-bing*) which 'represent coming together' (*daibiao tuanjie*). Although reunions on *zhongqiu jie* are not felt to be as compulsory as those during the new year, the festival is almost universally celebrated, and people do generally try to be with their families when it arrives. Here I want to discuss, however, one case in which a state institution effectively prevented many such reunions from occurring, and co-opted, at least partially, the symbolism of the festival. Hopefully my brief account of what occurred will dispel any notion of 'timeless' Chinese traditions of separation and reunion.

The institution to which I refer is an educational 'work-unit' (*danwei*), a teacher-training college (*shizhuan*) located in a market-town outside of a small city. Most of the students there come from the north China country-side – i.e. from villages like Dragon-head – and most can expect eventually to be posted back to rural areas. While at college, these students lead a highly structured existence, and it is widely assumed (both by students and staff) that such regimentation is particularly suitable for the training of teachers. Here, in the week before the mid-autumn festival, the only obvious festival-related activity consisted of people buying, both in the market-town and the nearby city, moon-cakes (*yuebing*) which they then ate and circulated amongst themselves in large quantities. It transpired that the college had organised its own mid-autumn festivities, and these were planned to coincide with celebrations of Teacher's Day (*laoshijie*). The students, many of whom lived close enough to home to easily spend the holiday there, might well have wished to do so; and they were, in fact, free to ask for leave (*qingjia*). But I was told that under the circumstances they 'wouldn't dare to' (*bugan*) because it would not look good, and in the event it appeared that almost all of them spent the mid-autumn festival participating in activities organised by the college.

These activities made for a rather fascinating combination. The day started with an early-morning assembly, in which a series of speeches praising education and current Communist Party leaders was made, be-tween which prizes were distributed to teachers and to senior academics (almost all of whom were wearing, even at this late date, Mao suits). This ceremonial was followed, to my amazement, by the showing of a dubbed version of 'The Professional', starring Jean-Claude Belmondo. Then came an enormous luncheon banquet in the college's dining hall (where normally only very meagre food was on offer). As the students ate off to the side, the teachers gathered around round tables to share a meal which was exceptionally grand by college standards, and which included chicken, prawns, sausages, mountain greens, and steamed rice buns. They drank beer and rice wine, and went from table to table to *pengbei*, 'clink glasses'. As the banquet started to get rowdy, the teacher next to me pointed out, with considerable irony, that such affairs are 'not scientific' (*bu kexue*) because of the waste involved. The meal was followed in the afternoon by parties, held in each department of the college, which centred on very long variety 'programmes' (*jiemu*).

But the grand collective event took place in the evening. Staff and students – over 1000 people – gathered outside in an enormous circle on the college's playing fields to watch yet another long programme of entertainments, ranging from ballroom dancing, to karaoke singing, to gymnastics. From the fields they could, in traditional fashion, admire the moon, and at the centre of everything was a great bonfire. After some hours of entertainments, i.e. at the end of the programme, the students formed large human chains around this bonfire. To the accompaniment of loudly amplified disco music, and I think to the dismay of college officials (who soon tried to calm things down), they began to race in increasingly wild circles around the flame. Their chains broke up, they rejoined hands, and the atmosphere was decidedly tense and electric (the contrast with the everyday demeanor of the teacher-trainees could not have been more extreme). Finally the music was stopped, the party ended abruptly, and in the darkness the somewhat over-excited students dutifully carried chairs from the playing fields back up into their classrooms.

In closing this chapter, I give this account of a relatively minor event for two reasons. First, and most obviously, because it is one example of a state institution intervening in a 'traditional' festival of reunion and, if nothing else, keeping its charges (the students) from returning home for it. But second, because it shows how very complex such an intervention is in practice. Within the work-unit itself, celebrations of the mid-autumn festival clearly borrowed from traditional observances: people ate 'mooncakes', and they gathered together outside in the evening to enjoy the moon – although not, of course, with their own families. As I noted, the mid-autumn celebrations were also here rather untraditionally merged with events marking Teacher's Day, including a banquet during which standard Chinese notions of commensality were invoked. Bear in mind, however, that the celebration of education, and of the achievements of teachers, itself has a complex and changing history in revolutionary China. Many of the teachers enjoying the Teacher's Day banquet, and the college's ersatz mid-autumn celebrations, had spent years in the countryside during the Cultural Revolution – the height of Chinese anti-traditionalism – because of their dubious profession. Now their own students will enter this profession at a time when it is officially praised and yet often openly scorned by the public (because teachers are so badly paid).

For students in the college, often away from home for the first time, and sometimes genuinely suffering for this separation, friendship takes on a great importance. (As I will discuss in the next chapter, the idioms of separation and reunion are also 'traditionally' crucial to the constitution of Chinese friendship and comradeship.) And when the college intervenes in the mid-autumn festival, and family reunions are replaced with collegial events, this produces precisely a gathering together of friends (something which can take on a momentum of its own). This gathering together – part of a newly realised mid-autumn festival of reunion – may thus be linked, in complex ways, to the history in modern China and Taiwan of the relationship between families and the state, via the medium of schooling. In short, it can be seen as a minor (if very complicated) example of the explicit and long-standing attempt by Chinese nationalists to replace kinship solidarity with comradeship and citizenship – often with unexpected results (Stafford 1992, 1995).

And I should stress that *all* the 'traditional' festive practices of separation and reunion which I have so far discussed, and which I will later discuss, should similarly be seen in the context of modern history. It is important to recognise that neither Angang nor Dragon-head (nor indeed any Chinese or Taiwanese locality) has been cut off from the transformations which are reformulating the parameters of the Chinese separation constraint. These transformations include very diverse phenomena: the growth of Chinese investment networks (which have fuelled international migration, but which have also sometimes brought 'sojourners' right back to their 'native places'); the dramatic post-war improvement in economic performance (which has, for example, made elaborate festival celebrations affordable for many in the Taiwanese, and more recently Chinese, countryside); the increase in women's mobility (a process which sometimes enables daughters, long before marriage, to separate from their natal homes); and the engagement of many 'dispersed' Chinese communities – arguably including those in Taiwan – in defining for themselves new forms of Chinese, and sometimes even non-Chinese, cultural identity (cf. Tu 1994). As I said at the beginning of this chapter: reunions may well be desirable – and calendrical festivals repeatedly underline their desirability – but history has a way (a very complicated way) of interfering with them.

2   The etiquette of parting and return

During the 'turning of the year' in Dragon-head and Angang, moments of separation and reunion are very numerous – but they are also obviously of different kinds. For example, 'inviting' the ancestors to leave their graves and to return home (*qinghuilai*) is a relatively sombre and formalised business, while many post-new year reunion banquets are informal, and often even drunken and rowdy, affairs. In the case of ancestral visits, the exact moments of their 'arrival' and 'departure' are matters of considerable concern, but their actual *presence* in homes is usually marked rather simply and not much commented upon. By contrast, the arrival and departure of friends and guests may, in certain (although by no means all) circumstances, prompt little obvious reaction, whereas the time actually spent together with them is normally a focus of much greater interest and attention. More generally – and of course not only during festival periods – the arrivals and departures of different kinds of spirits (gods, ancestors, ghosts) and different kinds of persons (kin, friends, guests) are handled in strikingly different ways.

In this chapter, I'll begin to unravel the complex Chinese etiquette of parting and return, starting with the 'greeting' (*jie*) and 'sending-off' (*song*) of guests. Then I'll turn to the ways in which people who either live together, or who know each other very well, handle such matters. Part of the interest of this comparison lies in an apparent contradiction: that the public elaboration of partings and returns seems, in many circumstances, inversely proportional to the emotional or social closeness of the attachments in question. As I'll discuss, this is related to the fact that formal 'politeness' (*keqi*) or 'etiquette' (*li*) – to the extent that it is practised in places like Dragon-head and Angang – may be seen as contrary to the easy informality which should normally obtain in certain kinds of relationships. Within these relationships, a lasting and genuine separation is sometimes made to seem *impossible*, and minor occasions of leave-taking are therefore handled with seeming indifference. Meanwhile, to complicate matters further, it is also sometimes the case that separation and distance, even among the very closest of kin, are seen to be desirable states.

Detaining (*liu*), and sending-off (*song*) guests

In both Dragon-head and Angang, when guests (*keren, laibin*), and es-pecially 'honoured guests' (*guibin*), but sometimes also friends and relatives, have been visiting a home and are on the point of departure, several rather formulaic things are normally said and done. (Note that this formulaic 'polite', or *keqi*, behaviour is also engaged in by city-dwellers in China and Taiwan and, in some cases, may be taken to greater extremes by them.) First, guests will usually be encouraged to delay leaving, out of politeness, regardless of whether or not this delay is in fact expected or even hoped for. Someone who pays a visit several hours before meal-time (and most visitors will avoid this unless they are specifically invited for a meal) will usually be encouraged to leave after, rather than before, the meal is eaten. 'First eat, then go!' the host will say. Someone who pays a visit in the evening may be encouraged, assuming that they do not live nearby, to return home in the morning, rather than on the same night. And an overnight guest will often be asked to delay his return home for as long as possible, if not indefinitely.

All of this is part of the process of 'detaining' (*liu*) guests, i.e. of delaying the moment of their departure. Out of politeness, a guest should be detained (*liu*), or at least made to feel that a proper amount of detaining is taking place, until he states emphatically that he must indeed go and that there is no possibility of his staying. It would be somewhat rude for the host to accept a guest's departure and the subsequent separation too lightly and without complaint. The guest, meanwhile, almost always insists on leaving, knowing perfectly well that he is being detained simply or primarily out of politeness, and that in any case the separation is inevitable and probably even desirable.

Once it is made clear that the guest does in fact intend to leave, the host will usually insist on sending him off (*song, songbie, songxing*); this is something which, again, is done out of a sense that it is the polite thing to do. And if the host is *not* going to send off his guest – whether out of a sense of informality, or because he is busy, or because he wants to manifest his superiority through such a snub – he will often apologise for this fact by apologetically saying 'I'm not sending you off' (*busong ni*). In any case, the guest will politely *protest* at the possibility of being sent-off, implying that he doesn't after all deserve such good treatment. In these circumstances a very typical style of conversation is held, somewhat along these lines:

GUEST: Well, now I really should go.
HOST: What are you so anxious about? (*You shenme zhaoji?*)
GUEST: I have some business at home.

HOST: Sit for a while.
GUEST: No, but I really must go.
HOST: Well, ok. I won't detain you then. (*Hao, wo bu liu ni.*)
GUEST: See you later.
HOST: I'll send you off. (*Wo song ni.*)
GUEST: You don't need to send me off, carry on with your own business. (*Ni bie song, mang nide.*)
HOST: I'll send you off. (*Wo song ni.*)
GUEST: But you're busy! (*Ni mang!*)
HOST: Busy with what? Busy playing! I'll send you off! (*Mang shenme? Mangzhewanr! Wo song ni!*)

At some stage the guest will acquiesce and the host will accompany him, certainly to the front door, but usually to the 'outside gate' (*waimenr*) or the 'big outside gate' (*dawaimenr*) in front of the farmhouse compound. (In towns and cities the equivalent is to accompany a guest out onto the street.) To fail to do this may, depending on circumstance, indicate that the guest is not seen to be very important. Meanwhile, as they walk out onto the street or road the conversation continues:

GUEST: That's good enough, don't send me off any further, now go back! (*Hao, bu song, huiqu ba!*)
HOST: Yes, o.k.
GUEST: Don't send me off! (*Biesong!*)
HOST: Yes, yes.
GUEST: Go back!! (*Hui ba!!*)

Finally the host will stop and let the guest go on his way, but usually not before shouting the word *lai*, which means 'Come!' By this it is meant that the guest should 'Come again!' (*zailai*) as soon as possible for another visit. But it often sounds, at least to my ear, like an order for the guest to return *immediately*: 'Come!'

This standard routine, this double act, is often rather protracted and comical, and people recognise it to be so. Obviously there are many subtle variations on the parting scenario, depending on context, and depending on the relationship between host and guest. I have described the way one would probably behave with a relatively unfamiliar guest (*keren*), an outsider, or a superior, as opposed to a close friend or relative (see below). But I do think most people in Dragon-head and Angang would agree with these two general principles of leave-taking: first, that it is considered polite, and indeed perfectly natural, to 'detain' (*liu*) guests in the way I have described before letting them go, and, second, that it is also polite to insist on 'sending off' (*song*) guests once they have insisted on leaving. To put this differently, it is polite to at least pretend that you wish the moment of separation could be delayed for a while or even avoided altogether, and then – when the inevitable separation occurs – to prolong contact with guests by accompanying them outside of the house for a reasonable distance. From the standpoint of a guest, it is considered polite to protest at being either 'detained' or 'sent off' by one's hosts, and to modestly suggest that one doesn't merit the attention these processes imply. Finally, it is equally important for both sides to express the hope of an early reunion. (I should note that the words said on these occasions sometimes echo the classical tradition – which I will discuss in a later chapter on poetry and literature – through placing great emphasis on 'words of parting', *bieci*.)

A guest who stayed for any length of time in a family or community, again depending on status, could expect not only to be 'detained', but also to be 'invited' (*qing*) to informal or formal departure meals (organised by his hosts and by others), and to be given gifts (e.g. of local produce) upon leaving. (Note that this banquet-hosting and gift-giving would generally be reciprocal.) Here my own most recent departure from Dragon-head – where I am a friend, but also clearly an outsider and politely treated guest – may be informative. On this occasion I was invited to several thankfully relaxed and informal pre-departure meals, at which *jiaozi* (dumplings, the food of new year reunions) were eaten, and following which I was given small gifts of food to carry with me on my journey. Before, during, and after these meals I was repeatedly asked when I would be coming again, and instructed that when I did come again I must obviously bring my entire family with me 'to play' (*wanr*). One of my hosts then insisted on 'sending me off' (*song*) by accompanying me to the city from where I would catch my train, although this was strictly unnecessary since I had made the journey alone many times before (and I was, in any case, accompanied by other friends). Meanwhile another man, a friend who lived in the city and whose wife was very ill and had been hospitalised, apologised to me repeatedly, and over a period of several days, for the fact that he would not be able to 'send me off' at the train-station. His children were instructed to act as his 'representatives' (*daibiao*), and they treated me to a departure meal at his home before personally walking me to the train-station, and in fact literally onto the train, on their father's behalf.

This treatment recalled not only my departure some years earlier from Angang, in Taiwan, when I was given farewell banquets by friends, but also my arrival there. Very soon after I had moved to Angang, people began to make reference to my forthcoming *departure*. I had mixed feelings about this, because my 'forthcoming departure' wasn't scheduled to take place for almost two years, i.e. at the completion of my fieldwork. I recall in particular that one elderly *tousu* (a local Daoist 'master' or priest) repeated to me time and again, with considerable feeling: 'Once you have left, you must come back with your father and mother to Angang, and with your entire family, to play.' Almost every time we met he would say this. Obviously I was concerned that his words revealed an understandable desire to be got rid of this troublesome foreign anthropologist, which for all I know he certainly may have felt. As I will later discuss, one of the advantages of proper separation behaviour is that it provides an extremely polite means of getting rid of unwanted guests, and even getting rid of evil spirits and terrifying ghosts. But in retrospect, I see the priest's words as motivated primarily by politeness and decorum. It was, without doubt, polite for him to stress that when I finally *did* have to depart, I must certainly come back for reunion visits. But his words implied more than this: for the inevitability of separation, and the potential for reunion, were part and parcel of his way of conceptualising 'guests'.

Greeting (*jie*) guests

The moment when guests arrive and are 'greeted' (*jie*) is often, at least on the surface, rather less complicated than the convoluted and oft-delayed moments of departure. This of course depends, again, on the nature of the host/guest relationship. For example, if people in Dragon-head see a reasonably well-known visitor walking up the road to their house (or know that someone is about to arrive because the family dog starts barking), they will often walk outside – even out onto the road if warning-time allows – and 'greet' the visitor. Having joined him outside, they will accompany the visitor back through the door and into the house, where (especially during the winter) he will be invited to 'sit on the *kang*' (*shangkangzuo*). The *kang*, which is both 'warm' and symbolically 'inside', becomes a seat of honour for the guest, who will often decline to sit on it out of politeness and deference to the host, grabbing a stool to the side instead. The host usually then offers him something to eat (usually seeds or fruit), or invites him to smoke a cigarette. Someone who has not been seen for a long time may be greeted more extravagantly, but in general such moments of arrival are fairly low-key. However, it must be seen – and this is a crucial point – that the 'greeting' of guests is usually not restricted to the moment of arrival, but in fact merges with the way in which guests are 'joyfully welcomed' (*huanying*) for the *duration* of their stay. In other words, the measure of a 'greeting' is normally the quality of the *period of reunion* which follows it. And in very many cases (as should be clear from my discussion of the new year, but which will be amplified in the chapter on commensality) the evaluation of the reunion focuses importantly on the quality of the meals which mark it. In short, very often greetings *are* meals, and should be seen as such.

Diplomatic etiquette and 'guest ritual'

At this point in my discussion of the formal etiquette of parting and return, I wish to insert a political footnote. To a striking degree, I would suggest, the roles of contemporary Chinese and Taiwanese leaders (both at national and local levels) are conceptualised in terms of the etiquette of separation and reunion. This is illustrated by the remarkable extent to which television news in both Taiwan and China is taken up with reports which are literally about the *reception*, by officials, of foreign guests. This is, to say the least, a critical task of all Chinese leaders, and indeed it is arguably constitutive of their leadership. In other words, the national political narrative is a narrative of 'greeting' and 'sending-off'. Such a conceptualisation has historical precedents. As I'll discuss in the next chapter, Qing emperors were held to 'unite the entire realm' through imperial Grand Sacrifice – which centrally involved the welcoming and sending-off of ancestors and gods. But if Qing ritual served as one way of uniting the realm *internally*, it was also a way of doing so with reference to *external* powers, and here the idioms of separation and reunion come directly and repeatedly into play.

This is seen in James Hevia's recent account of the Macartney Embassy to China, and of Qing 'guest ritual' during it (Hevia 1995). This famous Embassy – famous primarily for having failed to advance British diplomatic interests in China – was the occasion for considerable court ritual. The reception of the British as they were 'channelled' towards and away from the imperial centre (i.e. as they were 'welcomed' and 'sent-off') was a matter of considerable concern for anxious Chinese officials along the way. Indeed, British accounts from the time express frustration that the Chinese attention to ritual was making it difficult for any substantive business to be transacted. And from the perspective of at least one British observer – Macartney himself – it was as if moments of 'greeting' and 'sending-off' were mysteriously more important to the Chinese than any actual state of diplomatic interaction:

> They *receive* us with the highest distinction, show us every external mark of favour and regard . . . entertain us with the choicest amusements, and express themselves greatly pleased with so splendid an embassy, commend our conduct and cajole us with compliments. Yet, in less than a couple of months, they plainly discover that they wish us gone, refuse our requests without reserve or compliance, precipitate our departure, and dismiss us dissatisfied; yet, *no sooner have we taken leave of them* than we find ourselves treated with more studied attention, more marked distinction, and less constraint than before. I must endeavor to unravel this mystery if I can. (cited in Hevia 1995: 114, emphasis added)

Is the 'mystery' merely a cultural one, explained in part by the Chinese attention to ceremonial greeting and sending-off? Accounts of the

Macartney Embassy have certainly tended to stress the role of cultural misunderstanding in the embassy's apparent failure. But Hevia, for one, is dissatisfied with the conclusion that Chinese officials were unable to respond positively to this early encounter with the British Empire simply because they were 'bound by ritual' and traditional pre-conceptualisations (in fact, they changed their rituals considerably in this particular case). Hevia argues instead that

> actors on both sides of the encounter were quite aware that what was at stake were competing and ultimately incompatible views of the meaning of sovereignty and the ways in which relations of power were constructed. Each attempted to impose its views on the other; neither was (at the time) successful. (Hevia 1995: 28)

In general, Qing Guest Ritual was a way of incorporating the 'lesser lords' of the Chinese periphery into the Qing orbit, and in the case of the British it became a way of (politely) sending them away from the Qing altogether. The British request to station an ambassador in Beijing was declined, and Macartney was put under polite, but intense, pressure to cut short his visit and to depart (Hevia 1995: 190). At that stage, it goes without saying, he was sent off – not so much because of a ritual logic, as because of a *political* one – but this was done, needless to say, with extreme politeness and 'marked distinction'.

What 'politeness' in sending-off and greeting represents

In this chapter and the last I have already drawn the attention of readers to several contexts in which separation and reunion, in *some* form, occupies the attention of people in Dragon-head and Angang, namely:

> the ritualised greeting (*jie*) and sending-off (*song*) of ancestors; the ritualised greeting (*jie*) and sending-off (*song*) of gods; formal and informal reunions (*tuanyuan*) with relatives, neighbours and friends during festivals; and the etiquette for greeting (*jie*) and sending-off (*song*) of guests (including diplomatic ones).

Coming across these examples, readers might easily be drawn to a conclusion along the following lines: that in China, elaborate greeting and sending-off is a way of expressing the importance of certain relationships – with gods, ancestors, relatives, friends, and guests – and a way of showing in public that these relationships are highly valued. Within limits this conclusion makes sense, and it is of course consistent with what I have already said about Chinese ways of conceptualising relations. Given the view that all relationships are always in spatial flux, it does make sense to say that moments of parting and return might be important, and, by extension, that *intensifying* these moments (through certain practices) is a good way of drawing attention to the most important social relationships.

But there are two interconnected problems with such a conclusion. First, it assumes a generically positive evaluation of politeness (*keqi*) and of ritual/etiquette (*li*), i.e. of the normative systems of 'good behaviour' which may be said to lie behind most of the manifestations of separation and reunion so far under discussion here. But as I have already noted, and will discuss further in the next section, there are many Chinese contexts in which 'politeness' is seen precisely as a *denial* of close relationships. The second problem, which flows directly from the first, comes from empirical observation of Chinese society. This reveals many contexts in which partings and returns involving precisely *the* most important relationships are allowed to pass with relatively little fuss, and sometimes with no comment at all.

Parting and return of relatives and close friends

In my account of Angang, I noted the extreme informality which marks relations between friends and neighbours there, many of whom also share a kinship relation of some kind. Doors to houses in Angang are routinely left wide open, and people are free to walk in and out of the homes of their friends and neighbours. Little fuss is made about this, and sometimes literally not a word will be said in passing (Stafford 1995: 34–7). Similarly, if people in Angang go away from the community for a short trip or come back from a short trip, it is often the case that very little, or even nothing at all, will be said or done in public at the moment when they leave or at the moment when they return. They are rarely 'detained' (*liu*). In short, everyday separations and reunions in that community often seem rather unimportant, or are even dealt with abruptly. To make a fuss over someone, to display the 'air of politeness' (*keqi*) with these friends and relations, would be seen as '*over*-politeness' (*tai keqi*), that is, as a denial of the close friendship, bordering with and overlapping with kinship, which villagers pride themselves on sharing. Given this perspective, it would obviously be completely wrong to assume that the lack of public display at moments of departure and return implies any lack of interest in these relationships.

Perhaps this resistance to 'politeness' will seem natural to readers, given that Angang is a small and especially close-knit community. But it is also true that apparently more significant moments of departure and return in Angang – for example when young people go away for long periods of study or work – are similarly treated in a low-key way. In such cases one might ask: what is being felt, if not shown? I was often told (and people in Dragon-head said similar things) that the overt displays of physical affection – i.e. kissing and hugging – which are assumed to accompany 'Western' partings and returns are, in Chinese eyes, very 'bad-looking', a further proof that 'we are not the same' (*women bu yiyang*). These statements are one indication of a more general principle: that it is felt inappropriate, and even vulgar, to show the 'inside' emotions felt between family and close friends on the 'outside', in public. In practice, this principle is constantly broken (e.g. in very public rows, or in the public – indeed electronically amplified – mourning at funerals). But such moments of parting and return are generally dealt with *in public* in a dignified, rather low-key – and at least superficially 'unemotional' – way.

Still, there are clear proofs of the seriousness with which such moments are taken. Consider again the example of a child or young person going away for school or work. It would undoubtedly seem very strange in Angang for, say, a mother to 'send-off' her children in the way that a household head would 'send-off' a guest – to flatter them with polite talk, and to 'detain' them, etc. But what *does* often happen is that concrete steps are taken to protect children on their journeys. In fact, one of the most common occasions for worship in Angang is in preparation for the journeys of children and young people (Stafford 1995: 45–7). To cite one example, I once accompanied a woman and her daughters to the local temple to Guan Yin (the Goddess of Mercy), because these daughters were about to depart on a journey. Small offerings were made to the goddess, who was asked (through the use of divination blocks) whether or not it would be safe to travel. Guan Yin was then asked to provide protection for the girls during their separation, and to ensure a safe return. But when they actually left Angang almost nothing was said – they simply left.

In Dragon-head, as in Angang, the attention given to separations and reunions involving close friends and relations is directly influenced by what might be called their rarity-value. I should make it clear that people who actually live together only exceptionally make an issue of arrivals and departures; for instance, children are generally not expected to say any-thing to their elders before leaving a room. On the other hand, children *may*, on occasion, be sent out to 'greet' and 'send off' their elders, especially their grandparents. But in general, close kin who are seen quite often, i.e. who by definition 'arrive' and 'depart' quite often (perhaps even several times in a single day), may be greeted and sent off without fuss or comment. By contrast, close relations who do *not* live together or live nearby, and who are thus seen only rarely, may find themselves effectively treated as guests in the matter of separations and reunions – although important distinctions do apply.

Let me illustrate this with the case of one woman who regularly received visits from the sons and daughters of her brothers, i.e. from her fraternal nieces and nephews – some of whom lived very nearby, and some of whom lived rather far away. The visits of *all* of these young people were a matter of formal obligation. Because the woman had effectively 'raised' (*yang*) her younger brothers upon the death of her mother – i.e. she had taken her mother's place – she was given by them the 'respectful nurturance' (*feng-yang*) which a mother (or foster-mother) could expect from her own children (or foster-children) in old age. One explicitly formulated aspect of this was that her brothers' children, i.e. her nieces and nephews, would regularly stop by to keep this woman, their *gumu* (father's sister), company. One brother lived only a few moments walk away, and his children, in particular his youngest son, would come by to visit with great regularity, virtually every day of the year.

These visits were exceptionally informal, and it seemed to me that part of the point was precisely to *show* how exceptionally informal relations between the two households were. When visiting his aunt in the evening – something which she very clearly loved – the youngest son would let himself into the house without comment (as he might have done at his own home) and stretch out on the *kang*. On a typical evening his aunt might be, for example, washing her hair in a big metal pan set out in the middle of the house. While lying there on the *kang*, the nephew would mercilessly tease his aunt's grandchildren (who lived with her) in the same manner in which he would tease his own nephews at his father's home. He would eat anything and everything available in the house (such as fruit or seeds) without comment, take cigarettes from packs lying about and smoke them without asking, change television channels if he wanted to watch something else (regardless of who might be watching), and so on. Then, as abruptly as he had 'taken over' his *gumu*'s house, he would stand up and walk away without a word.

In short, in spite of the high standard of his public manners, here he behaved in a way which would have been very rude if he had been a guest, and I believe that this woman (and her husband) were in fact *delighted* with this behaviour which implied that he thought of himself *completely* as a member of their family, a position which entitled him to dispense with 'politeness' (*keqi*) altogether. But it is important to recognise, again, that the underlying reason for this visit was a 'moral' one – i.e. the moral obligation which this young man's father had to the sister who had 'raised' (*yang*) him. In any case, in these everyday visits attention was directly focussed on the actual state of being together – which in this case was very intimate – rather than on the moments of parting or return as such. The young man's reappearance in the house was so taken for granted that nothing needed to be said when he did reappear; and his departure was usually equally abrupt and unremarkable – he would simply climb off the *kang* and walk out the front door (of course he was never 'sent off').

The woman's *second* brother lived, as I said, considerably further away (about one hour away by bicycle), and visits by his children were therefore a rarer event. When these children – two nieces and one nephew – came, they normally brought gifts for their aunt (e.g. fruit from the city market), and they were more likely to be invited to share meals (even if these were relatively modest affairs), more likely to stay overnight or at least to be asked to stay overnight, and more likely to depart bearing gifts (such as duck's eggs or tomatoes from their uncle's farm). These various practices are also, of course, typical of behaviour between hosts and guests, and this reflects in part the fact that these young people did not live in Dragon-head and had to journey to the village from the outside. They were never treated with formality, as such, but their visits were publicly marked in the ways I have indicated.

Especially rare (at the time of my fieldwork) were visits to *gumu*'s house by the second brother's son, who was serving in the military in a different province. When on holiday (e.g. during the lunar new year) he would return home to see his parents in the city, and when this happened he would always make the journey to Dragon-head in order to visit his various relatives, including his aunt. Because of their rarity-value, these visits were, not surprisingly, more of an occasion for his aunt and her family than the everyday or periodic visits of her other nephews and nieces, but on the surface at least they were dealt with informally. On arrival he would also simply walk into the house unannounced, and no particular fuss would be made over him. He would eventually be asked about his affairs, and to some extent he would become a centre of attention, but he was not subject to the kind of 'polite talk' (*keqihua*) which characterises encounters with guests. When he departed, he was never subjected to a formal 'sending-off' of the kind I have described above, and I have seen him leave his aunt's home for a separation due to last many months without a single word being spoken. (Except, in fact, to me. He said, 'I'm going home', turned, and left.)

Nevertheless, he was 'detained' (*liu*), in the sense that his aunt and uncle would sometimes encourage him not to rush away from Dragon-head. And the actual period of togetherness was marked by particular attention to the sharing of food, i.e. by commensality. During the course of his visits, he would share with his aunt and uncle meals on the family *kang* which they would have characterised as highly *informal*, i.e. as 'everyday family meals', in which they simply ate whatever was available. (Given the economic circumstances of their household, these meals often *were* quite simple, consisting of cabbage, eggs, and rice, and this differentiates them from meals for guests which are often *said*, out of modesty, to be simple, while in fact being quite lavish.) During these low-key meals, in which the spoken pressure to eat was almost completely absent, the young man (normally of limited appetite) would nevertheless eat a great deal, slowly and deliberately, and he would also consume large quantities of rice wine (he was a good drinker), during which his aunt or uncle would endeavour to 'accompany' (*pei*) him, i.e. to match him drink for drink. Note that, under the circumstances, his *willingness* to eat and drink a great deal was comparable to the behaviour of the nephew mentioned above (the one who effectively took over the house, teased the grandchildren, etc.) This was a kind of presumptuousness on his part, an overt display of familiarity unfettered by 'politeness', a willingness to eat them out of house and home, and it was something which his aunt and uncle were visibly delighted to observe.

These extended examples of visits clearly deal with relations of particular kinds (e.g. those between one woman and her nephews and nieces), and the visits themselves should be viewed in the context of specific personal histories (e.g. the obligation of these young people to an aunt who nurtured their fathers, the sustained absence of one nephew due to military service, etc.) But the examples do illustrate what I would take as the *normal* way of dealing with such visits, and with separations and reunions, between very close friends and relations. Especially in cases where these people live in close proximity, it is not necessary to make a fuss over arrivals or departures, and to do so would seem strange, as if one were treating these 'insiders' as 'outsiders'. In cases where (usually because of physical distance) they visit less often than those who live nearby, it is *more* acceptable to make a fuss over people who are 'insiders'. But even here there is a sort of compromise between the need to show, on the one hand, that such visits are remarkable (comparable to the visits of guests), and, on the other hand, the need to show that such visits are completely unremarkable, because the ongoing incorporation of the visitor into the life of those they visit is largely taken for granted. In other words, because emotional and/or practical separation *should* be impossible between those who are genuinely close, and genuinely engaged in each other's lives, a mere physical departure is, in this respect, inconsequential. To make too much of it would be to suggest otherwise.

In fact, in some contexts distance itself may even be seen to be desirable – as a way of not sullying the ideal of perfect family 'unity'. Here I should draw attention to the analysis of Chinese emotions put forward by Potter and Potter (1990). Drawing on material from Chengbu (in south China) and elsewhere, they suggest that an emotional, and sometimes physical, distance is *meant* to obtain in traditional father-son relationships:

a display of affection is dangerous to appropriate behavior in the relationship, which is optimally maintained when there is due distance between the two. If love is openly expressed, the form and strength of the relationship between the father and son are thought to be damaged. [. . .]
    Related to this belief is the view that distance, physical as well as social, is a *favorable circumstance* for the maintenance of [the] relationship. What is well preserved by distance is a relational ideal, and an abstract idea of connectedness, which cannot be tarnished by the inevitable stresses of daily contact. What cannot happen at a distance is the continuous recreation and experience of relationship that are regarded as essential if the social order is understood as continuously regenerated from within the self, rather than as having an abstract, independent existence. (Potter and Potter 1990: 190, emphasis added)

This passage highlights a considerable tension in attitudes towards separation and reunion in China. As the Potters suggest, 'distance' (emotional and physical) might help to preserve the 'relational ideal', but the 'relational ideal' is itself based precisely on the notion of non-separation. That is, fathers and sons are not meant to separate (in the sense of 'dividing the family'), and are meant instead to celebrate the moments of unity and reunion which explicitly affirm the fact of non-separation. In this sense, for them to be 'distant' is an impossibility.

The difficult separations of friendship, and 'retaining a memory'

In the matters of behaviour and etiquette I have been discussing, the distinction between closest relatives (i.e. those most clearly defined as 'insiders', such as one's own parents or children), and most distant guests (i.e. those most clearly defined as 'outsiders', e.g. visitors from afar) seems clear enough. In simplest terms, this is the distinction between *jiaren*, the members of one's own family, and *keren*, guests. But of course, many people fall somewhere in between – e.g. those in Dragon-head and Angang who are such good friends that they are, in many respects, treated as if they were family. As I have already suggested, the departure and return of such people is often not dealt with 'politely', and this lack of politeness is, in the circumstances, taken as a sign of familiarity and closeness. The kinds of close friendships I have in mind are primarily those between people who have lived alongside each other in rural communities for many years.

    But I should note that in certain other kinds of friendships – e.g. among those who do not live in close proximity, among those who do not see each other very often, and perhaps especially among those whose association is

primarily 'voluntary' – the problem of separation is sometimes very publicly discussed and elaborated. This is clearly seen in the treatment of same-
sex friendships among the young, e.g. among schoolmates (*tongxue*). (Here
my observations are primarily drawn from research in a middle-school,
zhongxue, in Angang, and from the northeastern Chinese teacher's college,
shizhuan, discussed in the last chapter.) These friendships are often treated
with a kind of open and somewhat stylised sentimentality which is different
from, on the one hand, the overtly polite but potentially insincere treatment of guests, and, on the other hand, from the silent but possibly deeply
meaningful treatment of relatives. By contrast, these friendships allow for
the overt expression of sentiment and emotions which are taken to be, and
often clearly are, genuine. But however genuine the emotions may be, it is
also true that they are often expressed in the terms of an orthodox aesthetics of friendship – which makes such expressions permissible. It is interesting to note that same-sex friends are allowed to display physical affection of
a kind that would be highly inappropriate among friends of the opposite
sex, and that they also often exchange letters and communications which
may be characterised as straightforwardly romantic. (For a fascinating
account of the formalised friendship ties among young women in Hunan,
and of the letters which passed between them, see Silber 1994).

When friends of this kind part, for example at school graduations, they
often do so with declarations of the 'eternal' (*yongyuan*) nature of the
relationship they have forged, e.g. with promises 'not to forget for all
eternity' (*yongyuan bu wangji*) what has passed between them. Notably, one
way of achieving this (i.e. of remembering for all eternity) is to have images
or objects which are left behind, and which therefore 'leave behind a
reminder' (*liu ge jinian*) of moments of togetherness and unity. Interestingly, this expression could also be translated as 'to detain a reminder' – this
liu is the same word which is used to describe the 'detaining', *liu*, of a guest.
These detained reminders include such things as tape recordings and
written traces (e.g. letters and poems), but perhaps most common are
photographic memorabilia. All of these 'traces' may be seen as ways of
overcoming separation through memory.

Here I will not have the space to fully explore the Chinese interest in
photography (an exceptionally interesting topic which merits careful
study), but it will be useful to mention several points for the sake of
discussion. When school-friends take an outing together, e.g. to visit a
mountain, it is almost always the case that they will take many photographs, but only exceptionally will these be of the mountain itself. Instead,
the photographs are of people, and usually not standing alone, but in every
possible combination of friends. The point, again, is to 'leave a reminder' of
the occasion. However, these photography sessions take place almost

regardless of the actual closeness of the friends in question, which means that the etiquette surrounding them can be as complicated as the etiquette of 'sending-off'. In fact, and this is my key point on the subject of photography, I would suggest that in these cases the etiquette is virtually the *same* as the etiquette of 'sending-off', because the underlying principle is the same. It is an honour to say to somebody that you want them to be in a photograph because it shows that you are their friend, and it also means that you take them seriously enough to want to 'be with them' – via the photograph – for as long as possible (protracted 'detaining' and 'sending-off' shows the same thing). But people often modestly decline to be photographed (just as they decline to be 'sent-off') and have to be literally dragged into the frame, much the same as they are dragged over to sit in places of honour at banquets. In extreme cases – where the 'friends' visiting a park do not know each other very well, or include important guests – the picture-taking almost doesn't happen for reasons of etiquette. People say they 'would not dare to presume' (*bugandang*) to be included in a group picture. All of this is a rather overblown imitation (for polite purposes) of the seemingly *genuine* desire of close friends to retain memorials – including photographs – of their friends, as a way of overcoming separation.

But I want to note that those sharing sentimentalised friendships of the kind described here – e.g. current or former schoolmates – generally have a relationship which is, in fact, directly threatened by separation. That is, they are often already living apart from each other (enjoying infrequent reunions, and meanwhile communicating by other means), or they are friends for whom separation is looming (for example, those together in school or military service). After they move apart, their reunions may become markedly 'hard to achieve' (*nande*). But if these friends could live in close and long-term proximity, I would suggest that their relations would become of the quasi-familial type I have described above, i.e. they would lose their stylised sentimentality. Instead, and quite unlike the situation obtaining on the inside of families, the permanence of these friendships needs to be proclaimed. Such 'proclamations', as I should note, often borrow from classical narratives of friendship and comradeship, i.e. from classical narratives of separation and reunion. As I'll later discuss, highly emotional Chinese classical poetry (frequently cited at moments of parting) very often focusses on 'separated' or 'separating' friends.

3   Greeting and sending-off the dead

My simplistic starting point – that separation and reunion are matters of great concern in China and Taiwan – has already been complicated in two significant ways. First, I suggested (in chapter one) that Chinese narratives of separation and reunion, however important and seemingly 'timeless', are in fact always embedded in history. This is clearly seen when state institutions explicitly intervene in their completion. I then went on to suggest (in chapter two) that the public elaboration of partings and returns in China is somewhat paradoxical: the most important relationships are often given the *least* attention in such matters. Following the argument put forward by Potter and Potter (1990), it might even be said that in certain relationships separation, which is often portrayed as if it were deeply problematic, is in fact highly desirable.

In this chapter, which focusses on examples of separations and reunions involving the dead, *both* of these complications will again come into play and their significance will thus be deepened. First (and to reverse my order), it be seen that separation from the dead is often viewed as a good, or at least necessary, thing, and more generally that separations and reunions involving different kinds of spirits engender complex, and often highly ambivalent, responses. Second, it will be seen that history, and specifically political history, has a way of interfering with separations and reunions which involve the dead. What does it mean for the state to intervene in such processes? Given the history of religion in late imperial and modern China, this question is of considerable relevance, and especially in light of the argument – which I will put forward here – that families and communities are importantly constituted or 'produced' through ritualised moments of separation and reunion. Before considering these matters, however, I must first explain the background to them, starting with the nature of the spirits from whom the living are – at least part of the time – meant to be separated.

Who are the dead?

As I've pointed out, in both Angang and Dragon-head, separations and reunions which involve the living and those which involve the dead share certain family resemblances. To put it simply, it is an important element of ritual or 'propriety', *li* – which in popular usage often simply means 'politeness' – that both the living and the dead should be appropriately 'greeted' (*jie*) in contexts of reunion, and appropriately 'sent off' (*song*) in contexts of separation. This similarity of treatment is perhaps not very surprising, because in Chinese popular religion and ancestral worship the boundary between life and death, and between mortals and immortals, is not always as clear-cut as it might at first seem (for general anthropological accounts of this religion see Ahern 1981a, Jordan 1985, Sangren 1987, and Feuchtwang 1992). As a number of writers have observed, the ways of dealing with spirits mirror, sometimes quite directly, ways of dealing with the living. Funerals and ancestral observances clearly reveal a concern to provide the deceased with things very like the things they needed while living (e.g. food, money, and housing).

Of course, as Feuchtwang stresses (1992: 1–24), this 'same treatment' is rarely in fact the same: it is rather part of the process of producing, through abstraction and distortion, a metaphorical 'theatre of memory' (1992: 20). The link between this theatre and what is seen to be 'real life' is thus highly complex. But most Chinese spirits – whether gods, ancestors, or ghosts – are at least *conceptualised* as spiritual manifestations of dead human beings, i.e. of ones formerly living in the 'real' (historical) world. For example, Chinese gods or 'bright spirits' (*shenming*), rather like the saints of Catholicism, are extraordinary human beings (sometimes extraordinary in quite devilish ways) whose exceptional characteristics and powers have made them the objects of widespread worship after their deaths. Ancestors are also human beings, but mostly much more ordinary ones, who upon death should become objects of worship *by definition*, i.e. by virtue of having produced and provided for their own descendants. In practice, however, many ordinary human beings die without descendants, or die with unfilial descendants, or die in circumstances which make their future worship unnecessary or impossible (cf. Ahern 1973). These variously unfortunate dead comprise one of the largest categories of ghosts (*gui*). While the most extraordinary ancestors may go on to become gods, the same is also true for dangerously powerful ghosts; both kinds of spirits are 'effective' (*ling*) and powerful.

These dead live in a world which is *somewhat* like the world of the living in certain key respects. The gods, for instance, are positioned in an imperial-style hierarchy, dressed in imperial-style robes, and their treatment is meant to be courtly – more or less like the treatment of government officials 'in the real world' (Ahern 1981a). That is, they are treated in a formal, straightforwardly bureaucratic style which mimics the procedures of an imperial court, and this imperial other world is also the space within which ancestors and ghosts are thought by many to move. Very significantly, all of these spirits require 'sustenance' (ancestors, for example, may become ghosts by virtue of not being fed), and they require 'money' (e.g. in order to bribe officials in the other world, or as a way of being themselves bribed). Like the living, the dead need 'housing' and 'clothing'. As revealed through spirit mediums and myths, they gossip and fight amongst themselves, and have fierce rivalries and attachments, including attachments to certain bodies of worshippers.

Now the question of such attachments is highly significant because spirits also have mobility, and this is a fundamental point. For the dead – although dead – very much *move* among the living, and have a powerful impact on events in this world. Their presence, which can never be taken for granted, may be a good or bad thing. As a result, the sending-off and greeting of the dead – a central means of expressing the quality of relations with them – becomes fantastically important, and is in fact one of the pivotal features of Chinese popular religion. I have already noted in chapter one the existence of explicit rituals of 'sending-off' and 'greeting' spirits, and in this chapter I will provide more examples of these. Beyond this, however, I will argue that *all* relationships with Chinese spirits are crucially focused – and given the hard-to-control mobility of spirits it could hardly be otherwise – on the processes of parting and return. With certain spirits, at certain times, 'summoning' and 'detaining' are crucial aims of worship. With other spirits, at other times, polite 'sending-off' is the goal. And in funerals, as we shall see, both kinds of ambition are expressed.

'Sending-off' (*song*) the gods

My first, and rather extraordinary, experience of a large-scale Taiwanese religious festival took place not in Angang, but in a fishing village located on an island in the Penghu chain (which lies between Taiwan and Fujian province).[1] This festival left me overwhelmed and confused, partly because there was more activity than one observer could possibly take in, spread over a number of days, and held at a number of different sites around the community. Thousands of visitors had descended on the small village. A series of noisy performances was being held on a stage adjacent to the local temple, and I was told that these were in honour of the temple's deity, i.e. they were for him to 'watch', although of course people could watch as well if they cared to (and so they did, day and night, in great numbers). The entertainments on offer included an electronically amplified 'traditional' opera, but also modern variety performances of various sorts, even including (before the police intervened) a coy strip-tease artist.

Alongside this, under a large tent, was a truly impressive display of sacrifice and consumption. Hundreds of fattened pigs had been slaughtered, and then laid out on tables for public viewing. These were first to be 'eaten' by the god, I was told, and then later by his followers – the residents of the local community and their guests – in an intricate cycle of banquets. In the temple itself, a steady stream of devotees offered incense and spirit money in front of the god's image, and for many hours a large group of Daoist priests and their assistants carried out an exhausting and endlessly repetitive ritual. Outside of the temple, a smaller group of priests were having a rather jolly-looking banquet (which, I was later told, they shared with potentially dangerous ghosts, as a way of keeping them happy and preoccupied). Occasionally, the crowds of onlookers would gather around a spirit medium (*jitong*) who had been possessed by the god. He would slash himself with swords and other weapons, and speak in hard-to-interpret tones – giving instructions about the conduct of the rituals. The other main attraction of the festival, and in the end apparently the most important one, was a large fishing vessel, beautifully decorated and filled to overflowing with offerings, which lay on the beach next to the ocean, and which was later due, before an audience of thousands, to be set aflame. Worshippers went there as well, both to admire its considerable beauty, and to leave yet more offerings for the god.

For a small and remote fishing village, it was an impressive and, of course, extremely expensive extravaganza. In my ignorance, and overwhelmed by all the activity, I kept seeking a simple explanation for what was taking place. Of course, I do not believe that such a festival could *have* a simple explanation (and such events certainly have complex theological underpinnings). But it was eventually explained to me in simple terms, and on several occasions, that the entire event had been set in motion by the words of a local spirit medium. This particular medium was able to speak for the god in whose honour the local temple had been constructed, and one day he announced that the god intended to leave the community. The spectacular festival – including the public performances, the complex rituals, the mass display of sacrifice and consumption – was then duly planned in his honour, as a way of sending him off (*song*) in the grandest possible style.

Near the end of the festival, the god's image was thus slowly and noisily paraded (by large teams of devotees) through the community and out towards the ocean, where it was ceremoniously installed on the decorated fishing vessel. This vessel, filled to overflowing with offerings, was then burnt to the ground – thus transmitting its contents, including the god, into the spiritual realms. But as it happened, this very grand sending-off was reportedly so satisfactory that at the end of the festival it was announced, again through the medium, that *the god intended to return to the village more or less immediately*, and to re-establish his residency, in which case a new image of him would certainly need to be made for the local temple. It went without saying that various preparations would need to be initiated at once in order to properly welcome him back again on his return.

'Summoning' (*qing*), 'receiving' (*jie*) and 'detaining' (*liu*) the gods

I've never again seen a comparably spectacular 'sending-off' for a god, but the underlying rationale for the festival is one that is perfectly ordinary and indeed fundamental in Chinese popular religion. First, as already noted, spiritual flux is taken for granted – there is no simple assumption that gods are omnipresent or static – and the movements of deities must be acknowledged and celebrated. They are *not* simply 'already there' in every household or village, and if they were, much of Chinese religious practice would lose its sense. Second, a large part of this practice is specifically directed towards encouraging gods to come into specific images, temples, households, and communities, and then encouraging them either to stay in place or to return repeatedly. For instance (to cite one of many examples which might be given), Choi Chi-cheung has discussed a *jiao* festival held in the New Territories of Hong Kong. This spectacular festival (the *jiao* is a grand ritual of renewal held periodically in all temples, and it has a very complex cosmological basis) requires, by definition, the *presence* of particular deities, and therefore commences with an invitation for them to descend (Choi 1995). But the same holds for the simplest forms of domestic worship. Feuchtwang, discussing domestic worship in Taiwan notes that it proceeds as follows: 'Facing outward, the worshipper invites the cieng-sin [gods], including T'u Ti Kung, in to his altar, and sees them off again after making offerings to them' (Feuchtwang 1974: 108).

In short, in Chinese popular religion – in both its grand and simple manifestations – gods and other spirits are constantly being 'summoned' (*qingshen*), they are greeted and received (*jieshen*), they are entertained and fed, and of course they are also sent off (*songshen*). But even their sending-off may be a way of trying to ensure (as in the case from Penghu outlined above) their future presence in a community. These may be seen as attempts to 'detain' them (*liu*), i.e. to hold them in place by treating them with special offerings and entertainments. It is as if the gods were long-term honoured guests in a community – but often rather short-tempered and unpredictable guests, who are just as likely as not to leave if they become bored or annoyed.

And what is divine presence? In Angang (as I have discussed in Stafford 1995: 153–65) one very frequent religious activity – carried out not only in public temples but also in many private households – is the *kng put*, a raucous 'god-carrying' ritual which ensures that carved images of gods are powerful objects (i.e. that they are imbued with the spirit and power of the god they represent). But one of the main purposes of the ritual is to attract the god into the statue in the first place.[2] On the day of the ritual, the god's image is placed in a small sedan chair slung between two bamboo poles. The sedan chair is then carried, throughout the day, by pairs of worshippers, while local Daoist masters (*tousu*) take turns chanting an 'invitation' to the god (*qingshen*). A charm placed at the back of the chair also 'invites the god', who is given offerings of food and money as an enticement. What is hoped for – at this stage of the ritual – is simply that the god will descend (*dao*), or arrive (*lai*), at which point those carrying his chair will be violently thrown to the ground. The ritual may be, and sometimes is, a total failure, when the god is shown not to have been properly 'entered' into the statue, thus leaving the household (at least temporarily) in possession of a useless piece of carved wood. But if it is a success, the god will repeatedly descend, literally knocking devotees to the ground, and at the end of the day he will show that he has indeed descended by protecting all of the participants as they walk across fire. The presence thereafter of the god in a particular home or temple, which is the goal of the ritual, helps ensure 'the absence of problems' (*pingan*).

The point of this activity, in short, is an *arrival*. And in my previous discussion of the *kng put* ritual I contrasted this arrival – in which 'a very pure thing (a "bright spirit") is given power, and triumphally brought into a home [or temple] by a large cross-section of the community' (1995: 153) – with the departure implied by funerals (when polluting corpses are carefully removed from the home). But here I want to stress something I may previously have understated, the fact that the *kng put* ritual *also* entails a departure – in fact, an entire journey – and that without this intervening period of separation the ritual would lose its logic.

I should explain that the *kng put* is closely related to ritualised 'tours of the boundaries' (*youjing*) which are a very common feature of Chinese and Taiwanese popular religion. In the *kng put*, as in most 'tours of the boundaries', the god's image is taken away from the altar and carried outside of the house (or temple) before being brought back in again.[3] The god's spiritual soldiers (*bing* and *jiang*) are ritually deployed (*diaoying*) to protect the god during these movements, which are explicitly conceptualised as a journey (*you*). In some cases, this journey is physically restricted to the space immediately in front of the temple or house, but it conceptually encompasses a much larger domain, and involves three crucial movements: (1) going outside (*wai*) of the house or temple, and then coming back inside (*nei*) again; (2) travelling, while outside, around the 'boundaries' (*jing*) of the community (as represented by the flags of the community's guardian spirits); and (3) travelling through the 'seven stars' (*qixing*) of Daoism (here represented by seven small fires or one large one). Note that in the course of the *kng put* ritual, the god *arrives* only to immediately *depart*, whereas in the Penghu 'sending off' the god *departed* only to immediately *return*.

During the climatic fire-walking (*guohuo*) at the end of the ritual – an act in which a large cross-section of the community normally participates – the god protects all 'sincere' devotees. However, and this is a crucial point, the god is seen to have the power to provide this protection precisely because the *kng put* has taken place: the ritual has strengthened him. (Local people sometimes say it is a way of giving the god some exercise.) This logic is not unusual in Chinese popular religion. As many writers have noted, without displays of public support and popularity (often quite literally in the form of offerings) it is felt that the power of the gods will eventually fade away (see especially Sangren 1987, 1991). The god uses his power to protect the community, but the community arguably helps produce the power of the god in the first place through collective acts of worship. So, as Sangren notes in his discussion of one pilgrimage: 'the incense and offerings brought by pilgrims were at once requests for divine help, repayment for help rendered, and energy that somehow verified and contributed to *the creation of divine power*' (Sangren 1991: 70, emphasis added).

But what do such 'creative' rituals imply? If we accept that the power of Chinese gods is produced, in part, through acts of worship, then what I want to stress is that many of these acts relate to the movements of the gods, and specifically to their *separation from and reunion with various human communities*. Often this is very explicit, when gods are invited to communities or households (e.g. in the *kng put* ritual), and when they are sent off in grand style (e.g. in the sending-off of the Stove God, *songzao*, discussed in chapter one). It is explicit when they 'travel', as in the *kng put* ritual, around local 'boundaries', and lead their devotees in walking through the fires of the 'seven stars' (before bringing them safely home). It is also very explicit when images of gods are 'sent away', along with pilgrims, to be strengthened through journeys to more powerful sites of worship (Sangren 1991). In such pilgrimages, the images themselves, local representations of the god, must *go away*, in order to come into contact with greater power or efficacy (*ling*) – by being literally waved above an older, more powerful, incense holder – before *returning* triumphally to their own communities.[4]

Even the most routine acts of worship, such as everyday domestic offerings, are surely related to the underlying capacity of the gods to simply go away – and of the consequent need to keep them held in place through consistent ritual action. As I've noted, most requests to a god for assistance or protection will be prefaced with a request for the god to arrive in the first place. And a steady stream of *attractive* incense and food (both of which are 'fragrant', *xiang*, and therefore capable of mediating between material and immaterial worlds), along with money, entertainments, and so on, are intended to detain (*liu*) the gods for as long as possible – and also are used to send them on their way (*song*) when the occasion necessarily arises. In sum, and remaining entirely true to the logic of Chinese ritual, we could say that the gods are importantly produced through explicit processes of separation and reunion. And this doubtlessly implies as well the manifestation, through ritualised narratives of parting and return, of ritual communities as communities, and of families as families.

Qing imperial ritual

The extent to which rituals may be seen – explicitly – 'to define the borders' of various Chinese collectivities, and then to *unite* such collectivities, is clearly illustrated in historical accounts of imperial ritual. Here I draw on Angela Zito's recent study of Qing Grand Sacrifice in the eighteenth century. Zito examines in detail debates among the Chinese literati about the protocol and meaning of these rites. Although the rituals conducted by the emperor were extremely complex, and the subject of much heated reflection and politicisation, on one level their aim was straightforward: '*to unite the entire realm*' (Zito 1997: 3). This unification was ritually achieved through sacrifices to Heaven and Earth which 'showed the emperor as the link between the two'; sacrifices to Ancestors which 'displayed the emperor . . . as the prime exemplar of filiality'; and sacrifices at the Altar of Soil and

Grain which 'cast him as the whole of his imperial parts, social and geographic' (1997: 2–3). Zito stresses the conceptual continuities between these various rites, noting that 'An important element in the power of the cycle was the way a *single ceremonial order* connoted themes associated with all four sacrifices' (1997: 186, emphasis added).

A key aspect of this single ceremonial order was a 'recursive' ritual pattern which should, by now, be familiar to readers of this book:

> The beginning of this recursive figure was signalled by the emperor's emergence from his palace; its end by his return. In between, the spirits were invited, then sent off; the emperor approached the altar and then walked away, and so forth. (1997: 187)

In other words, the detail of Grand Sacrifice itself was built around patterned and 'recursive' movements of parting and return. Here it may help to cite a few details. The emperor began the process by going into seclusion. Officials from the Ministry of Rites then made offerings, and invited 'the spirits of Heaven and the ancestors to *descend*' into the spirit tablets which represent them (*qing shenwei*) (1997: 188, emphasis added). The emperor, secluded, was informed when the spirits had 'taken their places', and was invited to emerge in order to make the offerings to them (1997: 188). Bullocks were burnt in a furnace 'to *welcome* the spirits [*yingshen*] whose presence was marked by music played in each segment until they inspired the rest of the offerings from a final massive fire in the furnace and *departed*' (1997: 189, emphasis added). Before this departure the spirits – in front of whom the emperor and others prostrated themselves fully (*ketou*) – were entertained with offerings of incense, jade, silk, meat, wine, music, etc (1997: 190–8). Once the essence of the food offerings had been 'inspired' by the spirits, 'human participants' – but not the emperor – ate 'the material leavings' (1997: 198). The spirits were then sent off (*songshen*), 'with a full prostration, as they were welcomed' (1997: 198), and the offerings to them were burnt. The emperor then returned to his palace, where officials who had not participated in the ritual were 'lined up to welcome' him (1997: 199).

Here I want to stress that the rituals of Grand Sacrifice, based on this 'single ceremonial order', were ultimately ascribed a political function: that of 'uniting the entire realm'. This unification was made possible through the totalising structure of the rituals themselves, which revealed the emperor as the crucial link between all aspects of the realm, and indeed of the cosmos, i.e. as the person who brought Heaven and Earth together. The rituals (patterned around separation and reunion) thus obviously helped legitimise and naturalise imperial power, but also served, more specifically, as a conceptual focus for the very existence of a unified Chinese empire in the first place. By analogy, the same and similar rituals 'unify' smaller units within the empire, including localities, lineages, and even domestic units.

Spirit mediums and the danger of summoning the dead

Many of the rituals of greeting and sending-off I have so far discussed – for example, the greeting of the ancestors in Dragon-head, the sending-off of a god in Penghu, and, for that matter, the routine ways of dealing with honoured guests – are in certain respects very controlled and polite processes. The whole intention is to show respect by a proper adherence to the forms of ritual/etiquette (*li*). In some ways this is also true of the *kng put* ritual held in Angang (during which 'respectful' offerings are made to the god). But at certain moments the *kng put* ritual is also very violent and boisterous, and it clearly shows that the arrival of a god may be seen as a potentially disturbing and even dangerous thing (cf. Feuchtwang's discussion (1992), cited earlier, of the 'demonic' side of Chinese popular religion). In the *kng put* the god is first sent away (taken on a tour) so that he may return even stronger (and in fact 'cleaner', i.e. more pure) than before. This is, however, a dangerous process, in part because a spiritual manoeuvre of any kind implies potential contact with a whole range of spirits and forces, including demons and ghosts. But also, more simply, because *all* spirits of the dead, however benign, are also potentially dangerous for those with whom they come in contact.

The experience of spirit mediums is an interesting case in point (for general discussions of spirit mediums see Elliott 1990, Jordan 1985, M. Wolf 1990, and Stafford 1995: 122–43). Perhaps the most immediate and palpable sense in which gods may 'arrive' (*lai*) in a human community is by entering the bodies of its spirit mediums. I say this is the most immediate because when gods do this it becomes possible for villagers to communicate very directly with them (about even the most intimate matters), to hear their voices, and to see them act in the world (e.g. by watching them write out 'imperial decrees' on altar-tops and charm paper). Through mediumship, devotees also have direct proof, via the words of the spirit medium, that the gods are aware of what transpires in this particular place, which again gives a kind of immediacy to their presence. In short, the basic job of mediums, in conjunction with their helpers and with priests, is to *summon* the gods. But the state of possession – which may be useful for the community, or for individual worshippers – is not thought to be something which mediums desire, and in fact it is thought, in some ways, to be something they would prefer to avoid at all costs. For the power of the god is often said to be simultaneously saving them from death (it is routinely said that they would have died had the god not saved them), and sending them to it (it is said that possession takes a dramatic toll on their health and longevity). Again, contact with the spirits of the dead – once they have arrived – is, in some cases, desirable, but also a dangerous and disturbing thing.

Sending off the dead (*songzang*)

That this is true is perhaps never clearer than during funerals, *zangli*, the rites for the newly deceased, i.e. those who have recently crossed the 'great boundary', *daxian* (cf. Wu 1994). These are seen to be extremely dangerous occasions, much more dangerous than rituals such as the *kng put* (Watson 1982). It should be stressed, of course, that following death, and in part through funerary rituals, most of the dead become progressively *less* dangerous. And as polluting corpses are transformed into esteemed ancestors, the desirability of separation from them becomes less acute. I have previously discussed funerals in Angang (Stafford 1995: 146–53), and funerals are of course already well-documented in the anthropological literature on China (see especially Watson and Rawski 1988).

Here I simply want to draw attention to two, perhaps obvious, things. The first is that the initial funeral rites are primarily concerned with the careful separation from the home of a highly polluting and dangerous object: the corpse (again cf. Watson 1982). The expression *song* ('to deliver' or 'to send off'), with which readers should by now be familiar, is once again used in this context. To attend a funeral, and to participate in a funeral procession, is to 'send off for burial' (*songzang* or *songsang*), and those who do this particular form of sending-off are themselves vulnerable to spiritual harm, inevitably taking on pollution during the event. But while separation from polluting corpses is seen as a desirable and necessary thing, the symbolism of Chinese funeral rites stresses *both* connection and disconnection between the living and the dead (cf. Thompson 1988: 71–108). For example, in the Taiwanese ritual of 'the cutting' described by Ahern (1973: 170–4), a priest ties a string to the wrist of the corpse, and then passes it through the hands of a line of mourners, linking them to it. But the string is then cut so that each mourner holds a separate piece, which is then burnt to ashes. As Ahern observes:

Some informants told me that the string-cutting ritual signifies separation between the living and the dead. 'The rope that stretches between the corpse and the living is cut to keep the dead away from his descendants so he will not come back and cause trouble for them later on.' (Ahern 1973: 172)

Feuchtwang similarly notes the following practices which serve to keep the dead 'firmly apart':

Into [the incense container for the deceased], or into the coffin with the corpse, is placed a boiled egg or a stone. The message conveyed by the egg, as repeated to me, is 'When this egg hatches you may join your descendants'; and by the stone, 'When this stone powders (or melts) you can return to your family.' (1974: 120)

But having been separated in various ways, the dead gradually become ancestors – not least because of the steps taken during the funeral itself – and are then periodically welcomed back *(jie)* into the home for moments of reunion *(tuanyuan)*. The entire way of dealing with the family dead shows the significance of the idioms of separation and reunion within the Chinese ancestral cult. In short, relations with ancestors are ambivalently structured around an original 'departure' (upon death) and a series of subsequent – albeit temporary – 'returns'. Such visitations are proof of the ongoing significance of the ancestors, for as Watson observes: 'Death does not terminate relationships of reciprocity among the Chinese, it simply transforms these ties and often makes them stronger' (Watson 1988: 9).

The second point about funerals to which I wish to draw attention is that the rites themselves comprise a journey for the deceased. Emily (Martin) Ahern's account of funeral performances in Ch'inan (Taiwan) stresses their unambiguously 'journey'-like structure:

All of these performances are said to act out the travels of the dead person to the underworld. The chase around the table represents the first stages of the trip, when the deceased rides a horse that carries paper money for him to spend when he needs it. The spinning torches are to "open the gate" *(khui-mng)* for him. [. . .]
The next event marks the arrival of the deceased at the gates of the underworld. The paper figure of the deceased is moved to the central, elevated table. Then someone, usually the priest . . . reads out from a document prepared beforehand the deceased's name and address, and then the names of his or her ascendants and descendants. People said the information was read out so the underworld officials would be able to identify the new arrival. [. . .]
The final major performance . . . both completes the travels of the dead person into the underworld and establishes firmly that he will be secure from any harm. (Ahern 1973: 223)

Furthermore, the conflation of death with a journey of this kind has been extant in China for centuries. Wu Hung has, for instance, translated the following funerary inscription from an ancient tomb in Shandong province as follows:

On the twenty-fourth day of the eighth month,
    in the first year of the Yuanjia reign period [151 A.D.]
We completed this tomb chamber
    to send you *(song)*, the honourable member of the family,
    off on your journey. (Wu 1994: 93)

To participate in a Chinese funeral is to literally enact such a journey, and to accompany the dead to the bridge to the spiritual world. In the funerals I attended in Angang, children and others physically mimed this journey while Daoist experts performed a musical description of their progress. In many funerals for women, this re-enacts the famous story of the filial son Mulian, which has been endlessly reproduced in the form of operas and various texts (cf. the discussions in Judd 1994b and Seaman 1981). The story itself is a classic account of separation and loss. Mulian's mother, having failed to live up to the standards of Buddhism, is upon her death consigned to a terrible punishment in hell. Mulian travels first to heaven and then to hell in search of his lost mother. He finds her, and because of his extraordinary efforts and interventions she is released from the gates of hell, reincarnated, and – eventually – allowed to reside in heaven. The funeral versions re-enact some of this drama, and outline the ultimate goal: the safe arrival of the deceased in a peaceful and happy afterlife.

Funerals thus comprise an explicit 'sending-off' (*song*) for the dead, and an explicit journey which they themselves must complete. But, more to the point, to provide the dead with a proper funeral – which includes, by definition, a journey to the spiritual world – is one of the greatest obligations of survivors, whatever the risks may be (as illustrated in the story of Mulian). As Johnson notes of Hakka funerals in the New Territories:

People assured me repeatedly that one of their concerns was that the soul not become lost, and that it should be able to find its way back to its former earthly home, to its grave, and to its tablet in the home or ancestral hall. (Johnson 1999)

If care is not taken, the dead will become ghosts and suffer terribly, but they will also bring suffering to the living. By contrast, properly buried and worshipped ancestors – by definition those properly 'sent off' and then routinely 'welcomed back' – bring blessings to their descendants.

The respectful and disrespectful 'reception' (*jie*) of ghosts

The ambivalence with which the dead are in general viewed, as reflected in the careful treatment of both gods and ancestors, is seen once more in the different ways of dealing with ghosts (*gui*). Because this topic has also been addressed extensively in the literature (for overviews see Jordan 1985 and Weller 1987), I will only comment on it briefly here. Unlike gods, one would expect ghosts to be very unwelcome visitors, because they are said to be the source of many troubles in this world. This is primarily because they are unhappy – about their hunger, about their untimely or violent deaths, etc. – and uncared for. But this logic also implies, by extension, that if they can be made to be happy, for instance through the provision of food and other offerings, they are less likely to cause trouble. There are many different types of ghosts and demons, and so this principle of appeasement does not necessarily always apply: considerable efforts are sometimes made to simply 'kill' (*sha*) them and be done with it. But it is nevertheless true that ghosts are also often formally welcomed (*jie*) and treated with polite respect, in the hopes that this will pacify them.

For instance, in describing the elaborate 'sending-off' ritual held in Penghu (above), I noted that a number of priests were stationed *outside* of the temple. Here they sat at a table holding a full-scale banquet for the 'good brothers', *hao xiongdi*, a polite euphemism for ghosts. A ritual of this kind is intended both to distract the 'good brothers' and to effectively keep them happy. Similar offerings to ghosts are also periodically made at temples and private homes in Angang. Again, they are 'invited' to eat, albeit *outside* of the home, often on the road running in front of it. This polite 'reception' of ghosts obviously echoes, in certain ways, the polite treatment of guests, ancestors, and gods. But in the case of ghosts the point is ultimately not to welcome them in, but rather to send them – in pacified mood – on their way. There is no question of trying to detain them. (However, I should also note that sometimes ghosts and demons are actively worshipped and petitioned for favours, because they are felt to be particularly powerful spirits, danger and efficacy here being closely intertwined.)

In general, however, very active ritual steps are taken to *prevent* the entry of ghosts into particular communities and houses, and to defend individuals in the community from the harm they may cause. This takes a great many forms, amongst which are the display of divine charms to curse away evil spirits, and the posting of door-gods to defend the entrance-ways of houses and temples (see chapter four). At a very general level, all Chinese religious rituals are aimed at protecting people from harm, and this is, for example, very clearly true of the *kng put*. During the ritual itself, the Daoist masters, while calling out the invitation to the god, will be taking many steps to prevent the entry of evil spirits into the household. They use whips to scare them away, and swords to kill them, and deploy entire armies of spirit soldiers to do the same. These actions surely underline, in dramatic form, that polite greeting (*jie*) is not the only mode of dealing with dangerous outsiders in Chinese popular religion.

But the fact is that ghosts are treated with considerable ambivalence. The most explicit manifestation of this is during the Chinese 'ghost festival' or 'universal salvation rites' (*pu tu*), i.e. when unhappy souls are freed from the underworld – literally released from its gates – to wander the earth for the seventh lunar month (see Weller's extended discussion (1987)). A number of religious rituals are conducted for their benefit during this time, and they are made numerous offerings, especially of food, by the living. As one of Weller's informants put it:

We invite the ghosts to a meal once each year, because they are wild ghosts, living a bitter life in the underworld. It doesn't matter if you don't worship. Asking people to dinner is just a courtesy; without this feeling of courtesy, there's no point having company. (Weller 1987: 67)

But Weller suggests that these apparently 'kindly' rituals and practices are subject to very different kinds of interpretation (e.g. by specialists and non-specialists), and to considerable ambivalence. Pitiful ghosts may need to be fed, but many other kinds of ghosts are, as I have already said, dramatically exorcised, or killed in militaristic rituals.

History and agency in the 'greeting' and 'sending-off' of the dead

In bringing together the diverse material presented here on 'greeting' and 'sending off' the dead, it is important to recall something which was pointed out at the beginning of this chapter: namely, the underlying continuity between dramatically different categories of Chinese spirits. The diverse means for dealing with the movements of these different spirits – the extravagant sending-off of powerful or 'effective' deities, the respectful greeting of esteemed ancestors, the dangerous expulsion of polluting corpses, the charitable feeding of wandering ghosts – can similarly be seen to have an underlying continuity. For once it is accepted that the dead *continue to move*, then it is consistent – and in the logic of this system even imperative – to greet and send them off properly. Sometimes this propriety occurs in a manner 'appropriate to the living', but in any case (e.g. when ghosts need to be 'killed' in a violent bloodbath), the rituals are seen to be necessary.

What, then, is done when these necessary rituals become *impossible*? What happens, for instance, when the state intervenes to make 'reunions' with the family dead illegal and therefore dangerous? As I have already discussed in chapter one, the issue of sending-off and greeting ancestors and gods is currently a central feature of the lunar new year celebrations in Dragon-head on mainland China. The Taiwanese rituals cited in this chapter, including funeral rituals, are certainly, at a minimum, consistent with the *logic* of this popular (mainland) Chinese religion. In some cases, the relevant practices are more or less identical. But most of the original material in this chapter comes from Angang and elsewhere in Taiwan, rather than from Dragon-head. Why? In part because popular religion was more an explicit focus of my own research there than it was in mainland

China. As a result, I participated in funerals, and spent a considerable amount of time visiting temples and spirit medium altars, etc., things I never really sought to do in and around Dragon-head. But the fact is that public religious activity is *much* less pronounced in Dragon-head than in Angang, and this is largely the result of a political history.

It is hardly necessary to spell this out, because the political campaigns in revolutionary China against all aspects of 'feudal culture', including religion, are perfectly well known. It may, however, be worth rethinking these campaigns in light of my thesis about separation and reunion. For in temporarily shutting down most domestic and public ritual observances, the state was effectively terminating the narrative of alternating separation and reunion with the dead (and also often with the living) in China. As I have been arguing, this narrative lies at the core of Chinese popular religion, and to stop the rituals of parting and return – themselves arguably *constitutive* of divine power – is therefore as good a way as any of killing the ancestors and gods. But how effective and conclusive was this intervention?

Jing Jun has addressed this issue in his impressive analysis of the longer history of one very painful moment in 1960 for the people of Dachuan (a village in Gansu province). This is when, due to a dam-building project, they were made to abandon their community, including homes, the local temple, and the tombs of their ancestors:

They hastily dug up the graves of immediate ancestors and close relatives, and, in violation of all tradition, unceremoniously threw bones in cement sacks or whatever other containers they could find for reburial on higher ground. 'It was no time for being proper about such things,' an elderly villager recalled years later. Nor did they have the physical strength to save older graves; the trauma of dislocation was exacerbated by a debilitating famine, the worst in modern Chinese history. (Jing 1996: 2)

This terrible dislocation did not make ancestral worship – its cycle of visits and counter-visits – impossible, but along with the anti-superstition campaigns which culminated in the Cultural Revolution, it certainly made it more complicated and dangerous. Private observances were sustained, but only with the rebuilding of the communal temple in 1991, over thirty years later, did *public* ancestral observances take place in Dachuan again, and then in a modified and still rather discreet form. As Jing observes, what is found today is not a simple 'return to tradition', but rather something entirely new. For while this new ritual practice incorporates elements of tradition, it equally memorialises the intervening local history, including the traumatic history of displacement, and of the revolution 'against culture' which momentarily halted public reunions with the ancestors.

The analytical weight to be given to a state intervention of this kind depends, of course, on how significant we think such reunions (and separations) are in the first place. I've argued above that they are very significant indeed: central aspects of the 'creation' of divine power, and crucial realisations of the link between spirits and particular communities. In this sense, as Sangren has argued, collective participation in religious rituals helps to constitute or produce local history and local social relations (Sangren 1987, 1991). In other words, while such rituals are arguably 'alienating' – i.e. they portray, in Sangren's terms, the source of individual and collective creativity as resting outside of human control – they are simultaneously *productive*: productive, in complex ways, of both collective and individual identities.

But this raises a difficult question. If collective processes of separation and reunion are taken to be productive in this sense, who should be seen as the agents of them? (Bear in mind, to state the obvious, that the agencies involved in the collective ritualised 'sending-off' of a corpse during a Chinese funeral, are very different from the agencies involved in infant separations of the kinds discussed by Bowlby et al). At one level, the agents of rituals are presumably 'entire communities', who show (not least of all to each other) their capacity for mounting the necessary celebrations. The enormous 'sending-off' ritual in Penghu, with which I began this chapter, is a case in point. The very ability of the community to produce that spectacular event was a sign, to the outside world, that the community acted as one. If we begin, however, to consider the entire complex of separations and reunions in Chinese social life, then the idea of communities as the agents of separation and reunion does not hold up very well. In the case of ancestral returns, for instance, we might be inclined to say that the agents are 'families' rather than communities. But the key rituals are often performed exclusively by *men*, and (as I will later discuss) the relationship of women to these processes is often highly ambivalent.

In any case, at this point I simply want to draw attention to the issue of agency, which could be reformulated as follows: if rituals of separation and reunion are helping to 'produce Chinese communities' (in the Durkheimian sense), then what do these communities consist in? This relates directly to a second question: how do the rituals and practices of separation and reunion contribute to the production of 'boundaries', and therefore of communities, in Chinese and Taiwanese social life? In this chapter I noted that rituals (such as the *kng put*) importantly involve 'inspections' of communal boundaries, and their logic implies the protection of everything within such boundaries. Indeed, the notions of 'inside' (*nei*) and 'outside' (*wai*) carry a great symbolic significance in China, not only in their cosmological and theological senses, but also in the flow of everyday life. This is clearly seen in the treatment of walls, doors, and gates, i.e. of the boundaries between inside and outside – and this is the subject of the next chapter.

4   The ambivalent threshold

When various people – say friends, or honoured guests – arrive and depart in China, they of course must normally do so via 'doors'. And while this seems perfectly natural, it has some intriguing implications, not the least of which is that doors themselves become very significant features of the Chinese social landscape. The Chinese word which is used to mean both 'door' (as in the door to a house or a room), and 'gate' (for instance the gate to a farmhouse compound or animal enclosure), is *men*. The same term also covers the many large and symbolically important public gates (or arches) found throughout China – such as the Gate of Heavenly Peace, Tian'anmen. It can in fact be argued that the symbolic centre of modern China, Tian'anmen, is not the famous square (*gongchang*) at the heart of Beijing, but rather the famous gate (*men*) which looks down upon it. For as Angela Zito has pointed out, imperial architecture (i.e. the architecture of imperial cities, palaces, and sacred sites in China) greatly emphasised not only walls, which served to delineate inside and outside (see also Hay 1994), but also gates which, as 'mediating spaces' (Zito 1997: 140), played a crucial role in imperial ritual activity:

> The size and ornamentation of these massive gates far exceed anything called for by their mundane function. Beijing, containing as it did the Son of Heaven, ultimate source of *wen*, order, 'civilization', possessed the most impressive gates in the kingdom. The Outer City had ten, the Inner City eleven. The Imperial City and the Forbidden City walls each had four, one facing in each direction. Within, the doorways to all buildings were named and often marked with imperial calligraphy on the lintels. (1997: 139; see also Bray 1997: 92–3)

From massive imperial gates to modest farmhouse doors, virtually all Chinese *men* are carefully attended to, and often surrounded in some way by auspicious written 'words' (*zi*).

This elaboration raises the question of why doors and gates, as such, should play such prominent symbolic roles. Of course, all the many varieties of *men* share the characteristic of enclosing openings, that is, they frame an open space which might be passed through in either direction in the process of arriving and departing. Doors and gates thus constitute an 'open' borderline or threshold between the inside (*nei*) and the outside (*wai*). By definition, they serve as a mediating space between members of a household, a nation, and so on (i.e. members of any 'inside' group) and those in the 'outside' world.[1] For this reason, as I've already noted, the term *men* also means 'a family' or a subdivision of it. Jing Jun notes, for example, that the four Kong sublineages in the Gansu village of Dachuan are referred to as the 'four gates', *simen* (Jing 1996: 9). (By extension, the term *men* also means a 'school', 'group' or 'sect'.) As I've pointed out, the expression translated literally as 'stringing together doors' (*chuanmenr*, i.e. the reciprocal visits which take place during the lunar new year festival) may also be translated as 'stringing together families'; while 'returning to the door' (*huimenr*), i.e. the activity of women returning to their natal homes after marriage, may similarly be rendered as 'returning to the family'. Here an architectural metaphor 'stands for' a social grouping. In fact, Chinese houses in general, and not only their doors and gates, are taken as symbolic manifestations of families and of their internal and external relations (cf. Bray 1997).[2] But doors and gates seem *especially* important, and perhaps for obvious reasons, in relation to the processes of separation and reunion.

Given the Chinese way of conceptualising relationships which I have already outlined – i.e. starting from the assumption that all human and spiritual relationships are in spatial flux, and are importantly realised through processes of separation and reunion – it probably follows that doors and gates, the thresholds which the living and the dead must cross when arriving and departing, should become a focus of attention and concern. But 'persons' and 'spirits' are not the only things crossing thresholds. In the popular system of ideas commonly known as *fengshui* ('winds and waters'), both the natural landscape and the built environment are held to powerfully influence the fate of humans, precisely by virtue of the 'forces' which they also send flowing *into* or *away from* communities and homes. For this reason, as Bray notes, 'The Chinese house was designed as a magical shelter from wind or evil influences, a site that could channel cosmic energies (*qi*) for the benefit of its occupants' (1997: 60). These cosmic energies, along with the flow of good and bad spirits, and of welcome and unwelcome guests, may enter homes through gates and doors. Such entryways – which unlike people, spirits, and forces do *not* normally move – are thus stationary markers in the social landscape, fixed points against which desirable and undesirable movements may be gauged, and which may also serve (along with walls) as barriers to exit and entry.

Ancestral gates

Let me start by returning briefly to popular Chinese beliefs surrounding death and the return of the dead. In one of the discussions I held in northeastern China about such matters, an eighty-year-old woman stressed to me the importance of what was, for her, an obvious detail of funerary practice: the simple brick *men* (gate) which is placed (in this part of China) at the front of each burial mound. These mounds, I should stress, are normally very minimalist: a rounded pile of earth fronted *only* by a 3–brick 'gate'.

The woman asked, 'Are your graves the same as ours?'
'No,' I replied, and described them for her.
She seemed genuinely shocked by my description, and asked, 'You mean, they don't have gates?'
'No,' I admitted, 'they don't have gates.'

'Then how,' she asked, 'does the spirit get out?' After a pause for thought, during which I couldn't think of an answer, she looked me straight in the eye. 'You tell me,' she exclaimed, 'aren't you people strange!'

In Chapter one, I described the new year offerings made at the burial mounds belonging to Old Yang's family. These 'invitation' offerings initiated the subsequent movement of the ancestral spirits out through their burial mound gates (*men*), in front of which the offerings were displayed, through the newly decorated outside gates (*men*) of Old Yang's family compound, and finally through the newly decorated front door (*men*) of his house for the new year's eve family reunion meal (*chuxi tuanyuanfan*). As the elderly woman's comments suggest, it is not a minor detail that these spirits must pass through doors or gates.

More generally, a great deal of attention is given to what might be called the material circumstances of Chinese spirits. Although such spirits may have extraordinary powers, and may often be seen as 'beyond materiality' (*yin*), their presence may also be blocked or diverted by objects in the 'material' *yang* world, objects as simple as closed doors (or non-existent ones). But what exactly is this *presence* which is potentially divertible? At times, people speak as if their ancestors were singular agents – i.e. the kinds of agents, very person-like, who might walk in or out of a door, or eat offerings left out for them on a table, and whose actions might easily be blocked or cut off. But at other times, the ancestors are discussed as the source of a (much harder-to-define) flow, one which is specifically *not* meant to be discontinuous, i.e. which should *never* be cut off. This is the flow of patrilineal 'breath' or 'energy' (*qi*), and of ancestral blessings (*fu*). After the separation rites of funerals, which I discussed in the last chapter, the bones of the deceased are carefully placed in graves to ensure that they are 'comfortable' (shufu), after which they will (hopefully) direct, quite literally, the flow of fertility and good fortune back towards the living. If, however, they are not comfortable, or their spirits are not properly fed, or are simply forgotten, they may cause trouble, for example, by provoking the illness of a child.

But this may again, in some cases, be seen as a significantly 'material' matter, e.g. as a matter of the physical placement and comfort of graves. The daughter-in-law of the eighty-year-old woman mentioned above suggested as much to me. She despaired at her own bad fortune, which she attributed directly to the state of her husband's ancestral graves. These were badly positioned, she claimed, because her relatives had been terribly poor, as a result of which they were unable to arrange for more suitable burial sites. The graves were located near a water canal and a large rock – both unfortunate, as is commonly said, in geomantic terms – and as a result good luck had never flowed down into her home. People who have good graves, she said, become successful: they become 'officials' (guanliao). In order for this to happen, their homes, importantly including their household doors, must also be properly positioned to *receive* the blessings which have been directed their way. In both cases (the placement of graves, and the placement of homes) experts are called in to offer advice (fengshui xiansheng). I say all of this in order simply to note, again, that the good flow from ancestors is seen – for some informants quite literally – to *exit* from the 'gates' to ancestral tombs and then to *enter* through the openings in houses, i.e. through household gates and doors.

The boundary between heaven and earth

In Angang, such views about the *fengshui* of graves and houses are also commonly held, and experts advise on their proper alignment. But each household front doorway also serves, in addition, as a crucial marker of the boundary between Earth (and the families living and working on it) and Heaven. I should first explain that virtually every home in Angang has a domestic altar on which are often found carved statues of popular and powerful deities such as Guan Yin, Mazu, and San Taizi. But the *most* powerful deity – the Emperor of Heaven, Tiangong – is in fact *not* represented by a statue there. Instead a simple incense pot for him hangs from the ceiling above, and just inside, the front door. Note that even when carved images of deities *do* exist, the incense ash held within such 'simple' pots is thought to be the most genuine physical representation of divine power. Within the symbolic field of the household, the location of Tiangong's incense pot, however outwardly modest, is therefore a crucially important site. This pot, positioned over the doorway, is used exclusively for offerings to Tiangong, and offerings to him, unusually, are made facing *away* from the altar, and thus towards the *outside* of the home. That is, they are made facing out through the front door towards Heaven. The pot is placed high, so that worshippers must lift their eyes to Heaven and stretch upwards, often on tiptoe, when placing incense. Tiangong should then 'arrive' – even if only just – within the home to consume the attractive 'fragrance' (*xiang*) of this offering.

In part because of the absence of carved images for him, it is rather easy to forget the significance of Tiangong for people in Angang. Mediums only exceptionally speak on his behalf, and worshippers do not usually presume to develop the sort of intimate relationship with him which they often develop with lesser gods (through highly personal exchanges during spirit medium sessions). Nevertheless, the main offerings of the new year are given to Tiangong (it is in his name that pigs are slaughtered at the end of the year), and *every* act of worship is commenced by a show of respect to him, however simple. So let me stress: while the immediate *outside* of the door is marked, at the turning of the year, in a way which will hopefully attract blessings into the home (e.g. through the posting of auspicious poetry), the immediate *inside* of the door is notably the site where the most powerful of all the gods is worshipped, the god who has ultimate responsibility for the distribution of all blessings throughout the year.

Attracting the good

When doors are decorated to celebrate the arrival of 'good things' (*haoshi*), the beneficial side of the connection with ancestors, and gods such as Tiangong, is part of what is being celebrated. But it is also part of what is being *attracted*. I have already described, in chapter one, the way in which Old Yang and his neighbours in Dragon-head (and also people in Angang) decorated their homes for the lunar new year, and noted that particular attention was given to doors, gates, and windows. In fact, aside from the red lantern hung in front of the house, and several posters placed on the walls inside, Old Yang's new year decorations consisted *entirely* of the calligraphy (written on strips of paper) which was used to frame the doors, gates, and windows of his farmhouse compound. As I mentioned, the front door was framed with a *duilian* (matching couplet), and a similar couplet framed the outside gate (*waimen*). Smaller *duilian* and stickers were even posted around the gates to the enclosure in which his wife raised pigs (these proclaimed: 'Fat pigs fill the courtyard!').

But what is the significance of these *duilian*, which are an almost universal feature of new year celebrations in China, displayed by virtually every household, and then left in place until the end of the year? Obviously they are intended to be decorative and 'good-looking' (*haokan*), and most of those on show in Dragon-head (purchased from an expert calligrapher at the new year market) were in fact rather beautifully done in gold or black ink on red paper. They are also meant to add, through their messages, to the generally optimistic atmosphere of the festival; their poetic content is, without fail, exceptionally 'auspicious' in tone. But *duilian* are more than mere decoration, and their very elaboration surely draws attention to the fact that doors and gates *themselves* play an important role in the festival. From what I have already said, it should be clear why this might be the case. If the festival may be seen as a long sequence of separations and reunions – involving the ancestors, the gods, and one's relatives and friends – then doors and gates become, by definition, spaces through which these humans and spirits must pass. The decorations are therefore also partly intended (explicitly) as a way of 'greeting' (*ying* or *jie*) these spirits and humans upon arrival. They are also (explicitly) seen as a way of 'greeting the new year' itself (*yingnian*), and in particular the flows of energy and good fortune which may accompany the turning of the year.

But here I want briefly to discuss in more detail one characteristic of these decorations. It is not always the case that people in Dragon-head (or in Angang) understand the words in *duilian* (even those who are literate), because unfamiliar 'classical' expressions are sometimes used, and the characters (*zi*) are often written in a way which is too 'flourishing' or 'grassy' (*cao*) to be easily legible. In any case, it seemed to me that relatively little attention was given by most people to the actual content of *duilian* (although when buying them people might request or select different messages depending on their current preoccupations). In general, it is assumed that all new year *duilian* will be highly auspicious (*jixiang*) and extravagantly optimistic, and that their messages will celebrate fertility, wealth, and renewal. But those who can and do read the verses often point out one characteristic of them which derives from classical Chinese verse, namely the complex link between the opposed lines of a couplet. As with all classical Chinese poetry, in *duilian* the symmetrical relationships between characters and lines is highly regulated, and a crucial part of the poetic art is the manipulation of such relationships.

To cite one simple example, if a couplet's descending line begins (at the top right) with a noun such as 'heaven' (*tian*), the opposite descending line (on the left) would begin with an opposed noun such as 'earth' (*di*). This might be followed on the right by a position character such as 'upon' (*shang*), which would normally stand opposite another position character, such as 'below' (*xia*). When the standard couplet for the Stove God (cited above) is rendered literally, the symmetry becomes clear:

Descending	Ascending
Earth	Heaven
Protect	Speak
Peace-Peace	Good-Affairs

(That is, from the top right: 'Ascending to Heaven convey good news, descending to Earth protect the peace'.) The symmetry is also clearly seen in a literal rendering of Old Yang's new year *duilian*:

Arriving	Producing
Blessing	Wealth
Achieved-achieved	Everywhere-everywhere
Step	Year
Step	Year
High	Plenty

(That is: 'Prosperity increasing on all fronts, abundance year after year; Every blessing achieved to the full, glorious step after step'.)

Again, people often spontaneously point out these symmetrical relationships, which are a standard feature of highly structured Chinese poetic language. The auspicious words of *duilian*, posted before the new year arrives, obviously frame and highlight each gate and door. But they also arguably form, through their highly structured interconnections, auspicious 'nets' which stretch across them. One obvious purpose for this, as I have already said, is to greet the arrival of ancestors, gods, and humans, and to greet the arrival of what the verses themselves proclaim, namely: blessings, good fortune, wealth, and fertility. However, it is important to see that an auspicious message stretching across a door – indeed, anything auspicious placed in the vicinity of the door – could equally be intended to *block* the arrival of unwanted visitors or forces, i.e. to help those inside to 'avoid evil' (*bixie*). For as Bray observes:

The walls and gates that surrounded the family compound provided protection as well as privacy for its inmates, keeping out the ghosts and evil influences that could strike a family down with misfortune or disease. Both ghosts and evil influences were thought to travel in straight lines or 'arrows'. (Bray 1997: 92)

Deflecting the bad

I've already pointed out that during the 'ghost festival', i.e. the 'festival of universal salvation' (*pu tu*) which takes place during the seventh lunar month, elaborate offerings are made in Angang. These are for the spirits of those who have died in unfortunate ways, and who are not being properly worshipped at other times of the year. But in the context of this discussion of doors, gates and social space, two facts about the ghost festival are of particular interest. First, the immediate occasion for the festival is said to be the opening of the gates (*men*) of 'hell'. Hell itself is conceived of as a multi-layered purgatory, literally an 'earth prison' (*diyu*), behind the gates of which the 'unsaved' dead are trapped in torment (see Goodrich 1981). As Feuchtwang notes:

> The seventh month is the opening and closing of the doors of purgatory, the release of [gui], which mingle with the ancestors of the locality during the month until they are shut outside it again on the last day. (Feuchtwang 1974: 114)

The action of opening the gates therefore allows the spirits of the unhappy dead to wander upon the earth, and this is when they must be fed. However – and this is the second fact I wish to stress about the ghost festival – during the seventh month, offerings to ghosts are made *outside* the doors of family homes, and often on the road *outside* of main household gates. So while it is true that ghosts, having been allowed outside the gates of hell, are being fed and cared for during the 'festival of universal salvation' (they are, more specifically, being helped to achieve a salvation so far denied to them), they are certainly *not* being invited through household doorways, nor into family homes.

This denial of entrance to potentially disastrous spiritual guests is seen more explicitly in one simple step taken during funeral processions in Angang (and elsewhere). Evil spirits may congregate during any stage of the death rites – by definition a dangerous moment when the worlds of the living and the dead collide – but the *procession* itself, the occasion for moving the polluting corpse, is thought to be particularly dangerous. It is thought possible that the dead person's spirit might take the opportunity of their departure from the community to attack some local person who had become an enemy. As a precaution, when funeral processions pass through the community, all of the doors in the community are normally slammed shut.

But might such a door provide protection from spiritual harm without even being closed? A number of steps are taken to try to achieve this. For example, during the new year period in Dragon-head many families attach a small strip of unmarked red cloth to their outside gates – a simple action which is said *both* to attract good fortune to a home and to protect it from evil spirits and influences. At some homes, Daoist charms (*fu*) are displayed above doorways throughout the year, with a similar intention: to invite in good spirits and (explicitly) to curse away demons. Some families also hang from their portals small home-made charms of brightly coloured thread, which are widely made to celebrate *duanwujie* (the 'dragon boat festival'). These charms, which are usually intended to protect children from harm, when hung above doors serve as all-purpose good-luck tokens, and as ways of *deflecting* spiritual risks.

I might note that during *duanwujie*, branches from medicinal plants are also hung over most household doorways. This practice (which is often now described as a traditional 'hygenic' practice) relates to a legend in which such branches protected a village from slaughter at the hands of an invading army. I was told one version as follows:

In ancient times, during a war, some soldiers were preparing to destroy a small village. The soldiers came upon a woman with two children, one of whom was crying. They asked her if this crying child belonged to someone else, and she replied that the child's parents had died. The soldiers felt that she was a highly virtuous woman to care for this orphan, and warned her that her village was soon to be destroyed. But they said her own family would be spared if she hung certain plants over her door as a sign to the invaders. She returned to her village and immediately warned everyone else that they must take the same precautions. When the soldiers arrived, they were unable to distinguish the house of the virtuous mother from any other, and they dared not kill anyone, leaving the village in peace.

Medicinal branches, home-made charms, Daoist talismans, strips of red cloth: all of these are displayed around doors – above the new year *duilian* – and all may help to protect a household from evil (*bixie*).

In Angang, similar door-charms are displayed (especially the kind produced by Daoist masters and spirit mediums), and medicinal plants are also put over doorways during *duanwujie* as a protection against evil. But most of the doors leading into private homes are additionally protected by fearsome door-gods (*menshen*). These are normally represented by poster-images of the gods themselves – which are replicas of the large and often very beautiful images of door-gods painted by specialists on all main temple doors. Door-gods are spirit-warriors, guardians whose specific task is to provide protection for what lies inside, i.e. a family, or the temple and the gods residing in it (who in turn provide protection and prosperity to the community). Along with the armies of spiritual soldiers who always accompany deities, these door-gods are seen as important spiritual defenders of the community. As such, they receive their own offerings on a regular basis, and during major domestic and public rituals they (and their troops) will often be taken into account – through offerings made, in many cases, adjacent to the threshold itself.

The ambivalent threshold and the passage through life

In sum, doors, supplemented by talismans, medicinal plants, door-charms, and door-gods, are a protection against the evil lurking outside, a disincentive to entry. And they are simultaneously an incentive, through auspicious and welcoming charms and *duilian*, for the good which is outside to make its way in. The ancestors are welcomed in through doors, and the highest god is represented there. But doors slam shut during funerals, and charms above thresholds curse away spirits who might arrive, looking to cause harm. In these notions which relate to good and bad fortune, attention is repeatedly given to the door as a household boundary, i.e. as the clearest marker between the inside (*nei*) and the outside (*wai*) of a family home. Doors are therefore, in the end, a site of considerable ambivalence.

By way of closing this chapter, I want to discuss this ambivalent threshold with reference to the living, rather than the dead. Of course, unlike evil spirits, most 'people from outside' (*wailai de ren*) are gladly welcomed (or at least appear to be gladly welcomed) to cross the threshold into family homes. They are invited (*qing*) to enter through the front door, and this clearly represents a temporary domestic incorporation of someone from the outside (*wai*). As I've already described, while on the inside (*nei*) such guests are politely 'detained' (*liu*), although only exceptionally is it expected that they will in fact remain inside for very long. When the inevitable comes and they leave, they are escorted to the door, and often to the outside gate of the farmhouse compound, because this is the polite way to 'send off' a visitor – by walking with him to, and perhaps even beyond, the marker between inside and outside. This is certainly 'polite', but could it also be seen as way of ensuring that a guest does in fact leave? Recall that one Chinese *ideal* – expressed in the virtual sealing-off of every household for the passing of the year – is a state of reunion in which the family closes in upon itself. But every family also needs to have contact with other families, and the development of such contacts has been a central concern of all the families I've known in Dragon-head and Angang. Far from being closed in upon themselves, they have invested a great deal of energy in establishing widespread networks of friends and acquaintances; and they positively welcome guests from the outside on most occasions. But there is still a marked ambivalence about this, because it is known (and widely commented upon) that contact with the outside carries certain risks – not least because every new friendship, the production of a new 'semi-insider', implies obligation.[3]

A similar kind of ambivalence attaches to the question of what happens to people from the 'inside' when they go away. Although separation is, in theory, something which should 'never happen' in any substantive way within families, some kinds of separations are seen to be necessary or even desirable. For example, many families in modern rural China and Taiwan accept the necessity for their children to go away, at least for a while, to places where opportunities are greater. Sometimes they even express the hope that their children will 'become dragons' (chenglong) and eventually 'leap the dragon gate' (tiaolongmen): i.e. become successful by jumping over the gates which symbolically, and sometimes literally, separate the powerful from those outside. It is assumed that if this were to happen, they would then share their success, and the insider-access which accompanies it, with their own families. Making use of successful 'connections' of this kind (i.e. sharing in the success of kin, as well as friends and acquaintances) is often referred to in China as 'opening the back door' (kai houmen). (In other words, having leapt the 'dragon gate' into power, one is then, at least in theory, morally obliged to open the 'back door' to one's kin and friends.) But those who go away from home, while potential 'dragons', are also meanwhile at risk from all the bad things which may happen on the outside. For instance, they may come to physical harm (they might die and thus never return) or they may suffer financial hardship. They will inevitably develop and sustain relationships with people on the outside, some of which may be useful, but which may as well present a challenge to their standing (familial) obligations. Going away, crossing the threshold for a temporary or prolonged period of separation, is therefore understandably viewed with some ambivalence (Stafford 1995: 33–68).

In this regard – i.e. bearing in mind the observable ambivalence about the departure of children from home – it is interesting to note that the passage of children through life is itself conceived (at least in traditional terms) as the gradual process of 'crossing' (guo) through a series of dangerous gates or 'barriers': guan. As Henry Doré puts it:

Every child is destined to pass, in the early stages of its existence, through a series of [thirty] barriers, which occur either monthly or annually along the path of life. It is only when the last one has been passed, at the age of sixteen, that all danger is over. (Doré 1987: 45)

The impediments include the barrier of 'the devil's gate' (guimen guan), the barrier of 'the hundred days' (bairi guan), the barrier 'where life is shortened' (duanming guan), and twenty-seven others. But children are helped to negotiate these dangerous crossings by their families – who supply them with the ritual means to get past the series of gate-keepers. For example:

the crown of hair, fashioned on the head of children, is a passport or permit, thanks to which a child succeeds in escaping every annoyance on the part of the barrier-spirits, who molest youthful wayfarers on the road of life. (Doré 1987: 45)

It is of course interesting to compare this 'road of life' with the 'road of death' discussed in chapter three. In Chinese funerals, mourners 'send off' the deceased on a dangerous journey (a journey which importantly includes their passage through significant 'gates' or barriers of various kinds). The hope, however, is that successfully 'sent-off' ancestors will return – entering through household gates and doors – to bring blessings to their living descendants. Movement is integral to the conceptualisation of death. Similarly, children are helped along the road of life, and helped to surmount its difficulties and dangers (including the 'thirty barriers'). But the hope is that they will return – at least for symbolically important occasions – and perhaps when they do so they will even bring with them blessings and wealth for their families.

5   Commensality as reunion

In many of the specific examples I have thus far given of separation and reunion in China – for instance, the case in chapter two of the nephew who visits his father's sister, and quietly eats and drinks as his aunt strives to 'accompany' (*pei*) him – my descriptions have turned, often sooner rather than later, to the sharing of meals. Needless to say, more than food is being shared, and of course the centrality of food to Chinese culture makes it difficult, if not impossible, to discuss *any* major topic (whether kinship or religion or politics) without questions of eating and commensality coming into play (cf. Chang 1977 and Anderson 1988). Food is redundantly a central aspect of Chinese kinship symbolism: e.g. to be a family is to eat rice together, whereas to 'divide the family' (*fenjia*) is to divide the family's stove, and so on. Familial rituals of the life-cycle, perhaps especially the sending-off of the dead (*songzang*), entail food symbolism of a remarkable complexity and sophistication (cf. Thompson 1988). Local popular religion also routinely involves food-based sacrifice and commensality on a grand scale (cf. Ahern 1981; also see my discussion of the Penghu 'sending-off' in chapter three). Meanwhile, the 'art of social relationships' in China, at least in public and formal terms, is intimately linked to the arts of gift-giving (the gifts are often food) and banqueting (cf. Yan 1996 and Yang 1994). Banquets may be displays both of hierarchy and of equality (cf. J. Watson 1987), and they are, redundantly, the means by which social transitions (whether births, marriages, or new business agreements) are publicly acknowledged and effected.

Against the background of this all-pervasive food symbolism, my aim in this chapter will be to suggest that states of reunion, in China, are very often both conceptualised and experienced as states of commensality. To be 'reunited' and 'united' is to eat together, whereas the failure to eat together is not merely a symptom of 'separation', but is actually constitutive of it. (By extension, I might note, the failure to eat is taken as an expression of separation: the idiom 'hanging garments' – *yi dai jian kuan* – indicates the weight one loses through missing someone who is absent.) In short, commensality *is* reunion, and this fact has important implications for the central concerns of this book. For as I'll explain below, food is a fundamental element in two key systems of reciprocity – what I call the cycles of *yang* and *laiwang* – through which relatedness with kin and friends is both manifested and produced in China. These cycles, in turn, provide the underlying context within which the separation constraint is actually experienced by people in Angang and Dragon-head. In the next chapter, I'll argue that an appreciation of the workings of these two cycles, saturated as they are with food symbolism, gives us a new perspective on Chinese gender relations, one *not* afforded by Confucian and patrilineal ideologies. Through their hard work in the cycles of *yang* and *laiwang* (importantly including work towards the production of reunion commensality) women can be said to produce certain forms of Chinese relatedness. Perhaps contrary to expectations, this unquestionably gives them a central, indeed pivotal, role in the Chinese separation and reunion matrix.

Some foods of separation and reunion

Given the complexity of Chinese ideas about food, it is hardly surprising that foods should 'say something' about moments of parting and return. In some cases, this relates less to the food itself, than to what the *words* for certain foods sound like. It is said, for instance, that friends should avoid eating pears at a moment of parting, because the expression for 'dividing a pear' (*fenli*) sounds like one of the expressions for 'separating' (*fenli*). In other cases, the point is not the name of the food, as such, but rather what consuming it is taken to mean. For example, on their wedding days brides consume (along with many other symbolically significant foods) *liniangrou*, literally 'leaving-mother meat'. This is so they 'will not miss their mothers' (*bu hui xiang mama*) when they go to live with their husbands and parents-in-law. In various ways, then, ideas about food and feeding intersect with ideas about separation and reunion.

Two important examples of this are found in popular ideas about dumplings (*jiaozi*) and noodles (*miantiao*). When people in north China go away on a journey or arrive from one, these are the two foods which are most commonly shared with them. In Dragon-head I was told – although some people said this the other way around! – 'When sending-off, eat noodles; when greeting the wind, eat dumplings' (*songxing chi mian, jiefeng chi jiaozi*). That is, noodles (*miantiao*) should, at least in theory, be served to those who are departing on a journey, and dumplings (*jiaozi*) served to those who are arriving from one (i.e. when 'greeting the wind'). People point out that long and thin noodles 'represent' (*daibiao*) a peaceful journey, a 'road without problems' (*yilu pingan*), and that they more generally symbolise the unfolding of events in a smooth and untroubled way (*shunli*).

Long unbroken noodles also commonly represent, and are said to help ensure, 'long life' (*changshou*), and they are thus an all-purpose auspicious food. In these senses, noodles are a good thing for departing travellers to eat. But some people also serve them to arriving guests, because, well, they represent 'a smooth arrival'!

Dumplings (*jiaozi*) similarly serve as an all-purpose auspicious food, and people sometimes point out that the character *jiao* sounds the same as the first character in *jiaoxing*, 'lucky'. But because of their round shape, and because they must be rolled up, dumplings are more specifically said to represent reunion (*tuanyuan*). They are commonly fed to guests (and, in north China at least, to ancestors) upon arrival, i.e. at moments of return. But they are also often served at moments of *departure*. The explanation given to me for this is that dumplings, in the context of separation, stand for the *next* reunion, i.e. a future meeting, in advance. The considerable symbolic significance attached to dumplings, in some ways a rather humble food, is related in part to the way in which they are made (cf. Watson 1987: 398 fn.18). They are almost always produced by groups of friends and relatives in a time-consuming and sociable process which repeatedly suggests 'roundness' and 'completion' – and, by extension, 'reunion'. During this process, a large round ball of rice-flour is rolled out and cut into smaller round shapes, which are then wrapped around round pieces of filling, placed on a round bamboo tray, dumped into a round pot of boiling water, and then, finally, shared by a circle of people (who are usually sitting around a round table). During the new year, the outcome of this process of 'completion' of the dumplings is itself said to reflect family fortunes.[1] As I mentioned earlier in my account of the new year festival, most families also hide special 'auspicious' objects in their new year's eve *jiaozi*. The most common object is a small coin, and it is said that the person who ends up with the coin will 'strike it rich' (*facai*) in the coming year – or at least that they will have 'blessings' (*fu*) and 'encounter good fortune' (*zou haoyun*).

Reunion as commensality

Again: considerable importance is attached in North China to dumplings – a food which importantly 'symbolises reunion', and which is eaten at the key 'turning' point in the Chinese lunar calendar (i.e. on *chuxi*, new year's eve). And drawing in part, I would suggest, on the symbolism of this fundamental new year's eve reunion meal, *all* reunions in China are conceptualised as moments of commensality. To put this the other way around: a moment of commensality is always, by association with *chuxi*, a moment of reunion. The point I wish to stress is therefore not so much the symbolism of any food of reunion in particular, but rather the symbolism of eating together in general.

This symbolism holds both for the living and for the dead. Earlier I noted that 'greeting' (*jie*) and 'sending-off' (*song*) guests is often less important than the actual process of spending time together with them, and this usually implies being together for a 'reunion meal' (*tuanyuan fan*), as well as some form of subsequent entertainment or 'playing' (*wanr*). The meal which follows an arrival is what primarily constitutes the manner of 'greeting', and is the event to which guests will normally have been invited (*qing*). By contrast, as I pointed out, the exact moment of arrival and departure of spirits is usually highly elaborated (i.e. when they are literally 'greeted', *jie*, and 'sent on their way', *song*), whereas the period of being together with them often does not seem to provoke much explicit comment or obvious activity. But such a contrast is ultimately misleading, because spirits must also eat and be entertained, and they often 'join together' with humans – in extended moments of reunion – in order to do so.

This is most obvious in the case of meals shared between ancestors and their descendants, while it is perhaps less obvious in the offerings made to deities. But it should be noted that virtually all such offerings to spirits include 'food' of some kind – minimally the 'fragrance' (*xiang*) of incense which is consumed by spirits. For the duration of their residence in any community, spirits can expect to be given periodic, and sometimes very elaborate, offerings of food. Such offerings to gods are then typically redistributed and 'consumed' in some form by the communities which provided them in the first place (e.g. meat from collectively produced and sacrificed pigs is normally divided and eaten up by local people at the end of a religious festival). In other words, a form of sharing and reunion commensality takes place here as well. Out of deference, reunion commensality with spirits is normally indirect – humans only 'dare' (*gan*) to eat once the gods have already eaten their fill – but it is certainly a routine occurrence.

The aesthetics of commensality

If reunions both with the living and the dead are importantly conceptualised as moments of commensality, then it follows (given the significance in China of reunion itself) that considerable attention will be given to the forms which commensality takes. And indeed the Chinese aesthetics of food and of banqueting have been elaborated and developed to an exceptionally high degree. This extends to the behaviour of diners, and depending on the relationships between those attending any particular meal, such behaviour may change dramatically.

In chapter one, for instance, I described a cycle of reunion banquets which occupied seven sisters and their families. I noted that the sisters' husbands engaged together in the classic (semi-ritualised) forms of behaviour which are expected of men on such public occasions. This included the characteristic show of modesty by the host of any particular day's meal, who usually apologised repeatedly for the conditions of his home, and for the poor quality of the food he could provide. The brothers-in-law in attendance would then eat, and be under pressure to eat, large quantities of this supposedly 'sub-standard' food. They would drink large *and equal* quantities of alcohol, preferably powerful rice wine (drinking beer doesn't 'mean' as much). They would utter, during the meal, some of the formulaic phrases which are often heard on such occasions (although, of course, they also improvised around them). In particular they would say, in some form, that if any of them had difficulties (*kunan*) in the future, they would certainly be able to rely on the others for help. And they would then arrange, before any particular meal was allowed to come to an end, a future reunion meal.

During such banquets it is often said that the occasion of a particular get-together is 'rare' or *nande*, literally 'hard to achieve'. And when a reunion banquet genuinely *is* 'hard to achieve', or when a banquet is held in order to send someone off for a very long time, the point will be made repeatedly that people do not know when, or if, they will manage to meet again. They stress, in other words, the poignancy of the moment of reunion commensality. Everyone knows that it can't last forever, for 'every banquet must end' (*tianxia meiyou busan de yanxi*)[2] – they all end with a 'dispersal' (*san*).

But banquets of this kind *can* sometimes go on for a very long time indeed (many hours), and they often involve an exhausting and more or less non-stop public 'performance' (*jiemu*). It is hardly surprising, then, that many people think of them as rather hard work, in spite of the fact that they are meant to be happy (and/or poignant) occasions. In fact, many people dislike the whole business. A man once turned to me as we sat down together at the banquet table and said with a grimace, 'Time to start work again!' (*zai kaishi gongzuo*). The problem is that to refuse to participate fully in such a meal is to *reject* relatedness. I was told that eating or drinking only a small amount wasn't sufficient, that it wouldn't be 'enough to mean something' (*bu gou yisi*). But exactly what is it supposed to mean? In chapter two, I noted that the 'greeting' and 'sending-off' of honoured guests may be very elaborate, and that this is seen as a way of showing that a particular relationship is highly valued. However, in the case of the relationships which are arguably the *most* highly valued, greetings and sendings-off may be abrupt or simply pass in silence. Similarly, sharing food with guests is a way of showing that certain relationships are important, but this arguably takes place when such a thing *needs* to be shown, and where eating/drinking together can show it. In other words, classic 'banquet behaviour' is taken to extremes in certain situations, and often precisely in those cases where the support of those around the table for each other cannot entirely be taken for granted.

The contrast should, in theory, be seen in meals held between *brothers*. I attended several of these, or at least thought that I had done so, in Dragon-head. Such nominally 'brotherly' events can also be boisterous (especially those held at the beginning of the new year), but at most times they are subdued and low-key precisely because it is not seen to be necessary for close relatives to make a big show for each other during meals. On one such occasion, for example, I was specifically told that the drinking would not be forced, because 'We're all brothers, it isn't a big thing' (*women dou xiongdi, meiyou shi*). I was advised not to worry about eating or drinking more than I cared to, because 'Today there's no big performance' (*jintian meiyou jiemu*). In my recollection, this very pleasant meal, in which friendly affection was shown between the men in attendance, reflected the understated *certainty* of brotherly connections. However, on checking my notes more carefully I realised that those in attendance were in fact *not* brothers. Or rather, while three of them were, the other three were not – one was a brother-in-law, one a neighbour, and I was the sixth diner. The point, I think, for those in attendance was that close friendship allowed them to eat together 'in the fashion of brothers', i.e. without overblown and frankly tiresome displays of closeness.

This example takes us back to general questions of etiquette and aesthetics: what are the polite ways of dealing with partings and returns, and with the meals which symbolise reunion? And here there can be no simple answer, because by the time they reach adulthood, most people in China are genuine experts in these matters. It is moreover acknowledged that some individuals are true masters of the banqueting art. They know the aesthetics, including the aesthetics of the emotions associated with these contexts, very well. Perhaps the most difficult thing to convey, in this explicitly performative context, is sincerity, because it is well-known that the language of politeness (*keqihua*) – no matter how smoothly delivered – is often completely 'empty' (*kong*). For example, people may use, in the presence both of close friends *and* total strangers, the language of kinship to accompany a meal. They say 'treat us as your own family' (*gen ziji jia yiyang*), or 'we're all the same family' (*yijiaren*), or 'we're all brothers' (*dou xiongdi*), or 'don't behave like a guest' (*bu keqi*). But depending on context, and on the style in which such words were delivered, they might have very different meanings. They might be read as signs of the genuine closeness of good friends, or as knowingly stylised displays of politeness for absolute outsiders.

The cycle of laiwang

Having discussed reunion commensality and aesthetics in general terms, I now want to turn more specifically to the role of food in the production of relatedness. Here it will help to think of two ways in which kin and non-kin relationships are popularly conceptualised in China, the first of which I have referred to as the 'cycle of *laiwang*' (cf. my discussion in Stafford 2000). Note that in the anthropological literature, this cycle has often been discussed in relation to the issue of *guanxi*, i.e. the production of 'social connections' through gifts, favours, and banquets (again, see Yan 1996 and Yang 1994). The term *laiwang* – literally 'come and go' – is used to describe the movement back and forth of people who have a non-kin relationship of mutual assistance and (usually) friendship. People make comments such as 'I have *laiwang* with him', *wo gen ta you laiwang*, and this roughly means 'we go back and forth, helping each other'. The people with whom one has significant *laiwang* would certainly be seen or visited, if at all possible, during the period of 'stringing together doors'. And more generally, the idea of having such a relationship, and sustaining it, is closely tied to the reciprocal obligations which are part of 'ritual/etiquette', *li*. Someone with whom you have *laiwang* is very likely, in the countryside at least, to be someone you could count on not only to 'help you out' in general, but also to participate in your family's important ritual occasions.

The saying has it that *li shang wang lai*: 'courtesy demands reciprocity'. An alternative, and arguably more accurate, translation of this would be 'ceremonial (*li*) generates back-and-forth (*wang lai*)'. Just as having a relationship of mutual assistance implies attending and helping out with important ritual occasions, attending these important occasions implies having a relationship of mutual assistance. In Dragon-head, as elsewhere, these occasions include weddings, funerals, the celebrations which follow childbirth, and the building of new houses. Strictly speaking, the building of a new house is not a matter of *li*, but it is certainly a matter for reciprocal support, and is clearly part of the economy of *laiwang*. And the economic dimension is not at all secondary. For all of these 'ritual occasions' are decidedly (and sometimes phenomenally) expensive affairs, and they almost inevitably require collective assistance if they are to be dealt with properly. It is also the case that in all of these occasions of *li*, even including funerals and house-building, food and commensality are central concerns.

This much is well-known, and well-documented in the literature. But here I would like to stress that many of the occasions of *li*, in which relationships of *laiwang* are expressed – (including, by definition, their expression through moments of commensality) – involve some form of 'sending-off' and 'greeting'. 'Attending the ceremonial' (*ganli* or *suili*) as an expression of *laiwang* is therefore also a way of collectively meeting the expense of *properly* handling certain crucially important separations and reunions: the greeting of a new bride and of new affines (*yingqin*), the sending-off of a daughter to her new family (*songqin*), the reception into the community of a new child, the sending-off of the family deceased (*songzang*), and so on. On most such occasions, the community of support 'comes together' (*tuanjie*) to eat, in a moment of reunion commensality, through which they are *realised* as a community, before dispersing yet again. (Only in the case of funeral commensality is neighbourly participation normally restricted; but the community still underwrites the expenses.)

Of course, the extent to which people who say they have relations of *laiwang* with others actually *do* provide each other with mutual assistance varies considerably. The expression 'I have *laiwang* with him' is sometimes used to brag about would-be connections to people of influence. And even when ties of *laiwang* are realised, many people think of them as problematic. They often note, for example, the burden which 'attending the ceremonials' entails (specifically the burden of having neighbours repeatedly 'take money', *naqian*, for ritual occasions). Elsewhere I have given the example of an elderly man in Dragon-head who grudgingly attended a local wedding banquet and made a contribution – the smallest amount possible – to help the host family defray wedding-related expenses (Stafford 2000). Given his cynical view of the proceedings (which he saw as overblown, and almost certain to bring financial ruin down upon the family in question), I asked the man why he bothered to attend. He said that when he had recently been forced to build a new home (because of the imminent collapse of his old one), the father of the groom had given some help, as had many other friends and relatives. It was only right that he should therefore 'attend the ceremonial' (*ganli*) held by this man, thus helping his neighbour to pay for a wedding banquet which would be 'good-looking' enough for his new affines. While these two men did have a relationship of *laiwang*, it was clearly not a particularly intense or important one. And yet they would both have acknowledged that neighbourly support, of the kind they provided to each other, was an absolutely essential element of life in Dragon-head. To put this differently: although they might have wished to distance (or separate) themselves from their mutual obligations, instead they participated – however unenthusiastically – in the reunion commensality which marked the key moments of separation and reunion in the lives of their respective families.

In Angang, people are similarly expected to help each other out with family rituals, but here the mutual support importantly extends to collective religious rituals of separation and reunion. When private households (and also local temples) must undertake some elaborate ritual event – for example the celebration of a god's birthday, or the mounting of the *kng put* ritual (discussed in chapter three) – many people in the community will give support in the form of participation and/or cash gifts. Because such occasions share with funerals and weddings the characteristic of being expensive and complicated, people *need* help in order to be able to mount them. Donations given are dutifully recorded, and ritual accounts, which specify the exact amounts donated, are prominently displayed throughout the event. As I have already explained, this process of giving and participating relates to a circular logic in which the god's power (*ling*) is produced through the collective efforts of devotees. By making offerings, and by participating in rituals, devotees not only show that a deity is strong, they *make* him strong. The strong god thereafter provides protection for all his devotees.

This process extends directly to offerings of food. (Indeed, I was always struck by the extent to which preparations for large-scale rituals in Angang centred directly on the matter of food.) People individually and collectively give food offerings, the fragrance (*xiang*) of which is 'consumed' by the god. I should stress that the gods are actually in part *attracted* to particular communities by this very possibility. But in many cases these attractive offerings are then redistributed among devotees themselves – sometimes in banquet-style, sometimes in the form of an individual portioning-out – for immediate re-consumption (a process which is said to give them *pingan*, the 'absence of problems'). Note that this is obviously a way of achieving indirect commensality with the god, but it is also another form of collective commensality. Both the symbolism of food, and the idioms of separation and reunion, are immanent in the logical structure of such events: we collectively 'greet', 'detain', and 'send-off' the gods, and do so importantly through offerings of food, which *we* then collectively share in our (human) moments of commensality (again, cf. Ahern 1981b).

Hopefully this brief discussion will serve to highlight that the cycle of *laiwang*, a very commonly held way of conceptualising non-kin relationships, has implications not only for the discussion of commensality, but also for the discussion of separation and reunion. I would suggest that a very intense relationship of *laiwang* – i.e. one involving very frequent 'back and forth' and frequent mutual assistance – may obviate the need for display, because the relationship becomes mostly taken for granted. But there is another way of saying this. If the 'back and forth' between two people becomes very frequent, then this may also (quite literally) mean that their moments of separation and reunion, and of reunion commensality, become more frequent – by definition – and therefore that they require less elaboration. These moments become rather like the 'partings' and 'returns' involving people who live together throughout the year, or who eat together every day – in some senses rather unremarkable. And yet this everyday commensality has profound implications: it *makes* people be related, and for those who have eaten together often, reunion becomes virtually inevitable.

The cycle of *yang*

Here it helps to think briefly about a second (arguably much more fundamental) cycle, the cycle of *yang*, which centres primarily on the relationship between parents and children. (I have discussed this more fully in Stafford 1995:79–111 and Stafford 2000.) The cycle of *yang* (which means 'to raise/nurture') is a very involving system of mutual obligations between parents and children, and it centrally entails the provision and sharing of money and food. Parents *yang* their children, by providing them with housing, clothing, food, financial support, emotional inclusion, and 'education' (*jiaoyu*) of some kind. Parents should also see that their children are properly married. They can then expect to receive 'respectful support' (*fengyang* or *shanyang*) back from their children in old age, support which is again given partly in the form of money and food, but which also entails emotional and ritual inclusion, and other things as well. Upon death, they will, in theory, continue to receive 'money' and 'food' from their descendants via ancestral rituals. This cycle of *yang*, I would argue, rather than patrilineal connections, as such, is what makes people be related, i.e. it is what *produces* relatedness (not least through repeated commensality). I say it produces relatedness because in the absence of a 'true' kinship tie, the provision of *yang* can make people have all the obligations of kinship; whereas the failure of *yang*, in the presence of a 'natural' kinship tie, can lead to this tie being cut (Stafford 2000).

I should stress that this is only the merest outline of a very intricate and highly variable system. But the reciprocal obligations between the generations implied by the cycle of *yang* are seen in China to be absolutely fundamental and taken for granted, and in most contexts they do not require stating. Certainly parents and children do not need to engage in rowdy banquets with each other in order to display their loyalty, and in fact it is generally considered disrespectful for children to even 'dare' to eat with their parents on formal occasions. But this does not mean that food is unimportant in defining their relationships, and on the contrary it is central to this definition. In everyday terms, the slow building up of *yang* obligations is virtually indistinguishable from the provision of daily food. (The written character for *yang* notably contains the 'food' radical.) And in terms of special occasions, the key moments of ritual reunion between generations are also importantly defined in relation to food. The fact of the development of *yang* relationships over periods of many years – centrally through commensality – means that the ties binding generations within a family together are meant to be, and quite often in fact are, beyond question. This is certainly part of the background against which moments of parting and return involving close relatives may be dealt with simply or silently.[3]

In concluding this chapter, and in reflecting on commensality in the cycles of *yang* and *laiwang*, I want to return to the matters which will frame my concerns in the next two chapters: agency and historical consciousness in relation to processes of separation and reunion. Most of the key public moments of separation and reunion in one's life – e.g. reunions during the lunar new year and other festivals, those found in weddings, funerals, and religious rituals – are carried out either with, or with the assistance of, the people with whom one is fully implicated through cycles of *yang* and *laiwang*. In other words, these moments of separation and reunion help define one's place in an historical community. Simultaneously, it usually seems – at least on the surface – that the *public* agents of separation and reunion are men: they generally 'represent' (*daibiao*) the family in the most public moments of parting and return. But to say this is to ignore the constitutive roles women play in the cycles of *yang* and *laiwang*, i.e. the cycles which stand behind virtually all public processes of separation and reunion in China, and which arguably comprise the popular Chinese model of human relatedness.

6 Women and the obligation to return

Thus far in my account – and hopefully not too unwisely – I've largely deferred the direct consideration of gender, preferring to focus on it once readers had become familiar, through reading descriptions of processes related to separation and reunion, with the basic outlines of my approach. The danger with this strategy, of course, is that it may appear to make gender somehow *less* than basic to my concerns. But a consideration of the impact of separation and reunion on Chinese historical consciousness is inconceivable without a simultaneous consideration of gender. For almost all of the public processes associated with separation and reunion involve roles which are at least superficially, and often fundamentally, different for women and for men. (For anthropological discussions of gender in China see e.g. M. Wolf 1968 and 1972, Martin 1988, Judd 1994, Gates 1996, Bray 1997.) In what follows, I'll consider three possible evaluations of this difference in participation. In the first, processes of separation (e.g. ancestral reunions) are seen, quite simply, as the province of men. In the second, women are seen to participate, but usually in ways which are either behind-the-scenes or strikingly ambivalent (e.g. in wedding separations). However in the third evaluation, and for reasons I'll spell out below, women are seen to be at the heart of the Chinese separation and reunion matrix: they produce, in short, the emotional attachments which *compel* reunions of various kinds.

Men as the public agents of separation and reunion

Let me return briefly to the subject of the last chapter: reunion commensality. One morning during the period of 'stringing together doors' in Dragonhead, I spent time in the smoke-filled kitchen of Old Yang's home. Here his wife was hard at work, producing a meal for the day's guests. The guests, of course, were in the main *kang*-room – visiting, playing cards and *majiang*, smoking cigarettes, and generally relaxing. Although Old Yang is well-off by local standards, he lives quite modestly, not least because he is a cadre, and there would be no question of hiring outside help for such occasions.

110

(This had only been done for the weddings of his sons.) Instead it normally falls on Mrs Yang, with some intermittent help from her daughter, daughter-in-law, and sons, to shoulder the load, and much of it is very tiring and physical work. It implies spending hours every day bent over the wood-burning stove, either feeding the flame with firewood at ground level, or leaning over to stir food within the rounded cooking pan above. While sitting with her in the kitchen during this, I stated the obvious: that she was having to do a great deal of hard work. She pointed towards the *kang*-room to her left and said with a laugh: 'They're waiting, I'm working – that's the way it is. The women get worn out, while the men sit around and wait!'[1] Mrs Yang eventually joined the guests, briefly ate with them, and even shared a token glass of beer; but her role on those days was primarily behind-the-scenes, while her husband, as the 'household head' (*jiazhang*), represented the family out front.

The position of men as household heads or 'representatives' (*daibiao*) is perhaps illustrated even more clearly in the case I have given of the reunion banquets held for the families of seven sisters (cf. chapters one and five). As I noted, the relationship between these families was explicitly defined in terms of the siblingship of seven women. But when it came to the reunion banquets themselves, the *husbands* of the sisters were the key players. The men sat at the table of honour, the men ate and drank in unison, the men engaged in the speech-making which serves to solidify relations between families, and the men arranged the ongoing sequence of reunion banquets until it reached its conclusion. In short, the men, as 'household heads', were family representatives even during banquets which celebrated the connections between their wives, who were sisters. Meanwhile, the sisters them-selves – that is, excluding the ones preparing food on any given day – ate off to the side, usually much more quietly and quickly, before carrying on with their own visiting and games.

In the last chapter, I argued that reunion in China is conflated with commensality, and to this could be added that the commensality which is publicly elaborated and celebrated is largely, although not entirely, that between men. It follows from this that women's direct experience of reunion commensality is significantly different from the experience of men. Indeed, as soon as one begins to consider various manifestations of separation and reunion from the perspective of gender, this difference is repeated time and again. For example, in the new year offerings made at the burial mounds behind Old Yang's home, the participants were all young men: in this celebration of patrilineal continuity, there would be no question of sending a daughter or other woman to do the job. Women *do* participate in the new year ancestral reunion in various ways, but one of its crucial events – the 'invitation' extended for the spirits to emerge from their graves – is something that Old Yang's wife, daughter, and daughter-in-law will never even have seen.

In Angang, men also bear primary responsibility for 'inviting' (*qing*), 'greeting' (*jie*), and 'sending-off' (*song*) the ancestors, and they are normally the ones who have the most direct contact with gods on important ritual occasions (including rituals of 'greeting' and 'sending-off'). That is, whereas women are often responsible for everyday worship in homes and temples and spirit-medium altars, men will normally take the leading roles in rituals such as the *kng put*, or in major celebratory festivals. But this can be put even more strongly: women should, at least in theory, be *excluded* from the most direct and most important contact with gods and ancestors.[2] The primary justification for this is that women are 'unclean' (by virtue of menstruation and childbirth) and therefore unworthy to touch divine images and representations (cf. Ahern 1975, Seaman 1981). While men are periodically also 'unclean' through contact with death pollution, this problem is not seen to be an ongoing and everyday one, and most of the time they are free to take on the most important ritual obligations.

On a more everyday level in Dragon-head, the same pattern of gender-bias repeats itself – or at least appears to do so. Men are generally presumed to be the ones who deal with 'the outside' and make connections to it, while women are presumed (in spite of dramatic changes in the roles and statuses of rural Chinese women) to still be the ones who mostly deal with 'the inside' (*nei*), and whose duty it is to manage affairs of the hearth. This remains true even when women work on the outside. A man working away from the community (e.g. in a factory) is often expected to make useful connections for his family (in part through cycles of reunion commensality with his friends and colleagues), but there is a lower expectation of this when women work outside. And within the community itself, when some matter needs to be dealt with, it is normally men who will go to *formally* visit other men in order to sort things out. By definition, it thus falls to men to do most of the 'greeting' and 'sending-off' of local visitors. The same holds for honoured guests from the outside. When such an outsider (usually, and almost by definition, a man) arrives for a visit, men will normally take the lead in making polite statements and in hosting the meals which celebrate states of reunion with them.

In Angang, there is a considerable circulation of people throughout the community on a daily basis, especially in the evenings, as families (often including men, women and children) visit each other. But I was told by young women that their fathers and mothers would not allow them to go around visiting on their own because it is deemed inappropriate for a young woman to do such a thing. One woman told me that her father would be unhappy if she even went out at all in the evening, and more specifically that he would become angry (*shengqi*) if she ate at the homes of other people. By contrast, this is precisely what young men are *meant* to do – at least some of the time – with the result that they soon become experts at the little rituals of parting and return, including moments of reunion commensality, and at the small talk which accompanies them (Stafford 1995: 100–4).

Can women be agents of separation and reunion?

If these examples (and more could be given) are considered together – participation in public banquets, in key religious observances, in the purposeful 'visiting' of useful connections, and in the more everyday 'back and forth' between neighbours and friends – one striking conclusion begins to emerge, or at least appears to do so. This is that men are the primary agents of separation and reunion in China, while women participate only secondarily, and sometimes not at all.

Of course, it could be said that in the popular logic of separation and reunion, *families* (and sometimes *communities*) – rather than individual men or women – are the basic units of separation and reunion, and women may therefore be said to 'participate' as fully as men. And while this popular logic may well only show the effectiveness of kinship and gender ideologies in China, it is undoubtedly very widely held. That is, when a man goes to the ancestral graves in order to invite them home for a reunion, he does so not as an individual but on behalf of his entire family. When men organise rituals to send off gods, they do so on behalf of entire families and communities (and sometimes, as it happens, under the instructions of local women). When men share banquets together, thus cementing particular kinds of relationships, it is often assumed that each participant acts, ultimately, on behalf of his family.[3] Women may, of course, be highly ambivalent about these 'family' processes which are transacted by men 'on their behalf' – and some of which imply women's subordination at every turn. But in my experience (i.e. my experience in Angang and Dragon-head) they are usually no more so than men themselves. In any case, from this perspective it is 'obvious' and taken for granted that men are *family* representatives during most public process of separation and reunion.

It is also taken for granted that women will participate in various ways behind the scenes in such male-dominated affairs. Women bear a considerable responsibility, to provide the obvious example, in relation to food.

Returning to Mrs Yang's comment about new year visits ('They're waiting, I'm working!'), nobody doubts that women play an important role in reunion commensality through regularly producing the meals which are eaten by men, and through preparing the food offerings which are presented to gods and ancestors. In a context in which singular attention is given to eating and commensality as a way of producing relatedness, the way in which food is constituted could hardly be a trivial matter (see Bray 1997: 107–14). And yet, compared to the grandiose participation of men, this (and other behind-the-scenes and everyday efforts) will undoubtedly *seem* rather trivial, and perhaps only serve to underline women's secondary status.[4]

However, if we look more carefully at the participation of women in Chinese processes of separation and reunion, a different sort of picture begins to emerge: one in which they *do* in fact have important formal roles, but ones which are sometimes strikingly ambivalent.[5] For example, although 'sons' rather than 'daughters' are expected to be the chief mourners in traditional Chinese funerals, women are nevertheless very important participants in most funerary 'sendings-off' (*songzang*). But how should we evaluate their participation? James Watson has shown, for instance, that in Cantonese funerals one special duty of women (as daughters-in-law) is precisely to absorb death pollution from the corpse, in theory a highly degrading and dangerous activity (J. Watson 1982). This taking on of pollution may also, however, be interpreted as a way of channelling ancestral fertility directly into the production of an obviously necessary and highly valued thing: future descendants for a patriline. In turn, the woman who can actually bring these descendants into being – a married-in daughter-in-law, i.e. precisely the woman who takes on pollution during the funerary sending-off – is seen as both necessary and problematic. For this reason, a similar kind of ambivalence is manifested in women's participation in their own weddings, a crucial 'separation' which I will discuss at more length in the next section.

Sending-off and greeting the bride

In the rites of marriage . . . what is crucial is *physical movement*, symbolized above all in the transfer of the bride but realized also in the many comings and goings between the two houses that both precede and follow the central event. Space is now of the essence.   Maurice Freedman[6]

As is well known, women in patrilineal, virilocal China are said to 'marry out' (*chujia*). That is, after marriage they are meant to stay with the families of their husbands – who are said in this way to have 'obtained' them (*qu*) –

for the remainder of their lives (for discussions of marriage in China see Watson and Ebrey 1991; R. Watson 1985: 118–36). Not surprisingly then, the rites of marriage focus importantly on the removal of the bride from her natal home, and the main activity of the wedding itself consists primarily of a process of literal separation. Prior to or on the morning of the wedding day, the groom, along with his representatives, makes a journey away from his own home (usually the home of his parents) and towards the home of his fiancee's parents. This is called *yingqin*, 'receiving the bride' (literally 'receiving/greeting kin'). Once the groom has arrived, rituals of parting and separation take place during which the bride is meant, ideally, to show distress at the prospect of her imminent departure from her childhood surroundings, and more specifically from her parents and siblings.[7] Together they eat a meal of dumplings (to represent future affinal reunions) and, as mentioned earlier, the bride eats *liniangrou*, 'leaving- mother meat', so that she 'will not miss her mother' in the coming days. But as she leaves, the fact that she is, indeed, going away is repeatedly underlined. (In some places, water is poured onto the ground to symbolise the unrecoverability of a married-out daughter.)

Then the groom (together with his representatives), and the bride (together with her parents and other relatives, in some cases a great many of them), make the journey *back* to the groom's parent's home. This is called *songqin*, i.e. 'escorting the bride to the groom's family' (literally 'sending-off kin'). Freedman remarks of this practice:

if the villages [of the bride and groom] are close, or the wedding one of people who live as neighbors in a town, the procession takes a circuitous route; for the phase of transition must be well marked by duration. The phase is highly dangerous *and* it must not be cut short. (Freedman 1979: 266)

On arrival, the bride and groom are initially greeted (*jie*) in the way they were sent off by her natal community: with great bursts of firecrackers which resound throughout the countryside. In fact, the bride's entry to her new home is normally at first *blocked* by men holding long strings of firecrackers on poles – an ambivalent welcome which is meant to reflect the potential dangers of incorporating a new outsider. (Bear in mind, as well, that any journey-like ritual – e.g. an ancestral return, a *kng put*, a spirit medium possession – is potentially dangerous.) The bride and groom then eat special 'long-life noodles' (a food of greeting), and the hierarchy of generations is subsequently acknowledged through respectful bows in front of the ancestors and elders, who have been summoned to the occasion.

Following this, a great banquet is held for both sets of relatives and for their neighbours, friends and acquaintances (often numbering into the hundreds). Indeed, from the point of view of the majority of invited participants (who may not observe the small family rituals) the meal is the primary point of the occasion. It is obviously intended as a celebration of affinity and of the wedding itself, but I want to stress that it is, more simply and perhaps more significantly, a way of 'greeting' the new affines – who have, after all, *arrived* from a journey – in style. During the wedding banquet, the guests of highest honour are precisely these arriving outsiders, and specifically the senior relatives of the bride, who normally eat inside the house, while the groom's own parents humbly eat outside, sometimes even standing up on the furthest fringes of the celebration. But the quality of the meal and the number of guests are both taken as reflections of the status of the groom's family and community, and for this reason people will stretch their resources to breaking point in order to ensure a grand affair. After the meal, the bride's relatives depart, obviously leaving her behind, and the main business of the day – the separation of the bride from her natal home – has been accomplished.

Weddings are the prototypical joyous and auspicious event in China, and may thus appear to be the clearest example of the 'positive' participation of women in Chinese processes of separation and reunion. However, I should stress that brides may also be seen (especially in terms of traditional patrilineal ideology) as relatively passive agents during their own wedding-separations. Most of the key arrangements for weddings are typically handled by parents (who normally pay for the proceedings), and what is arguably celebrated on the day itself is not the tie between bride and groom, as such, but rather the new affinal link between two patrilineal groups. It should also be noted that wedding rituals – although happy events – serve as well to highlight the ambivalent position of 'out-marrying' women within Chinese patrilineal kinship. As Freedman puts it, weddings are occasions of both 'danger and joy', during which a bride's status as a 'necessary stranger' is symbolically marked (1979: 267).

Women and the separation constraint

But the seeming lack of agency women have with respect to their own weddings may be put in even stronger terms, for marriage-separations could be said to take place (or at least could be said to have *taken* place in the past) completely against the wishes of the bride. From the point of view of the bride's family, and in terms of strong patrilineal ideologies, this 'going out of the door', this 'sending-off' of an irrelevance and a burden, may even be seen – at least in theory[8] – as a perfectly good thing, whatever the bride may think. 'Bridal laments', previously sung by out-marrying daughters in certain parts of China, appear to have captured this sense very well:

Your enemy goes out from your dragon door
You will feel lucky when I am away.[9]

Elizabeth Johnson has studied lyrics of this kind extensively, and (drawing on the work of Fred Blake) she draws attention to the ways in which bridal laments – saturated as they are by images of separation and loss – closely parallel funeral laments also formerly sung by women in some parts of China. As she notes:

> The correspondence is appropriate, for the themes of the bridal laments are the injustices inflicted upon the singer by her parents and the matchmaker, the impending loss of her family and lineage sisters, and the misery she anticipates at the hands of her husband's family. The analogy of the wedding process with death is made explicit: the bride describes herself as being prepared for death, and the wedding process as the crossing of the yellow river that is the boundary between this life and the next. (Johnson 1988: 139; cf. Blake 1978, Johnson 1999, Martin 1988)

In the Hakka communities studied by Johnson, a bride being transported to her new home was said to emit the same highly dangerous 'killing airs' which are emitted by a corpse (Johnson 1999).

Drawing in part on material of this kind, Emily Martin has suggested that the perspectives of women on the key processes of life and death – as seen especially via their participation in weddings and funerals – may differ in important respects from those of men (Martin 1988). With respect to separation, this seems obviously true in one important sense: in classical patrilineal kinship, Chinese women (unlike men) face an explicit process of separation from their natal families, and one which can be, and in fact sometimes is, explicitly equated with the separation process of death. In other words, although of course both men and women die, and must inevitably confront the 'separation of death' from loved ones, for women the link of this to the 'separation of the living' is clearly and very dramatically illustrated in the context of their own marriages. Indeed, in some cases, the solution of women to the problem of marriage-separation (and more generally to the problem of taking on the morally-ambiguous status of sexually-active wives) has been to resist marriage altogether. (For a recent commentary on the literature concerning Chinese marriage resistance see Gates 1996: 177–203; cf. Topley 1975.)

Chinese weddings may thus seem very strange examples of 'auspicious' separations: ones in which parents seemingly *want* to get rid of their daughters (who are useless 'enemies'), and in which daughters themselves seemingly wish they could *resist* departure altogether (weddings are seen as a kind of 'death'). With respect to this, I want briefly to mention again Sangren's recent discussion of the seemingly contradictory or 'reciprocal' desires which sons and daughters may experience within traditional Chinese family dynamics. As I noted in the Introduction, in his analysis of mythology with regard to the themes of 'autonomy' and 'recognition', Sangren suggests that Chinese sons and daughters may come to desire dramatically different things:

> Chafing under the constraints of patriarchal authority and their privileged but *unchosen* role in establishing patrilineal continuity, (at least some) Chinese sons come to desire autonomy and freedom – . . . a separation – precisely because the family system binds sons so closely. Conversely, because the Chinese family system enjoins a daughter to marry out – another, in this case obligatory, separation – daughters come to desire that which the system denies them – in other words, inclusion . . . reunion, or recognition [Sangren 1999].

In short, while sons may want a 'separation' they can't have, daughters arguably don't want the 'separation' they are obliged to take. In Sangren's terms, mythological sons and daughters thus sometimes achieve 'recognition' from their parents in reciprocal ways: sons (initially) by separating themselves from parental contact and control (i.e. by being unruly sons), and daughters (initially) by refusing to be separated (i.e. by rejecting marriage).

Of course, as Sangren stresses, the relationship of images and representations of these kinds to the everyday reality of family life is very complex indeed. Certainly, the young women I knew in Angang and Dragon-head – all of whom would understand that Chinese daughters are meant to be sad on their wedding days – almost uniformly expressed a very strong desire to get married; and their parents – all of whom would know that Chinese parents are meant to prefer sons – almost uniformly expressed great sadness at the idea of losing their daughters (in any sense). How can this be explained?

It is, I think, routinely assumed that sons are preferred in China because of the palpable benefits – economic, religious, emotional – which they may bring. Conversely, it is routinely assumed that people prefer *not* to have daughters because they do not bring such benefits: they 'marry out' and become the concern of some other family. For this reason, it is said, daughters are not well-treated, i.e. they are less well loved, and the clear 'preference' is for sons. This may be true in some senses and in some cases, but the potential emotional cost to parents of separation from their daughters, in a society which repeatedly underscores the problem of separation, must also be taken into account. To have a daughter is to endure, at least in theory, an inevitable, and painful, separation. (Note that the poignancy of separation from daughters is beautifully expressed in the great Qing novel

The Story of the Stone, which virtually all Chinese parents would be familiar with in some form, and which I will discuss in chapter eight.) The problem, in other words, is arguably not one of loving daughters too little, as the expression 'son preference' may imply, but rather of loving them too much.

In Dragon-head and Angang I constantly observed displays of love and affection towards daughters – something I had (perhaps naively) not really expected to see in patrilineal China. Of course, there might be a number of other factors which could help to explain this 'unexpected' treatment of daughters. Neither Dragon-head nor Angang are the kinds of communities in which one encounters strong lineage organisations (as opposed to loose patrilineal networks), and as a result extreme versions of patrilineal ideology are not much in evidence. The treatment of daughters in Dragon-head and Angang in the 1980s and 1990s may also reflect modern changes in women's status.[10] These have come (in both mainland China and Taiwan) with successive political and social transformations, and can be phrased partly in economic terms: now daughters tend to marry late, and meanwhile to have improved job prospects. In the years *before* marriage they may therefore be in a position to provide substantive financial support to their parents. But perhaps even more significantly, there seemed little acknowledgement in Dragon-head and Angang that *after* marriage-separations – which are poignant moments to be sure – daughters would genuinely be lost to their parents.

Returning to the door

If separation on the wedding day really *were* the end of the story, then one could say that Chinese women genuinely do 'marry out', and that they separate permanently from one patrilineal family only in order to join another. But it is clearly the case that many if not most Chinese women now have ongoing and repeated reunions and dealings with their natal families after marriage, and that these are of considerable socio-economic significance (cf. Judd 1989 and 1994a). As I have already pointed out, women 'return to the door' (*huimenr*) for a reunion visit with their families almost immediately after marriage – on the third day. After this, virtually all 'married out' daughters will continue to return home each year, *hui niangjia* (literally 'return to mother's home'), during the new year festival (usually accompanied by their husbands and children). Most women also return to their natal homes on other occasions for visits and contacts of various kinds.

But even taking these examples into account, we might still be inclined to say that most Chinese women (at least in the normative pattern) leave their natal families and only periodically ('symbolically') return, whereas most Chinese men stay in their natal families for their entire lives and only periodically leave. In this sense, it is arguably true that women *are* perpetual outsiders (separated from their first family upon marriage, but then never fully integrated into their second). This status is symbolically reflected, for example, in processes of ancestral separation and reunion in which women are excluded from active agency. Furthermore, we might argue that there is a considerable ambivalence regarding the 'reunions' which involve women (as daughters and daughters-in-law). When a woman returns to her natal home, although it is treated by her in-laws as a proper and honourable thing, it might well also highlight the fact that she did, after all, initially *arrive* (in her husband's family) from the outside.

In both Dragon-head and Angang, however, the majority of married women I have known well had relations with their natal families which were much more significant than this rather limited practice of 'maintaining periodic reunions' would imply. This was especially true in Angang where, because of the high proportion of marriages which have taken place between residents of the community, it is extremely common for women to live a very short distance away from members of their own families. In many cases, they live only a brief walk from the homes of their parents, grandparents, siblings, etc., with the result that contact with them is virtually an everyday affair. In disputes with their husbands, or with their parents-in-law, they are able to call on these relatives for help; and many couples are as likely to depend on the wife's natal family as on his for support and assistance throughout the year.

The sample of families from which I draw my most intimate understandings of Chinese kinship – including the understanding that affinal ties are very important – is very small indeed, and it could of course not be assumed to reflect any general trends in Chinese kinship. If anything, it might reflect the experience of women in modern rural Chinese communities such as Dragon-head and Angang: where elaborate lineage institutions do not exist, where local inter-marriage is common, and where the ideologies of agnatic kinship are subsequently less dominant and extreme. But I cannot help but be struck by the fact that in virtually all of the cases I know well, the notion of a near-total 'separation' of Chinese women from their natal homes, and their isolation within a patrilineal unit, simply does not apply. Here I provide several outline examples of households from Dragon-head and Angang which help illustrate the central significance of ties reckoned through women (these details of residence are obviously those which applied at the time of my fieldwork):

Household 1   Headed by a couple who live surrounded by the wife's relatives, while the husband's relatives live far away and are very rarely seen. Their daughter, instead of being 'married-out', also lives, along with her husband and children, in the natal home. While both of these arrangements (the husband's separation from his patriline, the daughter's post-marital residence with her parents) are technically 'unusual', they simply carry on with life. (In my terms, they produce relatedness in the present through cycles of *yang* and *laiwang*.)

Household 2   A classically successful patrilineal family, in which the husband maintains very close and significant relations with his brothers and other patrilineal kin. However he also maintains significant ties both with his sister and her husband (i.e. his brother-in-law) and with his daughter and her husband (i.e. his son-in-law), *all* four of whom live very nearby in the same community. His wife's relatives live far away, however, and she has only periodic contact with them – she did truly 'separate' upon marriage.

Household 3   A couple with two young daughters and no sons; they have frequent dealings with the wife's relatives, who live nearby, whereas the husband's live further afield and are less often called upon. Although they complain about having no sons, the daughters are treated with enormous affection, and indeed their life primarily revolves around the two girls.

Household 4   A wealthy couple with two sons and a daughter. His parents having died, the husband maintains equally significant ties with his brother *and* with his sister (both of whom live nearby). But overall the couple probably have more dealings with his wife's family than with his, and they live in the part of the community where most of her kin (including her mother) reside. At the time of my fieldwork, they were investing more in the education of their daughter than in that of their sons – she seemed to be the smart one.

Household 5   A classically 'unsuccessful' family in patrilineal terms, and yet somehow a great success. The husband and wife – neither of them originally from the local community – are separated (he often lives away from home). They have four daughters but no sons (which is seen to be a disaster). However, the emotional and economic ties between mother and daughters (including the 'married-out' one) are especially close. For reasons of distance, however, there is fairly limited contact with the wife's natal family, and virtually none with her husband's.

Household 6   A couple with two sons and a daughter. Both husband and wife have relatives in the local community, but there is more everyday contact with her side, whereas his agnatic relatives are (according to him) 'of no use'. (This comment was made in relation to a religious ritual, during which many friends and neighbours came along to offer both financial and moral support.)

Household 7   A couple with four children (three daughters, one son). The husband was raised in another village by foster-parents, with whom he maintains friendly contact and some ritual connections. But they actually live alongside his wife's family, and have much more important and everyday contacts with them. Although the wife expresses special concern for her son (the youngest of her four children), the daughters are treated with tremendous affection by both of their parents.

Again, these examples provide what is perhaps only anecdotal, and certainly randomly gathered, evidence of the importance of Chinese women's ties to their natal families (something already amply illustrated in the anthropological literature). But in these cases, at the very least, we can see that the notions of women being 'separated' from their homes by the rites of marriage, or being undervalued as daughters, are – at least on the surface – rather misleading. At the same time, we can see hints – e.g. in the view that uxorilocal residence is 'unusual', or in the special concern given to a son – that the classical view of Chinese family life still holds in some respects. And this takes us back to very general issues related to the logic of Chinese kinship, and to the two cycles of reciprocity which I discussed in the last chapter: for here we can see the centrality of women in producing Chinese relatedness.

Women and the cycles of *yang* and *laiwang*

As James Watson has noted, the anthropological discussion of Chinese kinship has often been dominated by a 'lineage paradigm' inherited largely (and, at least in part, mistakenly) from Maurice Freedman (J. Watson 1986: 274). This paradigm tends to assume that patrilineal ideals are paramount in Chinese social organisation (i.e. that everything else follows on from them). It also normally assumes that Chinese kinship is fundamentally about formal, and usually descent-group-oriented, kinship, whereas everyday family and domestic life are treated as a different (i.e. non-kinship) matter. As I have discussed more fully elsewhere, there are at least two central problems with this formalist approach (Stafford 2000). The first is that by taking the strongest version of patrilineal ideologies as its guide, the lineage paradigm helps sustain the impression that Chinese kinship consists in inflexible and *given* relatedness, by contrast with systems of kinship which are seen to be processual and incorporative, and in which relatedness is seen to be 'creatively' produced by social agents. But ethnography conducted in China (e.g. on everyday family and domestic life, the sphere which has been excluded from the lineage paradigm's formalist definition of kinship) shows beyond doubt the importance of processual and creative aspects of Chinese relatedness – as seen in the cycles of *yang* and *laiwang*. A second problem with the lineage paradigm is that by assuming the inflexible and given nature of Chinese kinship, it tends to misconstrue the widely acknowledged and highly valued role of women in producing relatedness, often leaving in its place the mostly negative representations of women found in official lineage ideology.

Over the years, the lineage paradigm has been subject to successive critiques and reanalyses, with one of the most important contributions coming from the anthropologist Margery Wolf. Basing herself on intimate ethnography conducted in rural Taiwanese households, Wolf proposed an important addition to our understanding of Chinese kinship: the notion of the 'uterine family' (M. Wolf 1968, 1972, 1987). This family *within* a (patrilineal) family consists of a woman and her own children, and Wolf argued that women tend to work on behalf of this unit, striving in particular for strong emotional ties with their sons. This is partly in order to solidify their current position within larger (patrilineal) families – in which they are dangerous outsiders – and more specifically in order to ensure their own future security. Loyal sons can be counted on to support their ageing mothers.

But the model of the 'uterine family' – which has certain advantages and which contains, I believe, some extremely important insights – unfortunately also characterises the kinship roles of women in largely negative terms, and implies that women are quite happy to work against the interests of their husbands and the patrilines into which they have married. Some of these negative evaluations undoubtedly come directly from the statements of informants, and from Wolf's own experience of (often conflictual) family life in Taiwan and China. But in isolation they do, I would suggest, portray women's roles in a rather misleading light. In any case, Wolf has largely withdrawn the 'uterine family' model from consideration, suggesting it was only ever a way of 'accommodating to the patriarchal family' (M. Wolf 1987: 11); in other words, it was a means of dealing with male-dominated patrilineal kinship.

But I would suggest that a much more central and positively evaluated role for women in Chinese kinship exists, and this is revealed through examining the cycles of *yang* and *laiwang*. The cycle of *yang*, to repeat, is a very involving system of mutual obligations between parents and children, which centrally entails the transfer of money and the sharing of food. Parents provide their offspring with support and nurturance (*yang*) during childhood, and as a result can, in turn, expect to receive 'respectful' support and nurturance (*fengyang*) back from them upon retirement and in old age. In the classical view, this system of support is usually only treated as one aspect of orthodox 'filial obedience' (*xiao*), and indeed is often treated as the merely practical side of a system which is more importantly about profound moral principles. In my experience, however, people in rural

China are firmly focused on the practicalities of support, and on the everyday emotions of kinship, rather than on the abstract moral principles involved. In any case, my key point is this: in China, ties of kinship between parents and children are significantly *produced* and *reckoned* through *yang*. Such ties are *not* simply given by patrilineal descent.

However, because in theory (and often in practice) parents rely on their sons, rather than on their 'married out' daughters, for support and nurturance in old age (i.e. for *yang*), the fate of sons is generally assumed to be a matter of much greater concern than the fate of daughters. Indeed, once daughters are separated by the rituals of marriage, they are, it seems, removed from the cycle of *yang* altogether. But this formulation, I would suggest, overlooks the fact that much of the actual *work* of *yang* is carried out by women, and this is perfectly well-known to be the case. First, as I have just been saying, the notion of 'marrying out' is often truly notional, and parents and siblings very regularly maintain close ties to the daughter who 'leaves'. This may include a flow of substantial economic, emotional, and ritual support (again cf. Judd 1989, 1994a). Second, while it is true that sons in China generally do provide their parents with financial support (whereas there is less of an expectation that daughters will do so), it is in fact *daughters-in-law* who are often left to provide for the actual day-in and day-out nurturance (*yang*) of their husbands' parents. That is, they often feed and care for their parents-in-law throughout the year, and this is one of the primary obligations for a resident daughter-in-law. Third, and perhaps most importantly, virtually *all* married women (including of course those who do not reside with or near their husband's parents) are the primary, and sometimes exclusive, providers of the *yang* which is given to their own children, and which is therefore helping to tie these children not only to them, but also to a family (by extension, to a patriline). As Margery Wolf's work on the 'uterine family' suggests, children (perhaps especially sons) therefore often feel deeply obligated to their mothers, and closely tied to them *emotionally*; and the theme of these emotions and obligations is furthermore very highly elaborated in Chinese culture (cf. Stafford 1992, 1995: 69–78).

It may be true that in many cases more attention is given to the nurturance of sons than of daughters. It may be true that men normally underwrite the costs associated with the provision of *yang* to parents. But it will almost always be a woman – a mother or daughter-in-law – who is actually providing *yang*, in some cases simultaneously to her parents, her parents-in-law, her children and her grandchildren. In sum, *yang* is central to Chinese kinship, and to the production of Chinese relatedness, and *women*, rather than men – in spite of ideologies to the contrary – are the key agents

of it. This means, by extension, that when Chinese kinship is being celebrated – for example through men's 'invitations' to their ancestors, or
through men's reunion banquets with their brothers – the celebration is of
a form of kinship which is crucially constituted through the efforts of
women (even when this contribution is explicitly denied). Kinship-related
separations and reunions, including those which 'must not involve women',
thus in fact *always* involve women.

It is therefore striking that in many cases the person one actually *misses*
and feels compelled to *return* to, is the mother. When a woman leaves her
natal home via the wedding-separation, she eats 'departing-*mother* meat'
(*liniangrou*), not 'departing-father meat'. Her subsequent reunion visits to
her natal community at the new year are called 'returning to *mother's*
home' (*huiniangjia*). Her children will similarly call this a visit to '*maternal-
grandmother's* home' (*laolaojia*). And when children visit their *father's*
parents during the festival they will refer to this as visiting '*fraternal-
grandmother's* home' (*pojia* or *nainaijia*). (Interestingly, when pilgrims take
statues of gods to older temples, such visits are organised, according to
Sangren, around affinal, rather than agnatic metaphors: 'The deity images
. . . are similar to brides who return on a customary visit to their natal
homes'; Sangren 1983: 9.) Symbolically important reunions are therefore
often seen, at least in part, as returns to the women who – I would suggest –
largely produced through *yang* the sentiment and obligation which compels a return. To truly 'separate' would be to deny the importance of this
tie. In short, women are at the core of the Chinese 'separation and reunion'
matrix, and for their own children they arguably embody most acutely its
emotional problematics.

Women are often similarly engaged in the production of sentiment and
relatedness with non-kin, although their engagement here is perhaps less
obvious. This is seen in the cycle of *laiwang*, that is, in the 'back-and-forth'
flow of help and support which characterises relations between friends and
acquaintances (discussed in chapter five). Most of the formal business of
this cycle falls to men, although, as I have said, much of the burden of
preparing meals for the banquets which manifest *laiwang* falls to women.
To the extent to which these relations are constituted through reunion
commensality, the role of women is clearly often an important one. And in
many cases, especially those involving close friends and neighbours,
women may be as involved as their husbands in the direct production of
friendly ties and the maintenance of ongoing connections. A good illustration of this is found in popular religion – obviously a key manifestation of
local solidarity and communal strength in places like Angang. Here men
sometimes take leading public roles; but the whole system normally rests
on the ongoing efforts and devotion of women.

To take the 'representative' roles of men, during public occasions, as proof that men are the central agents of separations and reunions (and of the relationships which arise from them), would therefore be highly misleading. And to simply assume, following the popular conceptualisation, that 'families' are the agents of separation and reunion, would be to ignore the particular roles of women in these processes. Women have as much of a practical interest as men in the 'ritual' maintenance of the connections on which their families rely, and they are often heavily involved in such maintenance work, in part through their behind-the-scenes roles in the separations and reunions which both display the connections of *yang* and *laiwang*, and help to produce them in the first place.

7   Developing a sense of history

Perhaps at this late stage, patient readers will believe me when I say that Chinese relationships are importantly realised through alternating patterns of separation and reunion. But here let me put this differently: in China, the *story* of relations with kin, friends, and spirits is often in fact an account of successive partings and returns. This is illustrated in familial and communal narratives of unity and completion during calendrical festivals (chapter one); in the articulation of relations with guests and outsiders through courteous etiquette during arrivals and departures (chapter two); in local histories of producing and revealing divine power through the summoning and sending-off of gods (chapter three); in the memorialisation of the ancestral dead through journey-like funerals and journey-like returns (chapter three); in architectural details which highlight patterns of 'coming and going' (chapter four); and in meals and banquets which often theatricalise the bittersweet nature of reunion commensality (chapter five). When viewed through most of these illustrative practices, acting out the narrative of separation and reunion appears to be the business of men. But in the last chapter I've argued that women – as daughters who must leave, and as mothers to whom one must return – often embody the most compelling versions of this story (chapter 6). Through care received in the cycle of *yang*, children become increasingly obliged to make a 'return' to their mothers, and by extension to give back what is due to their families and their native places.

Bearing all of this in mind, I now want to return to an argument posed at the very beginning of this book: that the practices and idioms of separation and reunion have a great, indeed inescapable, impact on Chinese historical consciousness. They contribute, in other words, to the development – by people in places like Angang and Dragon-head – of a 'sense of themselves in history' (whether of the familial, local, or national kind). That is, they help give people a sense of their own relationship to, and personal agency within, a wider pattern of events.

Of course, as many anthropologists and historians have shown, in different places and times 'history' is itself conceptualised and rendered in different ways.[1] In the case of China, anthropologists have recently begun to explore the relationship of written history (which itself takes a number of distinctive forms) to other kinds of Chinese social remembrance (e.g. mourning and ancestral commemoration; cf. R Watson 1994 and Jing 1996), and more generally to what James Watson calls the 'orthopraxy' of ritual and everyday life (Watson 1988). Forms of Chinese remembrance and 'history' (in this broad sense) are not only uniquely Chinese in certain respects, but are also transformed through time. (For example, when calendrical festivals of memorialisation are *stopped* by revolutions.) It therefore follows – given this cultural and historical specificity – that Chinese children are not born with a generic sense of history, but rather that they must *develop* one in the context of changing notions of the past and of historical transmission. Given the active nature of learning, it also follows that they do not accomplish this by simply 'taking in' whatever kind of history currently surrounds them. Instead, they produce new historical understandings (and styles) for themselves, as part of a more general re-thinking of their cultural inheritance, and partly in light of new events and personal experiences.[2] (This is why, I should note, even a seemingly very 'conservative' sense of history can spring unexpected surprises in the real world.)

But how does this complex business *actually* happen? And how does it relate to the separation constraint? Infants in communities such as Angang and Dragon-head observably accumulate (as Bowlby would expect) emotional attachments to those on whom they depend. Thus begin personal emotional histories: perhaps with a bit of instinctive attachment. But of course this very subtle process takes place in a specifically Chinese context, and is shaped – among other things, not least of all the unique personalities of everyone involved! – by local methods of parenting. From birth, infants are immersed in complex cycles of *yang*. They receive specific kinds of care and nurturance from their parents and others (i.e. from those to whom they are becoming emotionally attached) via culturally defined processes which will help to frame their familial obligations throughout life. Simultaneously, these infants are immersed – as sideline observers, at the very least – in complex patterns and processes of separation and reunion (many of which themselves relate directly to familial cycles of *yang*, and to neighbourly cycles of *laiwang*). These patterns and processes, outlined in previous chapters, often have an explicitly 'temporal' dimension. Many are tied to specific moments in the lunar calendar, and to the question of 'fate' *in time*, and are thus at least quasi-historical. That is, they help children and others to situate themselves in relation to ongoing stories (i.e. local narratives) about the familial-communal past, present, and future. In this way – i.e. starting with infant attachments and the cycle of *yang* – the most intimate familial processes and emotions may be linked, via patterns of separation and reunion, to processes which involve much larger communities: from neighbourly networks of mutual support, to the collective national 'family'.

Of course, this is clearly not the only thing which makes 'the Chinese past' *thinkable* for children. On the contrary, as I'll discuss below, a whole range of historical references and traces are distributed, sometimes explicitly, sometimes in unexpected ways, among the ideas, practices, and objects encountered by children in their learning environments. Living in these environments, children begin to associate various images and accounts, and themselves, with certain time-frames. For example, some things are labelled 'ancient', *gudai*, a period itself divisible into dynastic cycles; while others relate to the period 'after liberation', *jiefang zhihou*, and so on. This process of temporalisation is facilitated by hearing of and reading about past events and eras (i.e. by being given ready-made historical narratives); but it is also shaped by children's own experience of the passage of time (e.g. their increasing grasp of the ageing processes and of what time *means*). But bear in mind that in China, both the everyday registering of diverse historical references, and the 'natural' experience of the ageing process, are framed – as I have been illustrating throughout this book – by the (often 'time-focussed') events and processes of daily and seasonal life. These events and processes (which are redundantly patterned around separation and reunion) imply not only notions of 'the past', but also notions of fertility, of child development, and of the reciprocal connexions between persons – i.e. notions central to the positioning of children and other human subjects in time (cf. Feuchtwang 1992: 1–60 and Gell 1992).[3] They comprise, in short, a kind of theory of history.

Old newspapers and ancient poetry

I want to start with two perhaps rather odd examples of historical traces found in mainland China. Many farmhouses in the northeast (including in Dragon-head) are literally wall-papered with history, in that pages from old official newspapers, magazines, manuals, and textbooks have been pasted on the walls which provide insulation from the bitter cold. Sitting in these farmhouses on *kang*s (fire-heated brick platform beds) it is therefore possible to read yellowing fragments of the story of modern China – even if that is not what the pages are there for. In one of these houses, my eyes were drawn to the following words of Chairman Mao, published near the end of the Great Proletarian Cultural Revolution:

In China, there is still a semi-feudal culture [*ban fengjian wenhua*], which is a reflection of a semi-feudal government, and a semi-feudal economy. It promotes respect for Confucius [*zun Kong*], reading of the classics [*du jing*], the old ethics [*jiu lijiao*], and the old thinking [*jiu sixiang*]. Those who are opposed to the new thinking and the new proletarian culture are its representatives... This reactionary culture is in the service of imperialism and of feudalism, and it is something which should be smashed and overthrown [*shi yinggai bei dadao de dongxi*].

I have in fact never seen anyone, other than myself, actually reading these farmhouse-wall newspapers. They are instead busy doing what is usually done on *kangs*: minding children, pestering adults, preparing food, mending clothes, playing *majiang*, drinking rice wine, smoking, talking, eating, sleeping. But at the time of their printing, Mao's words were a dramatic provocation. 'Smashing and overthrowing' took place across China, as people were attacked for their 'old thinking' and for their attachment to the 'old culture'. Children and young people – key players in the unfolding drama – took over schools, attacked parents and teachers, ridiculed both classical education and popular 'superstitions', and shouted the slogan *yue du yue fandong*: 'the more you study, the more you're reactionary!' Mao's yellowing rhetoric on the wall is an historical trace from this relatively recent period of upheaval, now bracketed off as a 'dark time'. But his words are also an evaluation of China's more distant history, a strident critique of the classical past, and its continued reactionary influence. (As I've noted, the Cultural Revolution may be seen to have stopped, at least temporarily, many of the 'traditional' processes of separation and reunion outlined in this book – including divine sendings-off, extravagant reunion commensality, and so on.)

On the morning in 1993 when I copied down Mao's prose, another reference to the classical past was being made on the same *kang*. A young father, having come to help his relatives (specifically, his wife's mother's mother) with the planting of maize, was teaching his four-year-old daughter to recite classical poetry, including a verse written by Li Po (Li Bai) during the Tang dynasty, i.e. over one thousand years ago:

> On the day of planting
> Sweat and seeds fell to the earth.
> Now this food in the centre of a pan:
> And who knows that every grain
> Is the fruit of bitter labour?

When children listen to, memorise, and recite such works (many of which are written in dense, classical language) they are sometimes said to 'hear without understanding' (*tingbudong*); and the four-year-old performed a whole series of them in the way one might rattle off nonsensical verse. But as they grow older, children learn that some verses, including this simple one, are at least indirectly about the sacrifices of parents. One young man glossed Li Po's words for me as follows: 'Everything you have is the result of your father and mother going through hardship' (fumu de xinku). He spontaneously cited the verse to illustrate the obligation of sons and daughters to 'respectfully support' (fengyang) elderly parents, as a repayment for the support and nurturance (yang) the parents have given them during childhood. Needless to say, this obligation (in part an obligation to return) helps explain why the girl's father was in his wife's mother's mother's home in the first place: he came back to fulfil his duties in the extended cycle of support by helping with the planting of maize. 'Teaching through poetry', shijiao, something I'll discuss more fully in chapter eight, is explicitly seen as one way of transmitting such values from the classical Chinese past.[4]

Now these examples of historical references around kangs (wallpaper which is not necessarily read, and poetry which is not necessarily understood) may seem unusual, if not wilfully idiosyncratic, but they help illustrate three points. First, that the form and content of references to the past around kangs is highly variable. I could cite more obvious (and perhaps more direct?) examples: history books, current newspapers which interpret past events, historical narratives on radio and television, and so on. However, and this is the second point, there is nothing obvious about the way in which young children respond to any kind of historical reference, no matter how explicit. From early childhood, a girl or boy (in their own farmhouse) encounters diffuse kinds of 'history' – perhaps in the form of unreadable or unread wallpaper, or in the form of incomprehensible poetry, half-watched television epics, etc. This sort of oblique exposure to learning-matter is arguably both typical of early childhood, and an important part of learning.[5] The third point is that the significance of these variously attended-to traces is of course contextual; even seeing them 'as history' depends on a developmental process. Through conversations with other children or adults, and eventually through reading, references to the past may be elaborated upon, and become explicitly 'historicised' (i.e. seen as historical). Such references become associated with particular dates, events, and eras, and with particular evaluations of the past. Here presumably the fact of your father never in your entire childhood saying a word about the wallpaper, while meanwhile repeatedly taking the trouble to teach you the poetry, becomes significant.

In this respect, it is worth noting that the two eras represented by the newspapers and the verses have an 'obvious' historical significance for many Chinese adults. To put this differently: the stories of these eras are especially evocative – part of the Chinese master narrative. The Tang Dynasty is often referred to as the height of Chinese civilisation (in terms of cultural creativity), while the Cultural Revolution is now seen as a kind of destructive low-point.[6] Li Po's poetry is seen as a national treasure from the classical era, and to teach it is to sustain a history in which the Chinese past is something to be honoured rather than overthrown. For this reason, it may seem remarkable to find Maoist rhetoric and classical poetry sitting, as it were, on the same *kang*. But note that to *find* it remarkable requires a certain perspective on history, a certain way of structuring (and evaluating) the old and the new. For the four-year-old girl, this kind of merging, which often happens in the flow of daily life, is presumably *not* remarkable – *unless*, for some reason, she learns to think otherwise. This might happen when she is told that the poetry is 'ancient' (*gudai*), and then hears that youthful Red Guards tried to smash everything 'ancient' during the Cultural Revolution. (Later, to complicate matters, she might learn that Mao in fact admired much classical poetry and calligraphy.) The fate of Chinese traditions, and her relationship to them, might then become explicit objects of reflection, as she developed a sense of Chinese history, and of herself in the flow of it.

Children in Angang grow up, along with their mainland counterparts, in the midst of narratives framed around processes of separation and reunion; and they are soon equally entangled in complex cycles of *yang* and *laiwang*. (For example, they routinely go off with their parents – as did the little girl in the northeast – to help relatives and friends with various matters including work and the key rituals of the life-cycle.) Many children in Angang also learn to recite classical Chinese poetry at some stage (either at home or at school), and they soon know the famous poets of the Tang dynasty, including Li Po. But their relationship to specific narratives of 'Chinese history' is often very different from that of children in Dragon-head (see chapter nine). The Kuomintang (KMT) government of Taiwan – although committed through its radical origins to the idea that Chinese culture in many ways *impeded* the development of a modern Chinese nation-state – ultimately positioned itself (against the Communists) as the defender of this culture. In Taiwan, Mao's attack on classical Chinese civilisation was therefore always *officially* seen as ideologically driven sacrilege – and there is little chance that his words from that 'dark time' would now be posted (except perhaps ironically) on farmhouse walls. Needless to say, much of China's classical past and its post-imperial (modern) history is rendered very differently in Angang and Dragon-head, e.g. in the schools which children from these communities must attend.

Childhood on *kangs*

But as I've already suggested, developing a sense of history is *not* restricted to formal learning about the Tang dynasty, or the Cultural Revolution. Instead, it takes place against the background of a 'whole symbolically structured environment' (to use Bourdieu's phrase)[7] – in which a great variety of historical and quasi-historical references exist. At the centre of this environment, in Dragon-head, is the kind of platform-bed found throughout north China: the *kang*. *Kang*s are heated by wood-burning kitchen stoves and, especially during the bitterly cold winter months, they are the setting for many kinds of activity. Family meals are often eaten on the *kang*, or immediately adjacent to it, after which, at night, the family sleep there, warmed by the lingering heat of the fire-wood used to cook the evening meal. Guests also often eat on the *kang*, and sometimes sleep on it, placed on the warmest side, and they are almost always entertained in this 'bedroom', in part because it is the warmest and most comfortable space in the house. On special occasions, the *kang* may overflow with visitors who often stay for many hours, eating, drinking, and playing cards and *majiang*. But in spite of these openings to the 'outside' (*wai*), the *kang* and the home are generally associated with women, whose domain remains primarily 'inside' (*nei*). During the day, women, including grandmothers, mind infants and children around the house, often on the *kang*. In fact many kinds of 'women's work' (*nuren gan de huo*) are done there, including the making and mending of children's clothes, breast-feeding, food-preparation, etc. So there are many potential associations between the house, the kitchen stove, the heat of firewood, the cooking of food, the warmth of the *kang*, women, conception, nurturance (i.e. the provision of *yang*), and children.

In this environment, one encounters a certain folk-model of child development, one which repeatedly stresses 'fate' (*mingyun*) and temporality, and which is arguably projected (along with various expectations) onto children by their elders. This folk-model is often said to be the province of 'old ladies' (*lao taitai*), and is usually of limited interest to children themselves. But note two things. First, that it is made up of a series of time-frames, histories, trajectories, and expectations against which children are measured, and against which they might eventually measure themselves. Second, that 'old ladies' – i.e. grandmothers, who often care for these self-same children throughout infancy – tend to carry great moral authority (they are the grandmothers to whom one returns).

That the *kang* is where children are meant to be conceived is emphasised in (carefully timed) ceremonies by the tradition known as 'pressing the *kang*' (*yakang*). During this, a small boy is placed on the *kang*, an action which is said to improve the chances that the newlyweds will have a son.

For this, 'a girl is of no use' (*yongbuzhao nuhair*). On the wedding night, the newlyweds also sit huddled together on the *kang* as their guests subject them to rough teasing (*naofang*) about sex. The wedding guests will already have eaten dates (*zao*) and pears (*lizi*), because these words together sound like *zao li zi*, 'to have a son quickly'. They will have eaten peanuts (*huasheng*) because this sounds like 'giving birth' (*sheng*) to 'variety' (*hua*), i.e. having both sons and daughters (a desirable outcome under the 'second child' birth policy in the countryside). The bride will have washed her face in water in which an onion has been placed, because 'onion' (*cong*) sounds like 'clever' (*congming*), and this act increases the odds that her offspring will be intelligent. In short, the small details of weddings, actions of the living, promote fertility, and help produce desirable characteristics in the unborn. While no efforts whatever are made to teach these ideas to children, children do loiter on the edges of such events, or run through rooms, watching and listening.

After a child is born, the mother is expected to remain in the house, on the *kang*, literally sitting out the first postnatal month (*zuo yuezi*). Children sooner or later witness or hear of this practice, which relates to the *burden* of motherhood – a redundant theme in Chinese culture – and to the subsequent obligations of sons and daughters.[8] People often avoid being the first to visit the home of a newborn child, because the infant is thought likely to take on the personal characteristics of the first visitor. (They modestly say they wouldn't wish their characteristics upon the child.) But a birth, and especially the birth of a son, is publicly celebrated at various timed intervals: usually after twelve days, one-month (*manyue*), one-hundred days (*baitianr*), and then most dramatically after one year (*manzhousui*). On this occasion, guests – the family's network of *laiwang* support – are invited for a large banquet. The child is placed on the *kang*, surrounded by a number of objects, each one representing a particular career or destiny. These usually include a book (for future scholars), scales (for traders), a stone (for hardworkers), money (for money-makers), and a steamed rice bun (for the child who will only be good at eating, not working). If not too terrified by the crowd gathering around to watch, the infant will grab one of these objects, indicating his or her future career. Several people told me the ritual is often 'reliable' (*biaozhun*), because the child does not 'understand things' (*bu dongshi*) and simply grabs the objects spontaneously.

When infants are taken, for the first time, to visit the home of a friend or relative, a 'long-life thread', *changmingxian*, with money on it, is usually placed around their necks. I was told this symbolises *baitou daolao*, 'achieve white-haired longevity'. But children, vulnerable to certain kinds of harm – remember that they must pass through many dangerous 'barriers' (*guan*) on the road of life – may require extra help in reaching that goal. For example, because of their very powerful or sensitive (*lingmin*) eyes they are kept away from the ancestral offerings which are made on the *kang*. They might see the ancestors eating food, and make some comment which would offend them (*maofan*). One woman told me that her nephew went through a long period of incessant crying, and that the child's grand-mother felt this was due to some *fanxie*, 'evil deed', from the past. The child was taken to a spirit medium, a *tiaodashenrde* (a 'spirit-dancer'), who traced the problem to an unhappy ancestor. The mother was instructed to visit one hundred homes in the vicinity, and to collect one hundred pieces of string. These were wound together and placed around the neck of the child 'in order to heal his illness' (*weile zhibing*), and to ensure his future protec-tion. Protecting children, and thus defending the cycle of filial obligation, is a central concern for most parents. This cycle is linked both to the ancestral past, and to the future, in which parents hope to be respectfully supported (*fengyang*) by their offspring. Such references to the flow of time, to diverse family-based histories, and to the reciprocal nature of human relationships, are very pervasive around *kang*s.

Many similar 'old lady' ideas about child-development (i.e. about children in the flow of time) are held in Angang: that minor rituals before, during and after weddings can help to induce fertility; that mother and child should remain in isolation after childbirth; that various timed intervals after birth should be marked with public celebrations; that various steps (importantly including the use of spirit mediums) can be taken to protect children from physical/spiritual harm. And yet the learning environment of children in Angang is very different from that found in Dragon-head. While people in Angang also normally sleep on platform-style beds, these are usually hidden from public view. Instead, guests are received in sitting rooms which are almost always dominated by large private altars, dramatically marking out each home as the site for ongoing ritual activity. I would say that in Angang these altars are the focal point of the symbolically structured environment. Children are regular participant-observers in rituals held at them, including those which involve spirit mediums. Starting from the *kang*-room: altar-room distinction, it follows that the learning environment of Angang varies in important ways from that found in Dragon-head.

The firecracker

But when I try to imagine – to go back to the case of Dragon-head – this symbolically dense environment from a child's perspective, i.e. to take the *kang* as the child's site for learning history, my description becomes much more diffuse, and my attention is drawn to sensations and emotions. These are not necessarily conscious or articulated, but may relate to intangible things about home which make it difficult – as is repeatedly said – to 'accustom' (*xiguan*) oneself to life in an unfamiliar place. (In other words: the place from which one 'ideally' doesn't wish to become separated, is the place to which one has become 'accustomed'.) Everything from toilet-training to misery-inducing family fights takes place on *kang*s, and life there often seems chaotic. Note however that certain childhood sensations and emotions may be repeated in time, and associated with specific seasons and recurrent events. The children growing up on *kang*s might, for instance, associate them with their oft-discussed (winter-time) warmth, and with the taste of food prepared by women in the kitchen stove. These taste-sensations are themselves patterned, because certain foods are eaten on specific occasions, and at certain times of year. Children might also associate *kang*s with the teasing they sometimes receive there at the hands of relatives and the friends of their parents. But the presence and absence of certain relatives and friends is associated with particular days and seasons.

For example, as I've described, the *kang* and its warmth are linked to the lunar new year activities, and to the chaotic sociability of the whole spring festival period. This is enacted in the 'bustle' (*renao*) of the reciprocal visits, the 'stringing together of doors' (*chuanmenr*), and the noisy drinking, eating and *majiang*-playing which takes place on and near warm *kang*s in the frozen first days of the first lunar month. At this time, as I've said, certain days are spent with patrilineal kin, then with affines, neighbours, old friends, work-comrades, and so on, until ideally the family has renewed, through commensality over a period of many days, an entire expanding network of obligation and support. This begins with the new year's eve (*chuxi*) ancestral reunion meal, itself a momentary denial of temporality, which simultaneously begins the new year and marks the passage of time (everyone becomes one year older on that night).

During this festival period, I found that children in Dragon-head (as in Angang) often spoke of two things. First, they often mentioned the gifts of money (*yasuiqian*) they receive from adults. The most important (and usually the largest) of these transfers, from parent to child on new year's eve, seems clearly linked to the obligation to support one's parents in the future (cf. Stafford 1995: 79–111). But children say no such thing, they only seem interested in the money. They also talk incessantly about firecrackers – which are said to frighten away evil spirits, and which form a central part of the tumultuous welcome given to the ancestors on new year's eve – discussing at length, between shooting them off, the number of explosions produced by various types. They relate this to their cost, and I also noticed that adults, while listening to the large-scale barrages (which are organised by grown men), often comment on the expense of this tradition. One woman said to me, at the end of a series of deafening explosions: 'Ten thousand *kuai* – finished!' (*wanle*). The resulting scraps of paper, which are said to represent the family's future prosperity, are swept into, rather than away from, the home. The two things children seem most interested in, gifts of money and firecrackers, thus share some important conceptual links; but children seem as uninterested in the meaning of the firecrackers as in the meaning of the money. In the days before and after the 'turning of the year', they nevertheless buy firecrackers, collect unspent ones from the ground, beg them from adults and, of course, shoot them off. The parents I met, who often expressed concern about the health and prospects of their children, did not prevent this, saying their children knew how to avoid getting hurt.

But with respect to this, let me describe what I take to have been a 'learning experience'. One day, during a post-new year neighbourly visit in Dragon-head, I noticed an increasingly restless boy sitting on the *kang*. Having lost his patience with his father, who was deeply involved in an interminable *majiang* game, this boy was being very rude to the adults. Children some-times find themselves with little to do when their parents become engrossed in long meals and gambling, and it was clear that the boy, who had already used up his collection of firecrackers, wanted to go home, and he went so far as to kick out at an elderly relative sitting on the *kang*, an unusually unfilial action. In spite of this, he was mostly ignored by the adults, who were caught up in their game. They may also have ignored him because people usually avoid arguments and the use of inauspicious language during the festival period. Negative words spoken at this time of year may have serious consequences. Eventually, one of the players, tiring of the stream of abuse, gave the boy some small firecrackers to entertain himself with. The boy ran outside and a few crackling noises could be heard, followed by a loud nearby bang. One of the firecrackers had exploded in his hand, and he raced, screaming, back into the house.

His mother, standing in the kitchen with some other women, rushed over and gave his hand a swift examination. It was black, red, and swollen, but she judged, as he howled, that it was not seriously damaged. She then scolded him, a common response to childhood injuries on the grounds that it is wrong to injure one's body, which is a kind of family property. The men playing *majiang*, to whom he had been so rude, paused for a moment to listen, whispering amongst themselves that it 'was not a serious matter' (*meiyou shi*). Again, this was perhaps a matter of not wanting, during the festival, to accept a bad omen as a bad omen. When the boy, still crying, re-joined them a few moments later, they began to tease him gently, saying he should by all means take more firecrackers outside to play with. He was obviously too frightened to do so, and continued to whimper in pain. As he began to calm down, his elders said that he was clearly a big man, and they jokingly invited him to join them in eating and drinking at a table next to the *kang*. Usually children would 'not dare' (*bugan*) to eat with their elders on a public occasion. To everyone's amusement he was however made to join them at the table, from which vantage-point he gave them resentful glances until, eventually, he began to cheer up, if only slightly. Later, having eaten some of the special new year's food on offer, and having drunk a large glass of beer, he rather happily reclined on the warm *kang* and fell asleep, as their game continued.

I'm fascinated by this case in which a fairly predictable 'unpredictable' thing, which shouldn't have happened during the new year, was simply incorporated into the flow of what *should* happen. The boy, in kicking an elder, and almost blowing off his own hand, was behaving extraordinarily badly. But his anti-social behaviour was met with the ultimate Chinese expression of sociability: eating and drinking around a table (i.e. with a moment of reunion commensality). Whether he really wanted to or not, and in spite of the normal hierarchies, the boy was cajoled into eating with the older men, who were acting out their 'connexions' (*guanxi*) through eating, drinking, and gambling. Then, slightly tipsy, the boy fell asleep in their midst on the warm *kang*. As I've been saying, the *kang* has many complex, and often time-related, associations. These include the warm sociability of the lunar new year, during which the dead join the living in commensality, having been *greeted* by a volley of exploding firecrackers. The boy's dramatic personal experience – which surely must have seemed completely singular – was thus merged, or made to merge, with a flow of (momentarily 'timeless') time, and with a pattern of ideas and events which is linked to the familial past.

Given the great number of firecrackers in China, and the great number of boys, this sort of drama might be expected to happen reasonably often. But for many children the lunar new year will be considerably less 'eventful', and simply involve sitting on the edge of a *kang*, feet dangling over the edge, listening for some hours to the slapping of *majiang* pieces. However, even to hear this noise, and to hear the rapid-fire joking which accompanies it, is surely to learn something about the relationships between the players, including one's own parents, and their mutual interdependence as relatives and friends, linked through a common past and a common future. A child will inevitably come to know about this, i.e. about the mechanisms of relatedness (including those which centrally involve *kangs*, food, money, and firecrackers) through which people come, in the passage of time, to be connected to one another. Through these mechanisms, I would suggest, children learn to situate themselves in particular historical communities.

Obviously, not every 'history lesson' relates directly to patterns of separation and reunion, but a great many of them do. For these patterns collectively comprise a series of powerful, and powerfully redundant, narratives. Children in Dragon-head learn, for instance, that they should – as a sign of respect – greet arriving elders and guests, walking out of the farmhouse to do so. They learn that certain foods mean reunion and 'completion'. They learn that they are often *not* welcome to join moments of reunion commensality, moments which sometimes imply, by definition, equality. They learn that parents make a fuss over departing guests but may be silent when they themselves depart from home. They learn that sending-off corpses and welcoming gods can be a dangerous business. They learn that daughters go away (*chujia*), while sons do not. They learn that women do not extend invitations to the ancestors at the family graves. They learn that doors are decorated for the new year, and that graves have doors. They learn that mothers do much of the hard everyday work of the cycles of *yang* and *laiwang*. But none of this is learnt generically, i.e. outside of the context of particular social relationships. The corpses are known and named corpses, the gods known and named gods, the mothers known and named mothers, the daughters known and named daughters, and the history of these names – and of the child's relation to them – is itself known.

Conclusion: a conservative sense of history?

But before becoming seduced by the coherence of this, it is important to remember the Maoist wall-paper – an 'over-looked' trace of China's volatility. Imagine that the boy, rather than hurting himself, had instead walked into the house, and thrown his firecracker into the midst of the *majiang*-playing elders on the *kang*! This may seem unimaginable, but these days much of what young people did during the Cultural Revolution seems equally unimaginable, and there are besides many other examples of 'confronting the elders' – breaking the cycle of separations and reunions – in modern Chinese familial *and* national history. In which case, the seeming conservatism of life on *kangs*, the capacity of that life to 'swallow up' events, and to control the young, perhaps needs closer examination. In particular, we might ask whether the seemingly conservative family sense of history is translatable in political terms.

I want to note, in this regard, some recent discussions of Chinese historical consciousness and cultural identity in the post-Mao era. One of the best-known contributions was made by William Jenner in a book called *The Tyranny of History*. Writing after the events of June 1989, Jenner argued that China was in an acute state of crisis which was, in a fundamental sense, an historical product:

What ties all aspects of the crisis together is the past: what has happened in the past and the past as perceived. Today's objective problems, like the subjective ones that make their solution even more difficult than they would be otherwise, were created under two thousand years of bureaucratic absolutism. The history of tyranny is matched by a tyranny of history: perceptions and thought patterns from the past bind living minds. (Jenner 1992: 1)

Jenner argued, in sum, that Chinese historical consciousness – which by definition permeates, and is a product of, all institutions and socio-cultural practices in China: from patrilineal kinship and the family, to the state bureaucracy, to Chinese literature and the system of writing – is deeply conservative.

But as Jenner is aware, an argument of this kind does raise some fundamental questions. Exactly who are the bearers of this conservative historical consciousness? Through precisely what mechanisms do they acquire it? In this regard I want to note two writers whose interests partly overlap with those of Jenner, the first of whom is the philosopher Tu Wei-ming. In a famous essay, Tu accepts that mainland China is indeed in a crisis with deep historical roots. However, he suggests that what he calls 'cultural China', far from being a unitary phenomenon, is now being shaped by very diverse communities. These obviously include: (1) people living in the Chinese mainland, as well as in Hong Kong, Taiwan and Singapore; but also: (2) those in the 'overseas Chinese' diaspora; and finally (3) the international communities of intellectuals and commentators who contribute to global debates about Chinese culture and identity. Tu's argument, in brief, is that the *periphery* of 'cultural China', rather than its centre, is now the driving force behind change:

Although realistically those who are on the periphery ... are seemingly helpless to affect any fundamental transformation of China proper, the center no longer has the ability, insight, or legitimate authority to dictate the agenda for cultural China. On the contrary, the transformative potential of the periphery is so great that it seems inevitable that it will significantly shape the intellectual discourse on cultural China for years to come. (Tu 1994: 33–4)

For Tu Wei-ming, then, the problem of conservatism in Chinese cultural identity and historical consciousness is primarily a problem of the *centre*, and is precisely one which the more imaginative periphery will help to overcome.

James Watson, in his post-1989 reflections, also accepts the crucial role of the international periphery in shaping the contemporary discourse on Chinese culture and identity, but his primary concern is with the divide between rural and urban populations within mainland China itself. Watson's argument, briefly, is that whereas most rural Chinese continue to practice (at least in modified form) the rituals, and to reproduce the folk-knowledge, which have classically defined Chinese cultural identity, this is no longer true of China's urban population:

[T]he cultural gap between rural and urban may be growing wider each year. The key symbols that helped hold China together (shared rites, folkloric traditions, a common notion of proper lifestyle) no longer have the same meaning they once had. (Watson 1992: 379)

Watson argues that this leaves modern Chinese identity up for 'renegotiation', which may suggest that the cultural/historical past is not weighing as heavily on the *urban* mainland Chinese present as Jenner and Tu have implied. But Watson goes on to note that many urban-dwellers themselves have the sense that China's problems have deep historical roots – and indeed they express pessimistic opinions rather similar to those expressed by Jenner in *The Tyranny of History*. Watson quotes one student in Beijing as saying:

We think there is something fundamentally wrong with our society. Everything has to be changed, especially the mentality of the Chinese people. This will take at least fifty years, maybe one hundred years. (1992: 380)

Watson himself sums up June 1989 as 'a disastrously violent reminder that the Chinese past is still very much alive in the present' (1992: 381).

In spite of their very different perspectives, these three authors – a historian, a philosopher, and an anthropologist – share with many people in China the view that history, both as a reality and as a perceived and represented reality, is a significant 'burden' on the Chinese present. My own view is that this conclusion partly represents the reproduction, in scholarly form, of the Chinese folk-model of history, i.e. of the popular Chinese model of the impact of the past on the present. And I would suggest that the tumultuous events of the past 150 years make this 'tyranny of history' thesis – in scholarly or popular forms – highly problematic. But the reproduction of this folk-model, which obviously *does* help to shape events in China, is itself an extremely interesting and important phenomenon. How does this happen? People in China and Taiwan often point out what to them seems an entirely 'obvious' fact: that China has a great *quantity* of history, much more than anyplace else. In theory, this history is knowable and debatable, but in practice it is mostly known only by experts who can master ancient texts, of which there are, again, a great quantity. For the layperson, then, much of 'Chinese history' is a fixed, largely unknowable, and non-negotiable thing.[9] People also often note that the difficulty with transforming China now is precisely that its history is *too long*, and also that it has *too many* people (*lishi tai chang, renkou tai da*). Personal or collective agency in the present, i.e. the ability to make something useful happen now, is seen to be limited by historical over-determination, including a population problem which is explicitly blamed (by almost everyone) on traditional values.[10] 'The past', no matter how venerated, is a burden.

In this chapter, I have sought to address the question which is raised most directly by Watson's contribution: namely, how do people in China develop a sense of history (conservative or otherwise) in the first place? Given the complex learning environment in which this occurs – only a fraction of which I have described here – this could never be said to proceed in a straightforward way. The historical references are too numerous, the symbolism too diffuse and complex, and the personal and sensual involvement in the whole process too subtle and direct to allow for simplistic explanations. But I have argued that the alternation between separation and reunion, which is explicitly highlighted in so many spheres of Chinese social life, contributes in significant ways to the development of Chinese historical consciousness. Within the flux of personal and collective history, this alternation helps define many of the most important, and most recognisable, events. In short, through constituting relationships, alternating patterns of separation and reunion in China become the substance of history.

Of course, it could be argued that this is simply about what happens inside families and localities (and furthermore only in the countryside), and that it cannot be linked to the ways in which children see themselves in relation to 'the Chinese past', to modern Chinese history, or to current national and international affairs. Indeed, it has been argued – if I can be allowed to summarise a highly complex discourse in my own terms – that familial narratives of separation and reunion have worked *against* (precisely) the narrative of Chinese national 'unity'. Briefly, during the late Qing Dynasty, Chinese scholars and activists (the intellectual ancestors of the KMT and CCP) tried to make sense of China's decline and subjugation. (The student Watson quotes above is following directly in the tradition of this old discourse.) Some argued, among other things, that Chinese familism, in spite of its virtues, undermined the development of nationalism. The traditional idea that a child cannot fail (to return to) the elders and the ancestors was thus seen as a source of *political* intransigence (cf. Stafford 1992, 1995). It was said that family-based narratives (by definition, narratives of separation and reunion) had a kind of priority for most Chinese over national narratives, and were a restraint on national historical progress.[11] But are these narratives really contradictory? In the two chapters following this one, I will show that they merge in crucial ways: in short, the national narrative *also* often draws very clearly and explicitly upon the idioms of separation and reunion.

But in closing this chapter I want to raise a question which is central to my concerns: in light of China's chaotic modern history, why do narratives of separation and reunion (in both their familial and national forms) remain so seductive? Here I want to provisionally suggest four reasons. First, because (like many successful symbolic elaborations) they are conveyed with remarkable single-mindedness: i.e. they are simply everywhere and impossible to miss in China. Second, because they hold, for most Chinese people, deeply personal associations. As illustrated in this chapter, these associations derive from the most intimate experiences of childhood and family life (where the separation constraint is first learned via the cycle of *yang*). Third, and following on from this, because they draw on *instinctive* human emotions related to attachment and separation, and, by extension to the universal problematics of autonomy and dependency. Finally, these narratives are seductive because they have, in China, such very long histories that their 'natural conclusions' must seem, to most Chinese, virtually inescapable. And this is the theme of the next chapter.

8   Classical narratives of separation and reunion

When seen through its distribution in time and space, the phenomenon Tu Wei-ming refers to as 'cultural China' seems an exceptional thing (Tu 1994). Taking Sperber's 'epidemiological' perspective on such matters (Sperber 1985), it is striking not only that many of the representations related to 'cultural China' are exceptionally widely-distributed among contemporary human populations, but also that many of these widely distributed representations have shown remarkable durability. That is, they have evolved and thus arguably 'survived' in some form for many centuries. Of course, this monolithic perspective on China can and probably should be brought into question; and anthropologists and historians have increasingly done so. They have stressed, for instance, the substantial historical and regional diversities of China (e.g. Faure and Siu 1995); and they have questioned essentialist definitions of 'Chinese identity' by drawing attention to the centrality in Chinese history of its non-Han populations (e.g. Constable 1996, Harrell 1995). This process of deconstruction is in the spirit of contemporary social science. However – and the implications of this cannot be ignored – the *narrative* of Chinese cultural uniformity in time and space retains a force of its own, regardless of its anthropological validity, and it has great appeal as a folk-model for many people who identify themselves as Chinese.

When such people must deal with moments of separation and reunion, they partly do so by drawing on culturally elaborated sets of ideas – variously described as 'traditional' (*chuantongde*), 'ancient' (*gudaide*), 'unchangeable' (*gaibuliaode*), and so on – about what constitutes proper behaviour during such moments. This proper behaviour implies as well an aesthetic sense – i.e. a sense not only of what needs be done, but also of the *style* in which it should be accomplished. And because separation and reunion are, in China, highly emotionally-charged topics, the aesthetics here extends to emotions: i.e. to a sense of how emotions should, or should not, be publicly and privately expressed during moments of parting and return.

But how are such behaviours, and the aesthetic sense which accompanies them, actually learned? Because certain kinds of separation and reunion

144

are constants in Chinese social life, everyone has opportunities (as I discussed in the last chapter) for developing expertise in dealing with them. But this learning experience is augmented by exposure to something else: a centuries-old written tradition within which moments of separation and reunion have a central place. I would suggest that this literature has a considerable impact on the aesthetics of separation and reunion in China – in part *directly*, because the tradition is very widely and popularly known (i.e. it is not simply the preserve of elites and scholars, and on the contrary is often transmitted almost universally through variants in 'popular culture'). But it also has an impact *indirectly*, because in China it is often implied (e.g. through the rituals of popular religion) that 'classical', 'imperial', 'elite' or 'textual' traditions are the ultimate source for models of proper earthly conduct – whether or not this ultimate source is actually comprehensible to the layman. This view may be held by those who never, for example, actually read classical poetry or literature, and by those whose knowledge of what used to transpire among the educated elite is strictly limited. As a result, this literature – an important element in the Chinese and Taiwanese 'symbolically structured environments' – has a significant impact on popular historical consciousness.

In this chapter – and rather bravely, I should think, since I have no special expertise in this highly specialist area – I want to cite a few rather obvious examples of this literature. I'll first discuss the great (and immensely popular) Qing dynasty novel *Hong lou meng*, before turning to classical (mostly Tang dynasty) poetry. While classical poetry may seem an esoteric source to use for this discussion, in post-Cultural Revolution China, as in contemporary Taiwan, such verses are widely known. As I pointed out in the last chapter, they are often memorised and recited (*beisong*) by children, even in the countryside, and the memorisation of poetry is explicitly seen as a method of transmitting Chinese cultural values, i.e. of 'teaching through poetry' (*shijiao*). The story and the characters of the novel *Hong lou meng*, in turn, are almost universally known because of their repeated transmission in popular forms (e.g. in television dramas). Both the ancient poetry and the Qing novel – completely obsessed as they are with the problem of human separation – help illustrate in the clearest possible terms many of the central themes of this book (including, as will become clear, the political ones).

A romantic novel of separation and reunion

Here everything is recorded precisely as it happened: partings and meetings [*li he*], sorrows and joys [*bei huan*], prosperity and decline [*xing shuai*]. I didn't add anything, or make anything up, for fear that my story would lose its authenticity [*qi zhen*].   Cao Xueqin, *Hong lou meng*[1]

Cao Xueqin's eighteenth-century romance *Hong lou meng* is routinely described as China's greatest novel. This may or may not be true, but it is certainly the case that Cao's wonderful work is exceedingly well-known, and that versions of it (including abridged editions, operas, and televised adaptations) have kept it very prominent in the public mind. (The book is normally translated either as *The Story of the Stone* or *The Dream of the Red Chamber*, and the chapter and page numbers below are from the brilliant translation by David Hawkes (Cao 1973)). I should point out that as a 'novel of (Chinese) manners', *Hong lou meng* by definition provides a great many concrete examples of the etiquette of parting and return – some of them hilarious in execution (e.g. the visit of the country-woman Granny Liu to her aristocratic relatives, in chapter six). But the general subject-matter of Cao's epic novel is the decline of an aristocratic family, the Jias, as seen largely through the eyes of a spoilt and precocious boy, Jia Bao-yu. In the course of the novel, Bao-yu comes to live (un-usually, to say the least) in Prospect Garden – an extraordinary 'garden of reunion' – surrounded by an adoring circle of his female cousins and maids, in what might be called a state of timeless or suspended unity and happi-ness. But time, decay (including the decay of family fortunes), separation and loss are nevertheless always looming in the background of this charmed space, as is the possibility that another, supernatural, world exists around and within it. Much of the dramatic tension of the novel arises from the awareness that the girls will inevitably age and 'marry out' to men they do not know.

So it happens that early in the novel, before the garden is built, one of the girls, Yuan-chun, is selected to become an Imperial Concubine, something which is, for her and for the entire family, a 'dazzling promotion' with profound consequences. Under these circumstances her separation from her natal family and absorption into the imperial household should be quite complete. However, thanks to the 'kindness of the emperor' she is allowed to return home after her marriage for occasional Visitations – the first of which takes place during the lantern festival, *yuanxiaojie*, one year after her marriage. This visit, the climax of the first part of the novel, requires on the part of her family an extraordinary and vastly expensive operation to ensure that the Imperial Concubine is properly *greeted*, and the impressive landscaped Prospect Garden is built for this very purpose. When the day of her visit arrives, the return of this daughter is celebrated, first, with a series of formal greetings and ceremonials, and then – in total privacy – with informal, highly emotional, and tearful reunions. But her male relatives are not allowed to look upon her at all, and as she interviews her father through a curtain she exclaims: 'What is the use of all this luxury and splendour ... if I am to be always separated from those I love...?' (p. 362).

During her stay, the Imperial Concubine is lavishly entertained in the reunion garden built to mark her visit; and as she walks through it she orders that the inscription on one memorial arch, which reads 'Precinct of the Celestial Visitant', should be changed to simply read 'The House of Reunion' (p. 359).

Following Yuan-Chun's tearful return to the Imperial Palace, she decrees that the garden built in her honour should not be wasted. It will instead become the residence of the family's young maidens, but also of the young boy Bao-yu – for whom the garden becomes a 'perfect' (and yet sometimes boring, and ultimately disappointing) home. Much of the action of the novel thereafter focuses on life in and around this space, and on the inevitable disruptions brought by separation and decline. Indeed, even before Yuan-Chun's imperial promotion and the building of the garden, a dying relative of the household predicts both the great event itself, and the generalised sorrow which will eventually descend upon the family (note the poignant reference to reunion banquet commensality):

Soon a remarkably happy event [*xi shi*] will take place, but one which will flare up like blazing cooking oil – as overstated as fresh flowers worn against embroidered cloth. It will be a transient joy, a passing moment of happiness. And when it comes, you must recall the old saying: 'Every banquet must end' [*sheng yan bu san*].[2]

In Cao's novel, the death of Qin-shi, the woman who makes this chilling prediction, and the subsequent lengthy and highly detailed account of her funerary 'sending-off' (in chapters thirteen, fourteen, and fifteen), directly – and I should think rather pointedly – precedes the joyous 'greeting' of the Imperial Concubine upon her return.

I want to stress again that the key setting for this great Chinese novel is a garden of *reunion*, and Cao Xueqin clearly establishes permanent unity as an ideal, and tragically unachievable, state. It is against this background that the tragedies of the novel occur. Chief among them is the course of the precocious Bao-yu's own love life. He hopes to marry Dai-yu, an adopted cousin living in the garden – one might say to keep her from being separated from him. But because of her delicate constitution, he is eventually obliged to marry instead another cousin in the garden, Bao-chai. On Bao-yu's wedding night, the delicate Dai-yu passes away, broken-hearted and virtually alone, thus irrevocably separating herself from her beloved. Very much later, in the ultimate and controversial conclusion of the epic novel (controversial in part because not written by Cao Xueqin himself), Bao-yu himself abandons his declining family. He literally separates himself from them in order to embrace Buddhism/Daoism, a religion which is otherwise known – significantly, given my concerns – as 'the gate of emptiness', *kongmen*.

That the theme of separation, and its relationship to the contingencies of fate, is central to Cao's concerns is clear from the novel's very first pages, before the main characters are even fully introduced. Let me cite a few examples of this. In chapter one, an ambitious young man, Jia Yu-cun, spends the 'mid-autumn' *festival of reunion* with his patron and sponsor. During their *reunion meal*, the patron offers support which will enable Yu-cun to advance his career. As a result, he abruptly leaves town the next morning, without even saying a proper goodbye (a *hasty departure*). A few months later (but still in Cao's first chapter!), the generous patron's only child, a daughter, is kidnapped (an *enforced separation*) – an event which again takes place precisely during a *festival of reunion* (*yuanxiaojie*, the 'lantern festival', i.e. when the Imperial Concubine will later *return* to her own natal home). Following their daughter's kidnapping, the patron and his wife become ill with grief, and they fall into total despair when their house burns down. Coming by chance upon a monk who chants about the futility of ambition (a *chance encounter*), the patron vanishes with him forever (another *hasty departure*). In chapter two, the ambitious young man, Jia Yu-cun, *re-unites with* and marries a beautiful young maiden upon whom – in the course of his earlier *abrupt departure* – he happened to have glanced in passing (another *chance encounter*). He then finds a job teaching the daughter of a man whose wife abruptly dies (an unexpected *death-separation*). Following this untimely death, Yu-cun's student, the daughter of the widower – she happens to be the character Dai-yu, later the delicate true love of Bao-yu's life, and a central figure in the novel – is sent (another *separation*), along with her ambitious young teacher, to the Rong mansion in the capital, i.e. to young Bao-yu's home. Here she is tearfully *greeted* by her relatives, and from this very odd sequence of events – which notably entails festivals of reunion, chance encounters, abrupt departures, kidnappings, love at first sight, and death – it happens that Dai-yu meets Bao-yu, and their own tragic cycle of meetings and partings is set in motion.

It is clear, then, that separation and reunion, as I have defined these terms, are central to Cao's concerns from the outset. Andrew Plaks has pointed out that images of forgetfulness and loss – undoubtedly metaphorical separations – are found in virtually every chapter (Plaks 1976: 74–5). And in considering the structure of the novel as a whole, Plaks draws attention to the 'ceaseless alternations' it exhibits 'along such axes as movement and stillness, union and separation, or prosperity and decline', alternations which 'make up the overlapping web of narration that comprises the dense texture of the novel' (1976: 6). He also points out that this texture is complemented by a pattern of 'seasonal and elemental periodicity'. And when taken together, Plaks suggests, these cumulative patterns of alternation and periodicity evoke:

an all-inclusive vision of the totality of existence that underlies and sheds a measure of 'meaning' upon the particular mimetic figures of the text. The fact that the characters in the novel most often fail to draw comfort from such a total vision ... serves to point up what we may call a 'tragic' disjunction of vision between the time-bound perspective of mortal sensitivity and the detemporalized structure of intelligibility that is by definition beyond the scope of mimetic representation. (1976: 6–7)

In other words, the characters of the novel, in the course of enacting their variously tragic and happy moments, *might* well draw comfort if they could adopt an 'all-inclusive' perspective on life, and on the crises experienced by them within it. However, the great difficulty for them of ever actually doing so (i.e. without detaching themselves completely from the normal flow of life, as Bao-yu eventually does through entering the 'gate of emptiness') is made clear in Cao's novel at every turn. In any case, let me stress again that the 'greatest Chinese novel' – an immensely popular one – is very clearly and explicitly focussed upon a reunion garden in which, for a moment, the problem of human separation is suspended.

I might add that in addition to providing many detailed descriptions of leave-taking behaviour, and of Chinese 'manners' more generally, *Hong lou meng* also clearly illustrates something else: the extent to which classical texts and poetry have been seen, in China, both as guides to proper behaviour and as philosophical source-matter. The young central characters of the novel – Bao-yu and the girls in the garden – repeatedly recite, refer to, and debate the merits of, ancient verses. They also write their own poetry (e.g. to commemorate the 'reunion garden'). Taking my cue from this, in what follows I will first illustrate, with a few brief examples, the extent to which Chinese poetry has focussed on the separation constraint. But such poetry is not merely sentimental, for it also often has, and is acknowledged to have, explicitly political connotations. At the end of the chapter I will provide one outstanding example of this.

Sending-off a friend with emotion

In noting the orientation of Chinese verse towards friendship, C. P. Fitzgerald observes that:

as the emotional crisis of friendship is the moment of separation, parting from a friend inspires many of the best poems in China. The circumstances of the poets' lives in China made such separations frequent and prolonged. (1986: 344)

That is to say, the occupation of many poets as members of the Chinese 'scholar class' implied travel, dislocation, and separation. As Fitzgerald also notes:

The immense distances of the Chinese Empire, the dangers of travel, and the inadequate means of communication made these partings a very real and often final separation of two friends, who might not meet again, at best, for many years. The fact explains and illuminates the frequent theme of leave-taking in Chinese poetry. (1986: 345)

Many verses deal quite specifically with the process of 'sending off' (*song*), and in so doing they provide contemporary readers with classical 'words of parting' (*bieci*).

For example, the Tang poet Li Po (701–762) – himself the subject, as I will later discuss, of a fascinating 'separation' verse – wrote the following lines as a leave-taking gift for his friend Wang Lun:

> I climb on board the ship, which begins to pull away;
> And suddenly from the shore I hear
> A rhythmic foot-step and singing.
> Peach-blossom Lake is a thousand feet deep;
> But this is nothing compared to the depth of Wang Lun's feeling
> When he sends me on my way![3]

Note that in his translation of this poem, Obata (1922: 67) renders the closing line: 'But it cannot compare, O Wang Lun, with the depth of your love for me.' In the original Chinese, however, it is specifically the deep emotion or feeling (*qing*) of the sending-off (*song*) which is highlighted (*buji Wang Lun song wo qing*). In other words, the warmth of the leave-taking expresses the relationship between the two men. The image portrayed is of a growing physical distance between friends which is suddenly bridged, if only momentarily, by the fading sound of Wang Lun tramping on the shore as he sings a farewell song to Li Po. (This can be compared with the 'retaining of memories', *liu ge jinian*, between friends described in chapter two.) A great many other classical verses deal in similar fashion with poignant moments of separation between friends.

Greeting a friend with food, drink, and modesty

Although separation is a frequent theme in classical poetry, many verses also deal directly with reunion, and with reunion commensality. The following Tang poem, by Tu Fu (a poet to be discussed below), is simply entitled 'The Guest Arrives' (*ke zhi*). It conveys not only the eagerness with which the guest is awaited, but also the host's sense of modesty about his own ability to properly greet a visitor. Specifically, he apologises – in ways which will already be familiar from chapter five – for the quality of the food and wine which will be served in their reunion meal:

The house, north and south, wet with spring water,
But every day only a flock of gulls arrive.
Seldom are the flower-paths swept for a coming guest;
Yet from today will I open the thatched gate for you.
Supper is only one dish, the market is far,
My home is poor, offering bad wine in broken cups.
Perhaps we'll share one with the old neighbour-man!
I'll shout to his side of the hedge, we'll drink up![4]

A longer verse by Tu Fu, 'To the Recluse, Wei Pa', addresses the poignancy of reunion commensality. That is, it deals both with the joy of reunion between friends, and with the sadness (and inevitability) of separation and death. It begins with these words (in a prose translation by David Hawkes):

Often in this life of ours we resemble, in our failure to meet, the Shen and Shang constellations, one of which rises as the other one sets. What lucky chance is it, then, that brings us together this evening under the light of this same lamp?

The verse goes on to comment on the passing of time, which is somehow exacerbated by the fact of separation:

Who could have guessed that it would be twenty years before I sat once more beneath your roof? Last time we parted you were still unmarried, but now here suddenly is a row of boys and girls who smilingly pay their respects to their father's old friend.

Of course, a reunion meal is hurriedly arranged in honour of this old friend, complete with 'spring chives cut in the rainy dark' and plenty of drink which is pressed on the visitor:

'Come, we don't meet often!' you hospitably urge, pouring out ten cupfuls in rapid succession. That I am still not drunk after ten cups of wine is due to the strength of the emotion which your unchanging friendship inspires. Tomorrow the Peak will lie between us, and each will be lost to the other, swallowed up in the world's affairs.[5]

Sending off loved ones in silence

Earlier I stressed the great variation in ways of dealing with separation and reunion, and suggested that in Angang and Dragon-head those involving close kin (and sometimes friends who live in close proximity) are often dealt with silently – and on the surface even abruptly. Note then a very different sort of verse about a moment of departure, 'Song of the wandering son' (*you zi yan*), written by Meng Jiao (751–814 A.D.). This describes a mother's fear of an extended separation from her son. But bear in mind that it was written by a man, and that the verse in fact expresses the emotions good sons should feel towards their mothers:

> The thread in the centre of a tender mother's hand,
> The garment worn by the wandering son.
> At the moment of departure, the close stitching
> Conveys her fear of a late return (*chichi gui*).
> How could this blade of grass – this child –
> Possibly repay (*bao*) maternal warmth?[6]

In this poem (a very popular and often-cited one), the pain of separation is heightened by anxiety about a 'late return'. But the emotion is expressed, again, not through words – and what words could express the emotions felt between mother and son? – but rather through the close stitching in the garment she makes for him. The son, a 'blade of grass', i.e. something vulnerable and in need of the 'springtime warmth' of maternal affection, cannot repay (*bao*) her, but is clearly obliged to make a 'return'.

But what about leave-taking involving husbands and wives – or indeed lovers? Here I should stress that a great deal of Chinese love poetry is also redundantly focussed on the problem of separation and loss. Given the psychological link between love and separation, this is perhaps unsurprising. But as Anne Birrell explains (in a volume which provides many excellent examples of the genre), the emphasis in Chinese love poetry on separation is also due to the discreet classical convention that the lover of any woman described in a poem should be *absent* – and therefore by definition greatly missed (Birrell 1986: 1–28). A rather wonderful early example is found in an anonymous poem – 'On, on, ever on and on' – from the first or second century A.D., which ends with the following lines:

> Longing for you makes one grow old,
> Years, months are suddenly grown late,
> Of rejection say no more,
> Let's try and get enough food.[7]

The arrival and departure of the gods

In chapter three and elsewhere, I've discussed the significance of rituals of separation and reunion within Chinese popular religion. As I noted, much of the activity of this religion would lose its sense if the spirits were not seen to have *mobility* – for many rituals relate directly to the 'arrival' and 'departure' of the dead. When ancestors are greeted in Dragon-head, or the Stove God is sent off (*songzao*), this is made manifest. And when, in Angang, spirit-mediums go into trance, they are explicitly summoning or 'inviting' (*qing*) the gods to make an appearance: that is, they are trying to make them 'descend' (*dao*). There is strong evidence that a very similar conceptualisation of divine mobility existed in ancient China, and a similar view of the role of mediums. K. C. Chang notes that verses in the *Ch'u Tz'u* (attributed to Qu Yuan, c. 340–278 B.C.) suggest 'that the basic role of a shaman ... was that of an intermediary who used alluring dance and music *to induce the deity to descend* (Chang 1983: 48, my emphasis). He cites in particular a verse from the *Ch'u Tz'u* (in translation from Hawkes) which illustrates beautifully the 'restless' nature of Chinese spirits. The verse describes a god (or spirit) suspended, as it were, over a community:

> The God [*ling*] has halted, swaying, above us,
> Shining with a persistent radiance.

But then the god vanishes:

> He yokes to his dragon car the steeds of god:
> Now he flies off to wander [*you*] around the sky.
> The god had just descended [*ji jiang*] in bright majesty,
> When off in a whirl he soared again, far into the clouds.[8]

A life determined by separation

Having given a few illustrative examples of 'separation' poetry, I now want to discuss one verse in more detail. This is Tu Fu's 'Dreaming of Li Po' – the opening lines of which I cited at the beginning of this book – and a poem which focuses directly on three themes which are central to my own concerns: separation as a human constraint, the relationship of separation to death, and the Chinese politics of separation and reunion. (Let me stress that these themes are all standard ones in Chinese classical poetry.) The choice of a verse by Tu Fu (712–770) for this illustrative role is not random – for he is routinely described, in popular discourse as well as in scholarly literature, as 'China's greatest poet' (e.g. in Chou 1995: 1, Graham 1965: 39, Hung 1952). Indeed, Eva Shan Chou has recently argued that the critical and popular reception of Tu Fu as a 'cultural icon' is unique, in part because it has tended to conflate the (mostly orthodox) moral-political values of his poetry with what are seen to be the genuine or 'sincere' emotions of the poet himself.[9]

But could this empathy with Tu Fu 'as a person' transcend cultural boundaries? It should, after all, be possible to forget, at least momentarily, the cultural and historical context in which Tu Fu wrote 'Dreaming of Li Po' – that is, to forget that it was written twelve-hundred years ago in Chinese, and in accordance with the conventions of classical Chinese poetry; to forget that it reflects specifically Chinese views of human attachments and relationships; to forget the political upheavals which inspired it and which also dramatically transformed Tu Fu's own life – and to engage instead in an unlearned reading of the translated verse. For most non-Chinese readers, 'Dreaming of Li Po' would perhaps then seem a literary text both strange (e.g. its closing line refers to 'water-dragons') and strangely familiar (at least so for a twelve-hundred-year-old verse). Readers might, for instance, be struck by the force of the opening lines which I have already cited: 'After the separation of death [*sibie*], one can eventually swallow back one's grief; but the separation of the living [*shengbie*] is an endless, unappeasable anxiety.' They might feel that in these lines Tu Fu had approached a 'familiar emotion', or even a 'universal truth': namely that ongoing separations among the living *do* provoke endless anxiety, and that separations of this kind perhaps *are* – somewhat counter-intuitively – more problematic for human beings than the separations of death.

But of course the verse *does* have an historical context: the dislocations brought about by the An Lu-Shan Rebellion, the repercussions of which deeply affected the Tang dynasty and contributed to its decline. Tu Fu was born into a relatively privileged background, but (after the start of the Rebellion) spent much of his later life on the move under difficult personal and financial circumstances. As Chou notes, 'Tu Fu himself never saw the end of war, and to the end of his life his poetry reflected the displacements and devastations of wartime' (1995: 4). His desire for a career in public service, momentarily realised, was ultimately frustrated, and he despaired of the fate of the divided empire. Meanwhile, he often lived separated from friends and loved ones, and as a result the political and the personal often merge in his poetry. As Tu Fu wrote near the end of his life:

> I dare not demand great lines of myself
> When worries come, I sing of separation[10]

A very specific context of separation informs the verse 'Dreaming of Li Po'. In about 745 A.D., the young and relatively unknown Tu Fu met Li Po, another brilliant poet, his senior, and already a famous man. Their brief association had a great impact on Tu Fu, who went on to write a number of tributes to his elder. David Hawkes points out that the life of Li Po, unlike that of Tu Fu, was *not* in general dramatically influenced by the An Lu-Shan rebellion. However in 757 Li Po *was* arrested (for associating with a prince who had anti-regime designs) and sent into an exile from which he was not expected to return. Although he was eventually given an amnesty, Hawkes says that when Tu Fu wrote 'Dreaming of Li Po' he undoubtedly thought of him 'as a condemned man whose banishment would probably cost him his life' (Hawkes 1967: 90).

In the verse (after the opening line about death-separations and life-separations) Tu Fu frets about his older, much-respected friend from whom he is separated by a great distance, but who has lately come into his dreams.

> That my old friend should come into my dream
> shows how constantly he is in my thoughts.

Tu Fu worries in particular that his dream-image of Li Po may in fact be the wandering (and very real) soul (*hun*) of his friend, who might already have died in exile. And so the poem concerns the 'separation of death' (*sibie*) and, explicitly, the close relationship of this to the 'separation of the living' (*shengbie*), from which it at times becomes almost indistinguishable:

> I fear that this is not the soul of the living man:
> the journey is so immeasurably far.
> When your soul left (*hunlai*), the maple woods were green:
> on its return (*hunfan*) the passes were black with night.

Although the tone of the verse is intensely personal and emotional, the separation being discussed is obviously a political one – Li Po has been sent into exile due to political intrigues – and one which symbolises, and is symptomatic of, a divided and crumbling empire. For this reason, the verse may also be read (along with much of classical Chinese poetry) as a commentary on the politics of the day:

> Lying now enmeshed in the net of the law,
> how did you find wings with which to fly here?
> The light of the sinking moon illumines every beam and rafter of my
>   chamber,
> and I half expect it to light up your face.
> The water is deep, the waves are wide:
> don't let the water-dragons get you![11]

Conclusion

In this chapter I have cited both *Hong lou meng* and the classical Chinese poetic canon in order to do three things. First, I wanted quite simply to draw attention to this literature, the existence of which serves to underline the long-standing concern in China with processes of separation and reunion. Second, I wanted to point out that this well-known literature continues to have a popular impact today – because, among other things, it provides models of socially appropriate behaviour during moments of parting and return. Third, I wanted to suggest that this literature has some direct and indirect political implications. At times (e.g. in the case of Tu Fu's 'Dreaming of Li Po'), poetry has been a way of discussing, more or less directly, the politics of the day (in this case the politics of Tang dynasty intrigues). But such poetry also 'remains contemporary', or at least has the potential to do so, through its metaphorical relationship to ongoing political developments. In the next chapter I will cite some examples in which classical poetry is quoted by modern politicians – i.e. in which it serves as a good, because highly emotive, source of political rhetoric. And as I said at the end of the last chapter, Chinese narratives of separation and reunion are potentially quite seductive: they have such long histories, as products of China's long dynastic heritage, that their conclusions – for those entangled in familial and national politics – must at times seem inescapable.

9   The politics of separation and reunion in China and Taiwan

> After a long period of unity, the empire must divide; and after a long period of division, the empire must unite (*tianxia shi hejiu bifen; fenjiu bihe*).   Opening line of *San Guo* (*The Romance of the Three Kingdoms*)

More than 1200 years ago, the Chinese poet Tu Fu used separation from an exiled friend as an emotion-laden metaphor for the problems of the Tang dynasty. But the resulting verse is far from unique. On the contrary, Chinese poets have routinely used emotive personal metaphors to discuss the politics of the day. In Bourdieu's terms, the analogies must seem 'irresistible', and modern Chinese narratives of national unity have also often drawn on the same and similar metaphors. In this chapter, I will suggest that the idioms of separation and reunion make for especially seductive political rhetoric in modern China and Taiwan, where they have many personal associations, and therefore a kind of natural legitimacy. But I will also hope to show that this seductive – or 'enchanting' – rhetoric has its limitations *in history*. This is so, first of all, because many people can be shown to have resisted its charms, i.e. they have 'gone away', in various senses, in spite of it. (Indeed, it can be argued that the separation/reunion matrix actually facilitates certain kinds of separation rather than making them more difficult.) Second, the very existence of historical communities (families, localities, nations) within which separations are problematic – and within which this rhetoric can therefore be *meaningful* – depends on an ongoing production of communal relatedness. When relatedness is allowed to lapse, the obligation to 'return', something which is never simply given, may begin to fade away.

Here my discussion will primarily focus (because of my own ethnographic interests) on the vexed 'Taiwan issue'. However, in order to illuminate my themes I will also draw briefly on material about Chinese patterns of migration (in which those separated from the homeland have often been assumed, in T'ien Ju-k'ang's phrase, to 'keep their eyes set on China' in the hope of a later return); and about Hong Kong's return in 1997 to Chinese sovereignty (during which classical imagery was often used in official pronouncements). It goes without saying that the political

156

status of Taiwan is a matter of great political sensitivity. The questions involved are far from straightforward, and I'll only supply a cursory outline of the background to them. I must stress as well that it isn't my intention to promote any political line, much less to put opinions into the mouths of people in Angang and Dragon-head. (The view from Angang is especially complex, and I couldn't imagine summarising it.) I simply want to discuss these matters in relation to my own theoretical and ethnographic interests, and perhaps in so doing to draw attention to connections which might otherwise be overlooked.

Two places

This book is comprised primarily of ethnographic material collected during research in two places: Angang and Dragon-head. Angang is a small township (*xiang*) in Taiwan, where almost all of the residents trace their descent to Han Chinese migrants from Quanzhou prefecture in Fujian province. At the time of my fieldwork, the economy of Angang rested primarily on a declining fishing trade and some nascent tourism. Dragon-head, in turn, is a small village (*cun*) near a market-town (*zhen*) in northeastern mainland China (in the large three-province region known as *Dongbei*). Most of the residents of Dragon-head earn their living from agriculture, and some have benefited nicely from China's post-Mao economic boom. Like people in Angang, most of them trace descent to Han Chinese migrants from somewhere else – in this case from Shandong province. With respect to this, I should note that by the late nineteenth century, Taiwan (where Angang is located) and northeastern China (where Dragon-head is located) did share, in spite of their different historical origins and trajectories, a converging political status: both were *outposts* of a (Manchu) Qing empire in terminal decline. Both then also became – albeit for different periods – Japanese *colonies*, and in fact many elderly people living in both Angang and Dragon-head can recall similar experiences of childhood under occupation.

But there are also a number of significant differences between these two places, and here I cite only a few. First, Angang is a fishing community in a semi-tropical climate, and as a result the regular patterns of work and of social life are very different from those found in Dragon-head, which is a farming community in a cold, sometimes frozen, part of northeastern China. Second, although standards of living in Angang are low relative to the rest of Taiwan, they are high compared with those in Dragon-head (from which vantage-point the wealth of most Taiwanese seems truly remarkable). Third, although literate people in both communities read the same Chinese characters (*hanzi*), everyone in Dragon-head speaks a version of the 'Mandarin' dialect as their first language, whereas most people in Angang speak it as a second language (it is the official language of both Taiwan and mainland China). In Angang, people normally speak *min'nanhua* (a Fujianese dialect) in their homes and among friends, and some older people do not properly speak 'the national language' at all. Fourth, in the region around Dragon-head the most important non-Han populations are comprised primarily of Koreans and Manchus (*manzu*), whereas in the region around Angang they are comprised primarily of Taiwan's Austronesian aborigines. (In both cases, the interaction between Han and non-Han has been of critical historical significance.) Fifth, popular religion (including the mounting of large and expensive festivals at temples, and the more or less everyday use of spirit mediums at private altars) plays an exceedingly prominent role in local social life in Angang; whereas in Dragon-head religion is a relatively sporadic, private – and sometimes even intentionally secret – matter. Sixth, in Angang, where children have a reasonable chance of advancing beyond primary school to higher education, schools and schooling are much more salient in both familial and collective life than they are in Dragon-head, where educational opportunities are for most people fairly limited.

Of course, some of the most striking differences between contemporary Angang and Dragon-head derive from the outcome of the Chinese civil war, in which the Communists (CCP) defeated the ruling Nationalists (KMT) – who subsequently retreated to Taiwan. As a result, for the past half-century Angang, along with the rest of Taiwan, has been ruled by a KMT-dominated government based in Taipei, whereas Dragon-head, along with the rest of mainland China, has been ruled by a CCP-dominated government in Beijing. During this time, i.e. within the life-span of my informants, many aspects of economic, social, and cultural life in Angang and Dragon-head have been dramatically shaped by official (and sometimes highly divergent) policies. For example, older people in Dragon-head have been through collectivisation and de-collectivisation, and have lived through the Great Leap Forward, the Cultural Revolution, and the post-Mao reform era of Deng Xiaoping. By contrast, those living in Angang have participated in Taiwan's post-war economic boom, and have lived through the New Life Campaigns, Taiwan's highly competitive (and often nationalistic) brand of schooling, and have been exposed to Western, especially American, cultural influences during a time when the mainland's door to the outside was very firmly shut. (For some interesting perspectives on post-war Taiwanese culture, see Harrell and Huang 1994.)

Chinese similarities

And yet: there are many similarities between life in Angang and life in Dragon-head, and of course more generally between life in Han Chinese communities in Taiwan and those in mainland China. My personal reaction to fieldwork in Dragon-head was to be constantly reminded of my fieldwork in Angang. This is hardly surprising. Commenting on his research in southern Taiwan and various locations in mainland China, Myron Cohen observes that 'even where differences in spoken language were most obvious, the Han Chinese [in the various fieldwork sites] shared traits so numerous as to readily place them in a culture area easily distinguished from those of nearby state civilizations in Asia' (Cohen 1994: 90).

The comparative material presented throughout this study is undoubtedly consistent with such a notion of Chinese cultural unity (or similarity) as reflected in 'shared traits'. I have shown that just as separation and reunion, as I have defined them, are matters of concern for the people in Dragon-head, so they are matters of concern for the people in Angang. In both places the movements of gods and ancestors prompt rituals of 'greeting' and 'sending-off' (the most important of which take place, in the two communities, at the same times of year). In both places the 'greeting' and 'sending-off' of guests is a major point of etiquette, while partings and returns which involve close relations may be dealt with abruptly or silently. In both places, reunions, including the key reunions of the lunar new year, are of profound importance, and are almost always marked by elaborate moments of commensality. In both places, doors and gates – the spaces through which people, spirits and 'forces' arrive and depart – receive careful attention, and are protected and decorated in similar fashion (e.g. with auspicious calligraphy). And so on.

Having located such continuities across space, it is not very difficult to locate them in time. As I have shown in the last chapter, classical Chinese verses (still widely read and studied both in the mainland and Taiwan) focus on moments of parting and return in ways which must seem, from the perspective of those in Angang and Dragon-head, distinctly familiar. While Cao Xue-qin's more recent 'novel of manners', *Hong lou meng*, is set in an aristocratic Qing family, everyone in Angang and Dragon-head would surely recognise the 'Chinese' practices, etiquettes, and emotions which he describes. Taking this and other evidence from the past (e.g. historical documentation about Qing imperial ritual), and linking it with evidence from present-day Angang and Dragon-head, it is not difficult to construct a mental image which 'unites China' – i.e. which by focussing on something important about these various Chinese times and places helps to give them conceptual unity. In this case, the 'something important' is the matrix of separation and reunion. But is this a misleading way of seeing things?

Separated from the ancestors

'Separation', in one form or another, has been a crucial factor in Taiwan's modern political history. Here one should bear in mind the status of the island – originally inhabited by Austronesian aborigines who still make up a significant minority of the population – as a relatively recent Han Chinese settlement frontier. (In what follows, I rely primarily on Shepherd's comprehensive history (1993) of Taiwanese political-economy from 1600–1800.) When Taiwan was ruled by the Dutch in the mid-seventeenth century (1624–61) there were probably no more than 50,000 Chinese on the entire island, and perhaps twice as many aborigines (Shepherd 1993: 86, 7). During Taiwan's subsequent (1661–83) occupation by the Ming loyalist Zheng Cheng-gong – who ousted the Dutch – the Chinese population more than doubled, boosted primarily by the arrival of soldiers and war refugees from the coastal provinces of southeastern China (Shepherd 1993: 96). It is important to stress that Zheng Cheng-gong was a (Han Chinese) Ming-loyalist, fighting to overthrow the (Manchu) Qing dynasty. This meant that Taiwan was for him – as it would later be for the KMT – a place of exile and military reconsolidation. Zheng's prize was the mainland, and when the Qing eventually forced his regime to surrender, many of the refugees and soldiers who had accompanied him to Taiwan 'eagerly returned to their mainland homes' (Shepherd 1993: 106).

In fact, at this point (late seventeenth century) it was the intention of at least some Qing officials to evacuate the *entire* Chinese population of Taiwan, i.e. to abandon the island altogether in order to focus on more pressing concerns (Shepherd 1993: 106). But Taiwan was not abandoned, and there followed instead a series of fluctuations in official policy to-wards Han settlement across the Straits. Significantly, family immigration (i.e. the movement to Taiwan of families rather than individual males) was forbidden in 1684, then allowed in 1732, forbidden in 1740, allowed in 1746, forbidden in 1748, allowed in 1760, and forbidden in 1761 (Shepherd 1993: 140–1). As Shepherd notes, these fluctuations mirrored official de-bates about how best to maintain control of a potentially troublesome frontier province. On the one hand, forbidding family immigration use-fully created:

a population of male laborers dependent on the government for access to families on the mainland. Filial obligations to parents and the duty to maintain ancestral sacrifices reinforced this dependence. (Shepherd 1993: 143)

This policy clearly relied on the (assumed) desire of migrants to *return* to their families and ancestors. But it was also argued that exactly the opposite policy, i.e. allowing family immigration, would help to diminish the considerable volatility of Taiwanese society. For example:

In a 1727 memorial requesting the lifting of the restrictions on family immigration, Governor-general Kao Ch'i-cho continued [the arguments of a previous advocate of aggressive Han colonization in Taiwan]. Kao found Taiwanese customs unruly, characterized by excessive drinking and gambling. Whereas immigrants in the old settled areas around Tainan had wives and families, those in the newly opened areas to the north and south had none, and the latter, 'whose hearts have nothing to remember with affection', were often involved in disturbances. Living in groups of 20 to 40 men, they spent their leisure and their income on gambling and drinking. When drinking and gambling exhausted their earnings, they turned to robbery. 'If each had a wife, inner and outer would be distinguished and there would be no confusion and disorder. If each had to support a wife, drinking and gambling would diminish. If each had to protect a household, robberies would decrease.' (Shepherd 1993: 149)

Behind both policy options we may discern a tension between two different, yet overlapping, ways of viewing Chinese attachments. In the first (and this would coincide with official orthodoxy), it is assumed that the (given) tie to ancestors and patrilineally defined homes is paramount: i.e. that in the hearts of good Chinese the significant return is to the ancestral graves – which are somehow 'always there'. (To ration such reunions is to keep people under control.) But in the second, it is assumed that Chinese people – some of whom may have forgotten their ancestors! – create their own most important attachments 'in the present' (in my terms through ongoing cycles of *yang* and *laiwang*). The significant returns are therefore often domestic and neo-local in orientation: i.e. towards the familial 'inside' (*nei*), and towards the places where relatedness is being produced *now*. (Allowing such reunions might encourage people to keep themselves under control.) While there is perhaps an ideological preference, even in popular conceptualisations, for the first ('patrilineal') model of attachments (e.g. for the narrative of the faithful migrant returning to make offerings at the ancestral shrine in his native place), it often seems that in practice the second ('creative') model of attachments predominates. Significantly, the second model also arguably allows more room for the incorporation, e.g. by marriage, of outsiders (including non-Han). By extension, and very significantly, it implies a much more fluid notion of 'Chinese identity'.

In any case, undoubtedly the most important fact about this era of policy fluctuations is that *illegal* immigration continued unchecked throughout it. People were leaving China in droves, and in time the Han population of

Taiwan increased (and was allowed to increase) markedly. This illustrates, if nothing else, that the presumed Chinese 'tie to home' – however strong, and however open to imperial manipulation – wasn't enough to keep a great many people from deciding to move away. Even when explicit policies were in place to *prevent* such movements they had a limited effect, not least because of the strong socio-economic 'push factors' which were encouraging people to depart. It should also be stressed that native-place ties, as such, were of variable significance among different mainland populations. For example, Mary Erbaugh has pointed out that although they were of considerable importance to many Han, the same cannot be said for the Hakka, who would simply 'dig up the ancestors' bones and carry them in jars to each new settlement' (Erbaugh 1996: 207). More generally, as Hill Gates observes:

The Chinese that many Westerners think of as home-bound, stuck in great-great-grandfather's mud, must have been rare. People in vast numbers were constantly on the move. (Gates 1996: 63)

But what, we might ask, did they *tell* themselves when moving? In other words, given a cultural context in which separation is portrayed as deeply problematic, what stories made migration acceptable? And what practices made it possible? Perhaps unsurprisingly, most migrants to Taiwan did not see themselves, nor did others see them, as having left home permanently. This was so for some very concrete reasons:

When male family members (travelling in groups of friends and kin) left home in search of economic opportunity, they retained important rights in and obligations to their natal families. A married man left behind a wife to serve his parents and care for his children. This minimized travel and living expenses and gave the sojourners greater flexibility in pursuing opportunities. The sojourner's definition of success was to *return* wealthy to family and native place. (Shepherd 1993: 311, original emphasis)

To put this differently, migration to Taiwan was normally conceptualised, at least in its initial stages, as a *non-separation*. And when migration eventually became (as it indeed became for many) a long-term reality, one's 'native place' might effectively be brought along as well:

Those who decided to relocate initiated chains of migration from their native places, recruiting kinsmen and neighbors to join them in their pioneering enterprise and gradually bringing over wives and dependent parents and children. (Shepherd 1993: 311)

This pattern of 'migration without separation' clearly raises some intriguing questions in relation to what I have called the separation constraint (for recent discussions in the field of Chinese migration studies see Pieke and

Mallee 1999). Much of the material in this book could be taken to imply
that separation is always a great *problem* in China, and that people will go
to great lengths to avoid it. However, as I have noted from the outset, many
separations are in fact desirable – e.g. when they are sociologically 'necessary' (as in the case of weddings), or when they help put some useful distance
between 'over-dependent' kin (such as fathers and sons). So it is with
migrations: the separations they imply are often desirable, e.g. economically advantageous, even when they entail high emotional costs. Ellen
Oxfeld, in her account of Chinese tanners in Calcutta, points out that the
'dispersal of family members over space [may be seen as] part of a strategy
through which economic and political risks are contained' (Oxfeld 1993:
11). It is moreover tempting to say that Chinese culture, far from making
such migrations impossible or difficult, actually facilitates them, not least
through idioms and practices which help people articulate and 'manage'
the problems (including the emotional problems) of spatial dislocation.
(Bear in mind that such idioms and practices can also give people a
legitimate means of leaving behind people and situations they might wish
to leave behind in any case.)

In discussing the Chinese living in Southeast Asia at the time of his
fieldwork in Sarawak (in the late 1940s), T'ien Ju-K'ang observed that they
did indeed seem to have strong emotional bonds to their mainland homes:

However many years they have stayed in the South Seas the China-born Chinese,
and many of the overseas born too, keep their eyes fixed on China and their hearts
set upon home. A Hainanese saying runs: 'The rivers and streams of Hainan go
far, far away to the oceans, but they always return at the last'. Dreaming of his
future the Chinese emigrant sees himself back in his own village giving a three
days' theatrical performance at the village temple, with a great banquet and
hundreds of fire-crackers, buying more land, building a fine new house, perhaps
engaging a beautiful concubine to care for his declining years. Sometimes the
dream comes true . . . (T'ien 1953: 9–10)

However T'ien makes three important points in this regard. First, that
the dream of return normally *doesn't* come true. Second, that having strong
'attachments to the homeland' is hardly unique to Chinese migrants.[1] And
third, that if and when such Chinese attachments *do* become or remain
particularly strong, it is surely for specific politico-economic reasons, and
not simply out of some primordial sense of loyalty.

And this takes us back to an explicitly political question: is there any
obvious reason why the (natural?) desire of a migrant to maintain ties with
his family and friends, to return home as a conquering hero, etc., should
translate itself into a *patriotic* attachment, as such? Is the analogy irresistible? Prasenjit Duara observes that in this century the ties of migrant
Chinese to China, as a homeland, have been an explicit object of narrative

exploitation. Following Wang Gungwu, Duara points out that *huaqiao* – the term which has come to be conventionally used for the 'Overseas Chinese' – literally means 'Chinese sojourner'; and that in nationalist usage the expression was intended to promote the idea that 'the primary loyalty of all Chinese', wherever they might be, 'was owed to China' (Duara 1997: 42). But according to Duara, nationalists working among the Overseas Chinese, and hoping to get financial support from them, actually found this a difficult line to promote: they had to struggle to 'secure and fix a sense of Chineseness' which could 'mobilize the emigrants to the national cause' (1997: 39). In short, this had *not* happened naturally – even though its effects later became 'naturalised' and 'dehistoricised' (i.e. taken-for-granted) – *nor* had a 'natural' resistance to separation from the ancestral land kept these people at home in the first place.

Forceful and peaceful reunification

Now back to Taiwan, the Han residents of which are not said to be *huaqiao* ('Chinese sojourners') for the obvious reason that since the war Taiwan has been seen (both by the KMT and the CCP) as an integral part of China. Still, histories of Chinese sojourning are highly relevant to my concerns, because after 1949 the KMT repeatedly stressed the links of Han Chinese in Taiwan both to the mainland in general, and to their ancestral 'places of origin' (*zuji*) in particular. Perhaps unsurprisingly, such native-place loyalties among Taiwanese have sometimes simply generated (and well before the arrival of the KMT) 'sub-ethnic' tensions, rather than a generalised Chinese patriotism.[2] But they nevertheless made possible the comparison of the most recent sizeable group of Chinese to arrive in Taiwan – the 'mainlanders' who accompanied Chiang Kai-shek into his post-1949 exile, some two million of them, about a quarter of whom were soldiers (Eastman et al. 1991: 352) – with their 'Taiwanese' predecessors there. The KMT also stressed that just as the patriotic Zheng Cheng-gong and his forces found themselves temporarily separated from the mainland during their seventeenth-century campaign to recover it, so too with Chiang Kai-shek. As Hill Gates has observed, once this separation became normalised – i.e. once it became clear that it would be a relatively long-term state of affairs – the question of how to occupy the separated mainlander population became a considerable concern. She suggests that many became the beneficiaries of what she calls a 'tributary mode of production' in Taiwan. The state, she argues, extracted surplus from the local economy and redistributed it amongst its own (overwhelmingly mainlander) functionaries (Gates 1996: 204–42; cf. Gates 1981). Needless to say, this extraction (and/or the perception of it), along with the suppression of virtually all local anti-KMT sentiment or activity, created tremendous resentment. It also arguably led many native Taiwanese to devalue precisely what the KMT ostensibly hoped to promote: their ties to the mainland (however see below).

But at the same time there was also undoubtedly considerable sympathy for the personal circumstances of some civil war exiles. As Gates observes:

No one can fail to share the pain of friends who left mother and father in [Shandong] 'for a few months,' and find themselves, thirty years later, in a still alien outpost, not knowing at New Year's whether they should address prayers to their parents' spirits. These personal tragedies lend an emotional color to the mainland recovery policy and make it *difficult to view objectively*. (Gates 1981: 266, fn.5, emphasis added)

Once again, personal separation-dilemmas became a metaphor for national division. And against this background the KMT promoted the 'liberation' of the mainland, however unrealistic, as a sacred responsibility: a necessary conclusion to the history of national division at the end of the civil war. Taiwan's de-facto status in the world, and the clear unlikelihood of the KMT ever actually recovering the mainland, did not, until very recently, alter this claim. At the time of my fieldwork in the late 1980s, the slogan 'unite China' (*tongyi zhongguo*) was found virtually everywhere in Taiwan – on everything from fishing boats to bottles of beer.

As I've already said, the background to the reunification issue is highly complex, and the diplomatic manoeuvring has been far from transparent. Matters have often seemed to rest on fire-power rather than 'narrative manipulation', as such, but in fact the two have often merged. In 1950, i.e. almost immediately following their victory in the civil war on the mainland, the CCP was preparing to take Taiwan from the KMT, when President Truman (in response, as it happens, to developments on the Korean peninsula) sent the Seventh Fleet to the Taiwan Straits in order to block the expected attack (Keith 1989: 44–5). China protested furiously to the UN Security Council about this action, which from the Chinese perspective of course constituted interference in its *internal* affairs (Keith 1989: 49–50). Since that time an uncomfortable stand-off has been in place, one in which the US, both implicitly and explicitly, has guaranteed the security of Taiwan.[3]

Beijing, for its part, has consistently sent out two messages: that Taiwan will be attacked if it tries to separate from China, but that a peaceful reunification of 'flesh and bone' is surely what everyone wants. As Deng Xiaoping put it:

we must work for the return of Taiwan to the motherland, for China's reunification. We will endeavour to attain this goal in the 1980s; it will be an ever-present and

important issue on our agenda, though there may be twists and turns in the course
of its development. (Deng 1984: 224)

As part of this general endeavour, China has sought (for the most part
successfully) to isolate Taiwan diplomatically as a rogue province. Indeed,
the KMT in Taiwan – for all its notable successes – has faced considerable
practical difficulties due to this isolation. This has also had significant
'ritual' implications, for as I noted in chapter two, the roles of Chinese
political leaders are often represented in terms of the etiquette of parting
and return. That is, the national political narrative importantly includes a
narrative of 'greeting' and 'sending-off' significant guests, a conceptualisation with long historical precedents. As the guests it *openly* receives have
become less and less important ones (at least in terms of their international
power and influence), Taipei might be said to have lost its legitimacy as the
ritual centre of the Chinese empire (or state). Note, however, that it might
well have developed, during the very same period, quite different forms of
legitimacy.

Sabre-rattling aside, the post-Mao, post-Chiang years have seen a sustained increase in substantive (especially economic) China-Taiwan links,
and things have often seemed on course for peaceful reunification. But
meanwhile something else has been happening in Taiwan. In the post-war
era, a significant ('native') Taiwanese middle-class emerged, and its wealth
gave it increasing political leverage. Post-Chiang political liberalisation
made possible the promotion of a distinctive Taiwanese cultural identity,
the championing of aboriginal rights, and – most dramatically – the open
advocacy of independence from the mainland. Many Taiwanese combined
such positions with the open expression of long-simmering hostility towards the KMT and the manner of its rule on Taiwan. (Although it should
be stressed that 'Taiwanese' views of the KMT have in fact always been
highly differentiated.)[4] Meanwhile, the KMT old-guard – mainlanders
separated from their mainland homes – long ago began to die out, and the
party has gone through a gradual process of 'Taiwanisation'. And now,
new forms of self-identification appear to be emerging in Taiwan, some of
which blur – not least because of fifty years of inter-marriage – the traditional mainlander: Taiwanese distinction.[5] Return visits to mainland 'places of origin', made possible by the lifting of travel restrictions in the 1980s,
have been disappointing for many, and such experiences have arguably
increased the perception that Taiwan and China are, on the whole, very
different sorts of places.

    Meanwhile, the stance of the post-Taiwanisation KMT has shifted in
complex ways, and increasingly to one which abandons the notion of 'one

China'. Whatever the underlying rationale for this public shift, it has prompted fury in Beijing. In 1995, China held naval manoeuvres in the Taiwan Straits which coincided with Taiwanese presidential elections – in which the issue of independence was at least implicitly on the agenda. In response, and in a historical echo of previous incidents, the US sent ships to the region. In an editorial published at the time (25 July 1995), the *People's Daily* declared that the 1.2 billion people of China would never allow 'the plot of "the independence of Taiwan"' to succeed, and condemned President Lee of Taiwan – himself a native Taiwanese, but the descendant of migrants from Fujian – as a 'criminal of the Chinese people throughout the ages'. (Bear in mind that this happened at a time when Taiwanese investment and tourism was flooding into China.)

President Lee's more recent comments (made in the summer of 1999), to the effect that Taiwan is now a separate state which should engage in state-to-state relations with China, have prompted an even more furious reaction. The *People's Daily* pointed out that Lee's very own 'lineage kin' (*zongqinmen*), in his very own 'ancestral place' (*zuji*) in Fujian province, had attacked him for his proposals. They said he should 'hold his horses at the edge of the precipice' (*xuan ya le ma*), lest he be seen as a 'stubborn and defiant son' (*wuni zi*) who had forgotten his ancestors.[6] A *People's Liberation Army Daily* commentary published the same week clearly shows the strength of feeling surrounding these issues. Here I'll cite edited extracts at length not least because they illustrate the salience, in rhetoric of this kind, of the notions of 'unity' and 'reunification':

In spite of divisions and reunifications [*fenfen hehe*] in China's 5000 years of history, gradual integration [*dayitong*] is still the major developmental trend. The ravages of war and the tearing apart of flesh and blood [*gurou fenli*] have occurred throughout Chinese history, and this has been a lesson to the sons and daughters of China [*zhonghua ernu*]. It has given the Chinese people both a strong sense of national coherence [*ningjuli*], and a tough spirit of solidarity [*tuanjie jingshen*]. By comparison with other peoples, *the Chinese have a much stronger national sentiment when it comes to treasuring unity* [*zhenzhong tongyi*] and upholding unity [*weihu tongyi*] . . .

The return [*huigui*] of Hong Kong, and the forthcoming return of Macao to the ancestral land's embrace [*huidao zuguo de huaibao*] have aroused the desire of the Chinese people to settle the Taiwan issue, to realise the total reunification of the ancestral land [*shixian zuguo wanquan tongyi*], and to rejuvenate the Chinese nation.

The commentary then goes on to attack President Lee's comments and proposals *vis-à-vis* the status of Taiwan, saying that he has

undermined national sovereignty and China's territorial integrity, betraying the interests of the nation, and stinging the hearts of the Chinese people. He can be called the number one filth of the nation . . . Those who uphold unity [*jianchi tongyi*] and oppose division [*fandui fenlie*] will prosper, while those who resist this historic trend will perish.[7]

Anthropology and Chinese unity

Taiwan is China – that at least is not in dispute . . .   Maurice Freedman[8]

In the field and in the armchair, we have come to know Taiwan as perhaps no other part of China. But in what sense is Taiwan really a part of China?

Emily Ahern and Hill Gates[9]

And here I wish to insert an anthropological footnote. Given the sensitivities surrounding the political status of Taiwan, it was probably inevitable that anthropologists would get caught in the cross-fire. They have been accused of conflating Taiwanese and Chinese culture, and therefore of inappropriately implying Chinese 'unity'.[10] On the other hand, if anthropologists were to say that Taiwan is not culturally 'Chinese', they would undoubtedly be accused of promoting Taiwanese independence. Of course, pointing out cultural continuities and discontinuities between distinct localities, a matter of considerable complexity, does not *have* to be a political game, but it is hard for it not to be turned into one.[11] Behind this issue lies the fact that for some five decades it has been relatively easy for anthropologists to conduct fieldwork in Taiwan, while it has (until quite recently) been impossible for them to do so in mainland China. Taiwan has undoubtedly been asked to serve, *on some level*, as a China 'substitute', and arguably even for those (myself included) who would strongly reject such a notion of substitutability. It is also true that in the post-war era, Taiwan – for all its dramatic changes – has often seemed not to be undergoing the sweeping *cultural* transformations imposed by the socialist revolution on the mainland. Perhaps on some level it seemed plausible, to borrow Keelung Hong's phrase, to 'look through' Taiwan in order to see an authentic version of a vanishing China: authentic because of Taiwan's perceived continuities with a Chinese (cultural) past.[12]

But I should stress that the modern Chinese politics of culture – as all anthropologists could not help but know – are certainly much too complicated to have supported such a fantasy for very long. This is not least because the very traditions on which *any* notion of Chinese 'cultural unity' must rely (whether in anthropological theory or in political rhetoric) are themselves far from timeless and unchangeable. On the contrary, throughout the twentieth century they were subject to repeated change and an explicit official anti-traditionalism (cf. Cohen 1994). While the CCP-directed version of this is widely-known, it is important to remember that the KMT also sought to transform Chinese culture (e.g. to combat 'superstition', and to transform kinship loyalties into patriotism). It is surely ironic that the two political movements which have argued most forcefully for Chinese reunification – not least on the grounds of a shared identity – both set about dismantling some of the very traditions which inculcated a common sense of Chinese identity in the first place (cf. Watson 1992). And then later – also ironically – anti-KMT activists on Taiwan reacted against this anti-traditionalism by becoming *supporters* of certain aspects of a traditional local culture which is arguably 'Chinese'. As Myron Cohen explains: 'In contrast to its fate on the mainland, traditional Chinese culture on Taiwan was transformed into a modern assertion of national identity, but in this case the identity was Taiwanese and the nationalism was linked to the movement for Taiwan independence' (Cohen 1994: 107).

In the midst of these complexities, anthropological data can obviously be exploited by all sides (i.e. through contributing to narratives of cultural unity *or* distinctiveness); but Sangren, for one, has suggested that the politics of identity are best left to others:

it is Chinese, Taiwanese, min'nan[13] people themselves who will determine the parameters and contextual significance of their variously defined and practiced identities; it is not for Western scholars to pass judgement upon which among the various possibilities has the greatest historical, cultural, 'objective', warrant. (Sangren 1998: 164–5)

However, Sangren also points out that anthropology *does* have an observer's role to play in shedding light on the process of identity construction itself:

perhaps most significantly by making explicit the ways that history and cultural identity are employed in situationally specific 'rhetorics of legitimacy' rhetorics that become part of emergent social realities. [Anthropologists can] record some of the possible fault lines, some of the issues that constitute the current context within which identity politics is conducted. (1998: 165)

As I have been saying throughout this book, one of the central narratives in Chinese and Taiwanese social and cultural life is the alternating pattern of separation and reunion. This extends to political rhetoric as well, where the narrative may become, in Sangren's terms, a powerful 'rhetoric of legitimacy', i.e. a means of legitimating specific modes of social power. My only 'political' aim here is simply to draw attention to this fact.

Contemporary Chinese rhetoric of separation and reunion

In recent Chinese discussions of the status of Taiwan, the connection between reunification with Hong Kong and reunification with Taiwan has always been close to the surface. Chinese politicians have repeatedly indicated that their way of handling the return of Hong Kong would prove that the policy of 'one country, two systems' was a workable option across the Taiwan Straits as well (cf. Cheung 1984: 3). It is worth noting Cheung's view that the leadership in Beijing was, at least initially, ambivalent about the implications of taking back Hong Kong from the British (in other words, their desire for reunification should *not* be taken for granted). He even suggests that they were probably only 'made aware of the implications of the expiry of the New Territories lease in 1997 by visiting British delegations' (Cheung 1984: 46). The eventual decision to re-integrate Hong Kong, and to do so on a rapid time-scale, was primarily motivated, according to Cheung, by the impact this would have *on the Taiwan question* itself (1984: 45–54).

The return of Hong Kong, when it did come, prompted a flurry of rhetoric which drew directly on classical images of separation and reunion. For example (and a great many other examples could be cited), just before the handover date the *People's Daily* published an article entitled 'The flower of the heart bursts with joy' (*xinhua nufang*). This pointed out that the region's new flag would have in the middle of it a red bauhinia flower which, by way of classical allusion, symbolises unity:

In the *Yiwen Leiju*, the chapter on filial sons, a story is recorded. Two brothers had decided to live separately and to divide the family property [*fenyi*]. But then one day they walked outside of their home and saw three red bauhinia flowers on the same stem. The foliage of these plants joined to form one unbroken shade. The brothers sighed: 'Even flowers rejoice to be united [*ju*], why should we separate?' They decided against their original plan and stayed together in harmony [*yong he*].[14]

The flag, with its evocative flower-design, is therefore, the paper says, the perfect symbol for a territory about to be reunited with the homeland. More than this, the flag 'has been loved by the people of Hong Kong since the decision [about its design] was publicised'. Three days later, the newspaper published a poem, 'Our Hong Kong', which set out the agonies of one hundred years of separation, and which included the following lines:

For one hundred years we have stared, with great intensity, across the
    water;
After one hundred years of waiting our garments hang loosely upon us . . .[15]

Note again that the idiom of 'garments hanging loosely' – *yi dai jian kuan* – is used to describe the weight one loses from missing someone during a prolonged separation.

Reports in the *People's Daily* of the post-handover celebrations in Beijing – edited extracts of which follow – also focussed repeatedly on the themes of separation and reunion. Note that these passages draw directly on idioms of kinship and commensality, and it is especially striking that the 'heartbreaking' separation of Hong Kong is conceptualised as being both a fraternal and a maternal separation:

Beijing has painstakingly prepared the first reunion feast [*diyi dun tuanyuan shengyan*] for a flesh-and-bone brother [*gurou xiongdi*] who has been separated for a hundred years. [. . .] On the evening of July 1st, 1997, in the Worker's Stadium in Beijing, the most moving night of reunion [*tuanyuan ye*] in the century was held! . . . The banners 'Nanjing Treaty' and 'Beijing Treaty' [symbolic of China's 'unequal treaties' with Western powers] were displayed on the stage – while shouts of 'Mother! Mother!' sent a heartbroken shiver through the crowd. Hong Kong was ripped apart from its mother [*xianggang congci shengsheng yu muqin wunai fenli*]! . . .

The emotions of the audience were stirred: an era has passed, and now there is hope for a peaceful reunion [*heping tongyi*]. Separated flesh-and-bone await reunification [*tuanyuan*] . . . Seeing the strong emotions of the crowd, an elderly man sitting next to me [i.e. next to the author of the *People's Daily* report] said, 'When we are celebrating the return of Hong Kong, we are missing Taiwan [*si taiwan*]. The people's glorious enterprise [*minzu daye*] of unifying the ancestral land [*zuguo tongyi*] is unstoppable!'[16]

I should point out that while this might be dismissed as mere propaganda, in my experience such powerful views (about reunification both with Hong Kong and with Taiwan) are quite commonly held in mainland China.[17] And I do also want to stress – indeed, this is one of the main points of this chapter – that the rhetoric of Chinese reunification, however seemingly overblown, draws explicitly and heavily on idioms which have deeply personal associations for many Chinese, including people in Dragon-head and Angang. To put this another way, a child who grows up experiencing Chinese 'separations and reunions' would – perhaps – be susceptible to the appeal of this rhetoric, or at least find its logic comprehensible. The power and emotional force of the Chinese separation and reunion idioms are perhaps such that they make political reunification *seem* inevitable, and (as I've already noted) this conclusion has, until recently, been scarcely debatable in Taiwan, much less in mainland China.

Distance and 'emotional indoctrination'

Now, however, to put it simply, some people in Taiwan oppose this way of thinking. In this respect, I want to cite a recent, and I think extremely interesting, article written by Li Fuzhong for one of the main Taiwanese newspapers, the *Central Daily News* (17 September 1997).[18] The article – which is entitled 'Demolish the bewitching screen of sentimental language' (*pojie ganxing yuyan mizhang*) – begins by noting a speech made by a mainland Chinese official on the occasion (precisely!) of the mid-autumn festival, i.e. during the 'moon-cake' festival of reunion (discussed in chapter one) when families should ideally gather together in the family courtyard to admire the moon:

On the eve of the mid-autumn festival, China's foreign secretary Qian Qichen delivered a speech to the Taiwanese people in which – as expected! – he 'dropped a booksack' [*diao shudai*] full of classical allusions. In order to add sentimental appeal [*ganqing suqiu*] to his political propaganda, he cited the Tang poet Zhang Jiuling:

The moon rises shimmering from the sea;
although far apart, we are together [*gong*] in admiring the moon above.

Li's article then goes on to set out, in fascinating language, the dangers for the Taiwanese inherent in this kind of speech-making:

In recent years, during official encounters between the two sides of the Straits, reciting poems has become the established practice . . . The recitation of poems serves to dazzle [*mihuo*] and stun [*zhenshe*] the adversary . . . In the diplomatic tug-of-war between the two sides, Chinese officials frequently play this consummate trick. Naturally it puts psychological pressure [*xinli yali*] on Taiwanese officials . . . But the China-Taiwan problem is a practical one, and one which greatly affects the interests of the Taiwanese people. If Taiwanese officials keep walking into the trap, choosing to negotiate through the bewitching screen of traditional Chinese language [*zhongguo chuantong de yuyan mizhang*], it is hard for us not to be outplayed. Besieged by the sentimental language of emotional indoctrination [*ganxing tongzhan yuyan*] used by Chinese officials, we should strengthen our immune systems [*mianyi xitong*]!

Here one should recall the standard interpretation of much classical Chinese verse: that poets such as Tu Fu used poetic metaphors, highly personal and emotive ones, to discuss – and help to overcome – the division and decline of the empire. And it is surely intriguing to compare this with the message of the commentary just cited, which calls on the Taiwanese people to *resist* (exactly) the poetic language of national unity. Of course nobody seriously imagines that rhetoric (or poetry) alone will determine the outcome of the 'Taiwan issue'. But everyone knows that *national* separation does have a *personal* (often highly emotional) dimension, and that the narrative of national unity therefore may indeed have, if properly framed, a strong sentimental appeal. For this enchanting narrative, as I have explained, draws on evocative associations with the practices and idioms of separation and reunion: on the mid-autumn festival of reunion, on the symbolism of reunion commensality, on classical poetry of leave-taking, and so on.

As I've already pointed out, however, it would be wrong to assume that Chinese narratives of separation and reunion – however powerful, and however deeply familiar – are irresistible in history. Just as the Chinese tie to family and home is *not* natural or given (and people certainly often find separation from their kin and neighbours an acceptable, or even desirable, state), it cannot be assumed that the attachment to the nation or 'ancestral land' is based on given and permanent loyalties. These must instead be produced and sustained, and always in specific historical contexts. Furthermore, as I've already suggested, the very existence of an historical community within which separation becomes problematic – i.e. the existence of a community within which the narratives of separation and reunion can be truly *meaningful* – depends on an ongoing production of communal relatedness. If relatedness is allowed to lapse (we might say: if there are too many separations and not enough reunions) then the obligation to 'return' may begin to fade away.

Here I might return briefly to the example of Chinese popular religion, as practiced in Angang and elsewhere. As I explained in chapter three, deities are key manifestations of local ritual productivity. That is, the localised power of particular gods is felt to derive, in part, from the cumulative ritual efforts of local worshippers. These efforts crucially involve the process of inviting or 'summoning' (*qing*) gods to descend to the community and into specific homes, where – having enjoyed local hospitality – they can then provide blessings and protection for all. But if the local people are *not* very good at summoning the gods, or not very serious about doing so, local images and statues of gods become less and less powerful. Eventually, as I was told, they 'amount to nothing' (*yuelaiyue meiyou*), because the gods simply stay away. Similarly, the neighbourly work of relatedness – the friendly cycle of *laiwang* – is known to be an ongoing process. If people want to have significant relations with non-kin, they generally must 'attend the rituals', i.e. literally show up for them, and otherwise participate fully in the joys and sorrows of life. Of course, the production of ties within families also requires ongoing, in fact never-ending, work: a child who fails to fulfill his obligations within the cycle of *yang* can be literally written out of a family estate. (Recall the charge against President Lee: that he has become a 'stubborn and defiant son', *wuni zi*. But why?) In short, relatedness is never simply given.

This has arguably become a part of the 'Taiwan problem'. For fifty years, the rhetoric of separation and reunion has implied that Chinese unity is inevitable. But sporadic official pronouncements of unity (rather like the dramatic greeting and sending-off of honoured guests) may be felt, perhaps understandably, to be rather empty of content. Where could the unity be seen? Meanwhile, people in Taiwan have been hard at work on the everyday – often private, often unremarked – production of *local* relatedness, furiously spinning out cycles of *yang* and *laiwang*. These cycles have significantly entangled 'mainlanders' with 'Taiwanese', Han with non-Han, and they have led directly to shifts in the perceived cultural identities of those now living in Taiwan. In other words, in a context of near-absolute separation over a period of many years, these people have arguably, and whatever the political consequences, started down the road of becoming something else.

Conclusion: the separation constraint

> We might almost say that social life does violence to the minds and bodies
> of individuals which they can sustain only for a time; and there comes a
> point when they must slow down and partially withdraw from it.
>
> Marcel Mauss[1]

I began this book by pointing out that in China, 'processes of separation
and reunion, epitomised in moments of parting and return which involve
both the living and the dead, are often a matter of great concern'. I also
promised to describe 'bit by bit', the Chinese fascination with separation
and its counterpart, reunion. In the chapters building up to this one, I have
dutifully described many practices and cultural objects – festivals, greetings, leave-takings, religious rituals, funerals, weddings, poems, banquets,
novels, doors, political speeches, and newspaper articles – which suggest,
when taken together, that separation is indeed a common theme, perhaps
even an obsession, in Chinese culture.

But is there anything unique about the Chinese focus on the separation
constraint? My argument from the outset, on the contrary, has been that
the *underlying* problem is a universal one: i.e. something given to humans in
their natural environments. Separation is unavoidable, and this has both
psychological and sociological implications. The universalist psychology
of Bowlby and others suggests that all human infants have instinctive
emotions related to processes of 'attachment'. Separation anxiety is integral to this: the natural response of infants to the loss (however temporary)
of those on whom they depend. By extension, such natural responses set the
psychological framework for adult life, during which our key emotional
crises may again be seen as effects of the separation constraint.

Of course behind this constraint – something which can be viewed
realistically, i.e. as a problem of literal 'departures' and 'arrivals' – lie very
complex questions of human relatedness. But actual processes of separation and reunion are themselves interesting (and important!) precisely
because they are often the most tangible manifestations of human autonomy and dependency. For this reason, the seemingly 'psychological' separ-

ation constraint, in all its rather literal expressions, has significant socio-logical implications. And this helps to explain why the rituals and practices of separation and reunion, far from being restricted to China, are found quite literally everywhere. Such rituals both express and explore issues of human relatedness, and in many cases they arguably produce (in the Durkheimian sense) the very collectivities within which separation has social and emotional significance.

Having invoked Durkheim, it is appropriate that I should acknowledge in this regard the work of Marcel Mauss. Mauss's rather wonderful classic, *Seasonal Variations of the Eskimo*, proposed, in brief, that patterns of collective concentration and dispersal (we might say reunion and separ-ation) are the very essence of human relatedness. In the summer, Mauss observed, Eskimo families lived far apart from one another, in individual (i.e. familial) tents scattered over very great distances. In the winter, how-ever, they lived in close proximity, and often in large multi-family units. Whereas during the summer dispersal there was virtually no religious activity whatever, in the winter the group, huddled together, lived 'in a state of continuous religious exaltation' (Mauss 1979: 57). Much of this activity centred on the *kashim* – an enlarged winter house in which there were 'no divisions or compartments but only a central hearth because the *kashim* is the communal house of the entire settlement' (1979: 45). This was 'always essentially *a public place* that [manifested] the unity of the group' (1979: 58, emphasis in original).

As James Fox observes in the forward to his translation of *Seasonal Variations*, there is a tension in Mauss's explanation of Eskimo concentra-tion and dispersal. On the one hand, there are clearly uniquely strong ecological factors which could explain, in quite simple terms, their pat-terns of housing, settlement and social activity. Mauss acknowledges these, and sometimes gives them prominence. But on the other hand, he observes that similar patterns are found in a great many societies, perhaps in *most* human collectivities. Surely almost everywhere, and regardless of ecological conditions: 'social life does not continue at the same level throughout the year; it goes through regular, successive phases of in-creased and decreased intensity, of activity and repose, of exertion and recuperation' (Fox 1979: 10).

But if the ecological explanation is put to the side, what could explain this pattern? Of the Eskimo, Mauss proposes that their dispersed summer-time recuperation may be *psychologically* necessary (Mauss 1979: 79). But he suggests that it is the intensely social winter period when people actually recognise and enact their crucial social attachments; in other words, this 'exertion' is *sociologically* necessary:

Winter is a season when Eskimo society is highly concentrated and in a state of continual excitement and hyperactivity. Because individuals are brought into close contact with one another, their social interactions become more frequent, more continuous and more coherent; ideas are exchanged; feelings are mutually revived and reinforced. By its existence and constant activity, *the group becomes more aware of itself* and assumes a more prominent place in the consciousness of individuals. Conversely in summer, social bonds are relaxed; fewer relationships are formed, and there are fewer people with whom to make them; and thus, psychologically, life slackens its pace. (1979: 76–7, emphasis added)

What I find most striking about this Durkheimian explanation is that Mauss, or so it seems to me, treats the state of winter-time unity as *the* moment of social recognition, rather than seeing the process of going apart and coming back together itself as constitutive of this recognition. He argues, in effect, that living together produces an awareness of society, and that living apart gives us a chance to recover from this awareness, in all its intensity. Whereas I would suggest – and surely this is what the ethnography being discussed by Mauss implies – that separation itself also provokes social recognition, not least by making possible the subsequent reunions in which human relatedness is there to be seen and celebrated anew.

Following on from ethnography of this kind, and from Mauss's discussion, it is not hard to see how the idioms of alternating separation and reunion – integral to the development of childhood attachments, of familial sentiments, of collective solidarities – could be extended to narratives of national unity. Again, this is not simply a Chinese tendency. As T'ien Ju K'ang observed, loving one's homeland – perhaps especially in contexts of displacement, conflict, and territorial division – is hardly unique to the 'Chinese sojourners'. On the contrary, we know that some of the last century's most intense emotional politics focussed, in totally different historical and socio-cultural contexts, on cases of national division and dispersal: in Germany, in Korea, in Cyprus, and so on. The 'Taiwan issue', for all its peculiarities, in fact embodies a very characteristic social dilemma. This is – if I may summarise it this way – the tension between autonomy and dependency, elevated from an individual concern, by way of evocative 'personal' idioms, to a central role in the ongoing narrative of national division and unity.

And this takes me back again to the question of universality: if the separation constraint is indeed universal, why should it be any more focussed-upon in China than elsewhere? The simplest response would be to say that it isn't: that Chinese children don't suffer from especially bad separation anxiety; that Chinese rituals of separation (e.g. wedding-separations and death-separations) simply follow near-universal patterns; that the Chinese politics of national unity and division are no more intense and emotional than those found in many places around the world. I could, of course, cite endless examples of separation as a theme in non-Chinese literature. The *Odyssey*, to give a famous instance, is clearly an epic of separation (anxiety) – the tale of a man living dangerously apart, until the very last possible moment, from his family and home:

> And when long years and seasons
> wheeling brought around that point of time
> ordained for him to make his passage homeward,
> trails and dangers, even so, attended him
> even in Ithaka, near those he loved.[2]

Or, to cite a more recent epic, recall that from the very first passage of *Remembrance of Things Past*, and the first traumatic departure of his mother, Proust is surely completely obsessed with separation – perhaps even more so than Cao Xueqin![3]

However I'd like to end this book by making a bit of a case for cultural specificity. While I don't think the personal emotions of separation are necessarily stronger in China than elsewhere (or at least I wouldn't know how to prove such a thing), I would suggest that one encounters there narratives and rituals of separation and reunion which are unusually *elaborate*, unusually *explicit*, and unusually *literal*. For instance, we could certainly say that narratives of separation are central to Christianity (e.g. in the story of the Fall, or in the account of Christ's exile on earth, etc.). But in Christian ritual we do not encounter what is seen at the very core of Chinese popular religion: a whole series of procedures for literally 'greeting' and 'sending-off' gods, acts which themselves effectively produce and sustain localised divine power.

As Feuchtwang (1992) and others have explained, the etiquette of such literal rituals draws on an 'imperial metaphor' – i.e. it seeks to re-enact (e.g. at a family altar) the proper behaviour of imperial agents. The simple procedures of 'greeting' and 'sending-off' in this religion therefore serve to connect, quite explicitly, the local world of everyday interactions, the religious world of divine interventions, and the political world of imperial (or state) control. This logical consistency or 'fit' extends as well to a more general Chinese world-view (or folk philosophical theory) in which all relationships – whether they involve emperors or peasants, spirits or forces – are always seen to be in a state of flux. This philosophical story, in other words, emphasises process and movement, and holds that relatedness in this cosmos is always, by definition, a matter of meetings and partings. This aspect of Chinese folk philosophy coincides, in turn, with an ancient historical/mythological tradition which provides many evocative, almost universally known, accounts of separation and reunion (from the Tang poetry of leave-taking, to the *San Guo* epic of national division, to the myth of Mulian's descent into hell, to the *Hong lou meng* garden of reunion). This narrative tradition helps make very tangible the abstractions of Chinese religion and philosophy – and indeed the abstractions of Chinese politics – by relating them directly to personal, or more correctly familial, experience.

It seems plausible to suggest that someone brought up in within the extremely coherent Chinese version of the separation and reunion matrix (i.e. living with the emotional dynamics of Chinese kinship, hearing the mythical narratives, enacting the religious rituals, and becoming engaged with the story of national division and unity) might become *especially* sensitised to the separation constraint. We might also suggest that the emotions of separation are actually *intensified* in China by the many explicit, and sometimes very moving, practices and idioms related to parting and return. But we should certainly bear in mind that in the end this 'making explicit' – not unlike Freud's famous *fort/da* game – may simply be a Chinese way of trying to ameliorate or control the problems posed for human relatedness, in all societies, by the inevitability of the separation constraint.

Notes

INTRODUCTION: AN ANTHOLOGY OF SEPARATION

1 From 'Dreaming of Li Po', translated by David Hawkes (1967: 87ff). The complete text of this verse will be discussed in chapter eight.

2 Radcliffe-Brown (1933: 117). I'd like to thank Peter Metcalfe for drawing my attention to this passage.

3 I say 'so-called' not out of disrespect for Chinese claims of sovereignty, but rather because this matter is one which clearly has important international implications.

4 As will become clear, 'separation' and 'reunion' are general glosses to cover a series of interconnected Chinese expressions and concepts. These include 'greeting' (*jie, yingjie, huanying*); 'sending-off' (*song, songbie, songxing*); 'bidding farewell' (*cibie, cixing*); 'words of parting' (*bieci, gaobie*); 'unite', 'union' and 'reunion' (*tongyi, tuanjie, tuanyuan, he*), 'separate', 'separation' (*bie, li, fen, fenbie, libie*); and so on.

5 Purely for the sake of the privacy of my informants, all place names and personal names in this book have been changed.

6 Freud suggests that this human 'death instinct' is revealed in attempts which are made (e.g. through compulsive repetition) to achieve a 'total draining of energy'. This expresses, he says, a desire for something (death) which is 'beyond' the pleasure principle (cf. Wollheim 1991: 179–86). This view has been rejected by many, including Bowlby (1978: 433–6) who suggests that it lacks any empirical validity.

7 I am grateful to Michael Lambek for drawing my attention to this work.

8 Daniel Stern, an author who assesses the difficulties at length, notes that:

> The [observation-based] discoveries of development psychology are dazzling, but they seem doomed to remain clinically sterile unless one is willing to make inferential leaps about what they might mean for the subjective life of the infant. And the psychoanalytic developmental theories about the nature of infant experience, which are essential for guiding clinical practice, seem to be less and less tenable and less interesting in light of the new information [based on empirical research] about infants. (Stern 1985: 5; cf. pp. 13–34)

9 While the issue of separation, or 'individuation', is central to Mahler's work, she does not conceive of the problem in realist terms. Briefly, she argues that infants, after an initial and brief form of 'autism', go through a 'symbiotic' phase of development, during which they are, from the point of view of the infant, effectively fused with their mothers. They then go through a crucial process of

'separation-individuation'; but this does not mean literal physical separation, as such:

> The most extreme separation reactions . . . seem to occur *not* in those children who have experienced actual physical separations, but in those in whom the symbiotic relationship was too exclusive and too parasitic, or in whom the mother did not accept the child's individuation and separation. (Mahler 1969: 225)

But if Mahler does not take separation literally, she nevertheless does give considerable weight to concrete interpersonal relations. That is, she foregrounds *observable* relations between infants and particular kinds of external objects (such as mothers who will neither accept nor enable separation), and not simply the internal imaginative state of the infant.

10 Trained in Kleinian psychoanalysis, Bowlby made use of key Freudian concepts and categories – although arguably with less subtlety than Freud himself – and like Freud was keenly interested in therapeutic practice. He also drew heavily on Darwinism, ethology, and early cognitive science. While his work has been influential in some circles, he was seen by many in the psychoanalytic movement as naively empiricist and positivist, and his theories were often met, according to Holmes, with 'outright opposition or polite indifference' (Holmes 1993: 5).

11 Bowlby's theories concerning the impact on children of separation from mother-figures have been strongly criticised on various grounds, notably by feminists (cf Holmes 1993: 45–51). It has also been suggested that Bowlby's emphasis on separation, as such, is misleading, and that he takes separation much too literally. Bowlby himself eventually acknowledged that terms such as 'separation', 'presence' and 'absence', are relative and therefore problematic in psychological usage. Ultimately, he said, the key issue in developmental terms was the 'accessibility and responsiveness', in both physical and emotional senses, of key attachment figures (1978: 42–3). Nevertheless, he arguably never shifted away from a fundamentally 'realist' approach to separation. Heinz Kohut's view, by way of contrast, is that infantile separation and other childhood traumas are not the *cause* of later problems in life, but that reactions to them are rather manifestations of underlying problems – i.e. they are flash-points:

> the gross events of childhood that appear to be the cause of the later disturbances will often turn out to be no more than crystallization points for intermediate memory systems, which, if pursued further, lead to truly basic insights about the genesis of the disturbance. (Kohut 1977: 187)

See also Daniel Stern's discussion of the limitations of attachment theory. While acknowledging that observation-based attachment theory *is* useful for predicting certain future relational trends – i.e. that one can predict the quality of a child's relationships in later childhood by observing the quality of their relationships in early childhood – Stern suggests that this is true only in rather culture-bound, non-specific and highly general senses (Stern 1985: 195–8).

12 See for example, Ainsworth et al. (1978), in which different kinds of separations are examined in carefully controlled circumstances, and in which some cross-cultural and ethological comparisons are made.

13 This rather idiosyncratic work – cited both by Bowlby and Carey – was reissued in a later edition as *The Discovery of Death in Childhood and After* (Anthony 1971).

14 Margaret Mahler's work also highlights the profound ambivalence of children towards separation. This is notably seen during what she calls the 'rapprochement' subphase of separation-individuation. As Greenberg and Mitchell note:

> Mahler describes the prevalent attitude of the child during this period as 'ambivalent', because of his apparently conflicting affective reactions toward his mother, alternating between periods of intense neediness and *powerful desires for separateness*. The child fears loss of the mother's love following his separation from her, on the one hand, and reengulfment in the symbiotic orbit resulting from his need for her, on the other. (1983: 278, emphasis added)

For Mahler, separation is perhaps something dreaded, but also simultaneously something strongly *desired*.

15 Interestingly, Bowlby later stopped using the Freudian notion of 'libidinal needs', instead referring to a 'desire for attachment', a shift which obviously has the effect of de-sexualising, in his theory, relations between parents and children (Bowlby 1989: 23, n.1).

16 More specifically, he differentiates his own Darwinism from Freud's Lamarckianism (Bowlby 1978: 449–53).

17 Firth 1972: 8.

18 As Rosaldo observes, however, 'cultural elaboration' alone does not necessarily equate with importance or salience or force (1993: 16). That is, the explicitness and elaboration of rituals (such as death rituals) does not mean that these rituals necessarily encompass everything, or even the most important things, which might be said about a subject such as death. By extension, a subject such as separation, which does not necessarily lend itself (the Chinese case notwithstanding) to explicit or elaborate rituals, might nevertheless be of central importance.

19 For example, the religious philosopher Eliade stresses that in many initiations the break with childhood is clearly and redundantly symbolised as a kind of death (bear in mind that for Eliade religion is above all a means of addressing the problem of human mortality). So in the Australian material he cites, mothers fear that their sons will *in fact* be killed during initiations, while the initiates are told that they will die. 'The very act of separation from their mothers', Eliade says, 'fills them with forebodings of death . . .' (1965: 9, cf. Bloch 1992: 9). But the death that arrives through this separation is metaphorical:

> The maternal universe was that of the profane world. The universe that the novices now enter is that of the sacred world. Between the two, there is a break, a rupture of continuity. Passing from the profane to the sacred world in some sort implies the experience of death; he who makes the passage dies to one life in order to gain access to another . . . [T]he novice dies to childhood and the irresponsibility of the child's existence – that is, profane existence – in order to gain access to a higher life, the life where participation in the sacred becomes possible. (Eliade 1965: 9)

Ritualised separation is therefore, for Eliade, not simply a way of symbolising death, but more importantly (as for Herdt and others, see below) a key element in the production of moral persons.

20 Le Vine incorporates this into a more general hypothesis:

> One hypothesis worth investigating is that the level and patterning of excitement in the first and second years of life influence the child's activity level, attention responses, learning of cognitive and language skills, and *emotional vulnerability to interpersonal discontinuities (e.g. separations and losses)* during that period and in the ensuing years. (1990: 465, emphasis added)

21 Whiting has similarly attempted to show that initiations everywhere are basically elaborations on Freudian problems. See the summary of this material in LaFontaine (1985: 102–16).

22 'The validity of Van Gennep's formulation as a descriptive framework for the structure of *rites de passage* has been confirmed by subsequent research, but the pattern which he identified has never been successfully accounted for in theoretical terms. Van Gennep himself made almost no attempt to do so, beyond the general affirmation that the phase-structure of the ritual reflects that of the social transitions it mediates . . .' (T. Turner 1977: 53).

1 TWO FESTIVALS OF REUNION

1 The significance of ongoing reciprocity between the living and the dead is already well-documented in the anthropological literature on China (e.g. Watson 1988, Thompson 1988), as is the significance of ongoing reciprocal ties among the living (e.g. Yang 1994, Yan 1996). Relationships of both kinds, as Göran Aijmer has noted, are symbolically enacted through 'the paying of visits and return visits and the presentation and counter-presentation of symbolic gifts' (1991: 180). More to the point, Aijmer argues that the *entire* Chinese ceremonial calendar is structured around such reciprocal visits and transactions (and in particular those between ancestors and their descendants), and the reunions and separations they imply. But this is undoubtedly most clearly seen during the lunar new year, when 'visiting becomes spectacularly important' (Aijmer 1991: 180).

2 There may be many reasons for emphasising this latter part of the festival *now*, not least of which is that increased prosperity has greatly intensified the process of 'stringing together doors' (and of banqueting in general), while ongoing official criticisms of 'feudal superstition' make some people anxious about discussing the key ancestral observances which take place on and around new year's eve. But whatever the reasons, much of what sinologists and anthropologists have found most interesting about the new year festival – namely, the rituals and ideals at its core and their cosmological, theological and moral significance – certainly seemed, at first glance, secondary to people in Dragonhead, if not a matter of relative indifference. By contrast, the business of eating, drinking and 'playing' (*wanr*) with family and friends seemed to be taken very seriously indeed.

3 *Sheng cai you fang nian nian yu; zhi fu de dao bu bu gao.*

4 For a fascinataing discussion of the collective nature of pig production, sacrifice, and consumption in Taiwan, see Ahern (1981b).

5 In this particular case, the sending-off of the goddesses coincided with the end-of-year offerings which are made to the Emperor of Heaven (Tiangong).

These offerings are exceptionally elaborate and involve, among other things, the slaughtering of a pig, the carcass of which is then displayed in front of the family altar, itself piled with special offerings of food and money for this most powerful – if distant – of the gods. Large imperial-style screens dominate the altar. It is significant, however, that the offerings to Tiangong are generally *not* described as a 'sending-off', perhaps in part because he is deemed to be so high and distant, relative to other gods, that his *presence* is more implied than manifested. He is not represented by images on family altars, but instead by a single incense holder above the door, and only very exceptionally does Tiangong 'arrive' to speak through a medium in Angang. As I will later discuss, his 'location' within the house, i.e. at the barrier between inside and outside, is highly significant. In any case, the offerings to him coincide with the end-of-year heavenly 'meeting' he convenes, and in some cases the deities being 'sent-off' for this meeting are worshipped simultaneously. Then, on the fourth day of the first lunar month when, I was told, these gods return from Heaven, they are 'greeted' (*jie*) with elaborate offerings, following which spirit medium sessions reveal what transpired between them (i.e. in Heaven) during their time away.

3 GREETING AND SENDING-OFF THE DEAD

1 I'd like to thank the research team from the Academia Sinica's Institute of Ethnology who very kindly allowed me to accompany them to this festival in 1987.

2 On one level, this should already have been accomplished, because the god will have been 'invited' into the statue through the Daoist techniques of 'entering the god' and 'opening the eyes' (*rushen, kaiguang*). But the *kng put* makes this presence both more immediate and more observable.

3 During the first part of the ritual, in the morning, the god's image (in the sedan chair) usually remains directly in front of the altar (and in this position the god's spirit begins to repeatedly 'descend'). But during the day, usually in the afternoon, the sedan chair (as if of its own volition) will dramatically move out of the house, dragging the chair-carriers behind.

4 As Sangren notes, these pilgrimages *of* the gods are organised around affinal, rather than agnatic, metaphors: 'the deity images . . . are similar to brides who return on a customary visit to their natal homes' (Sangren 1983: 9).

4 THE AMBIVALENT THRESHOLD

1 If Tian'anmen is the symbolic gateway into China, it is striking that the characters upon it proclaim both the permanent solidarity of the 'inside', i.e. of those within the People's Republic (*zhongguo renmin gongheguo wansui*), and the permanent unity of the 'outside', i.e. of all the people of the world (*shijie renmin da tuanjie wansui*).

2 As Bray observes:

The word for 'family', *jia*, also means a house or home (as in *jia xiong*, my elder brother – as opposed to other elder male relatives of the same generation – and *jia nei* or *jiazi*, the person inside the house, i.e. my wife). Other words that conflate the meaning of family or kin with that of the building in which a family resides are *fang*, or wing (as in *nei fang*, the women's quarters, and *fang qin*, agnates), and *shi*, house or room (*shi nei* is the person who has remained inside her room, that is, an unmarried daughter, a virgin; *shou shi*, literally 'to take a room', means to marry) (Bray 1997: 91, fn. 1)

3 Cf. Yang's comprehensive discussion (1994) of the complex, and often problematic, 'art of guanxi' and social relations in China.

5 COMMENSALITY AS REUNION

1 Note that a distinction is made in China between two categories of food: *fan*, which is usually rice, but may also be any grain-based product; and *cai*, the 'dishes' of vegetables and meat which are served with *fan*. This distinction is of considerable symbolic importance, and dumplings are notable for containing both *fan* (the wrapping) and *cai* (the filling). When people prepare their new year's dumplings they try to come out even on *fan* and *cai*, because it is said that if they run short of filling, then in the coming year they will have plenty of rice but run short of 'dishes', and vice versa.

2 Literally: 'Under heaven [usually meaning in China] there are no banquets which do not scatter [i.e. end with a dispersal].'

3 This silence leaves us with very complex questions related to food and the aesthetics of emotions. In China, it is arguably the case that displays of emotion are sometimes effectively displaced onto the medium of food, and that emotions are often expressed (both implicitly and explicitly) through shared moments of commensality. Obviously, some of the reunion meals I have already discussed involve rather grand displays of emotion (public pronouncements of great friendship), and things are often drunkenly said during such banquets which would not be said elsewhere. It is considered appropriate for this to happen, and people have fairly clear ideas about how such emotions should be expressed (again, some people are felt to have a great skill for it). But many other meals (including those held at certain moments of departure and return, e.g. those involving parents and their children) do *not* provoke such statements, and here the very fact of commensality speaks for itself, it is part of the ongoing commensality which defines relationships of *yang*. (Note that similarly, with intense relations of *laiwang* or 'back and forth', commensality begins to speak for itself, and speeches no longer need be made, except under extraordinary circumstances.)

6 WOMEN AND THE OBLIGATION TO RETURN

1 In fact, many of the guests waiting for food to appear on that particular day (as on all the days of 'stringing together doors') were women, who themselves make the rounds of visits when visitors are not expected in their own homes. And I can hardly believe that in making this comment Mrs Yang intended to criticise her own husband (as opposed to men in general) on the grounds of laziness, given that he scarcely ever stopped working. But the new year did increase her work-load, whereas for men the period is explicitly seen as a time for *not* working, and instead for visiting and 'playing', *wanr* (although recall that some men find this form of 'playing' quite burdensome).

2 I should point out that in Angang women appear to be comparatively active in public religion; for example, they carry statues of gods during rituals, something that wouldn't be allowed in many other Taiwanese communities.

3 This is true whether or not these families are physically present, and even when the business at hand seems to have nothing to do with family matters. The extent to which even 'personal' relationships may be subsumed to familial concerns is perhaps indirectly expressed in the saying: 'Many friends are many roads, many enemies are many walls'. (*Duo ge pengyou, duo tiao lu; duo ge yanjia, duo du qiang.*) The point of the expression is that friendships represent opportunities, whereas enmities represent barriers. But the 'enemies' in the saying are in fact 'feuding families', *yanjia*, and it is, I think, normally assumed that even one's most 'personal' friendships and conflicts are ultimately collective (i.e. familial) matters.

4 Indeed, people in Dragon-head and Angang – both men *and* women – often make statements which appear to confirm precisely this: the basic 'inferiority of women'. For example, they point out that Chinese people 'take men seriously and take women lightly' (*zhong nan qing nu*), or they say that a couple with daughters only (i.e. without sons) 'doesn't have a family' (*meiyou jia*), or they say that in China women are evidently 'a class below' (*xia yi deng*). Such statements clearly relate (and are directly related by informants) to patrilineal ideologies which explicitly devalue, and sometimes even totally deny, the roles of women in producing and reproducing families, which are seen ideally to consist of chains of men (cf. R. Watson 1985). To the extent to which women's productivity and fertility is acknowledged within these ideologies, it is portrayed as something which must be controlled, not least because it always comes from the 'outside' of a patrilineal unit, and is therefore seen as a potential threat. In light of this, women really *shouldn't*, after all, be allowed to handle the important family business of separation and reunion, except perhaps in an indirect or behind-the-scenes way.

5 In this respect, I should note Sangren's thought-provoking analysis of gender symbolism in Chinese popular religion (1983). As Sangren points out, many of the most popular Chinese deities, ones thought to possess great power, are female. And the myths associated with them – in which women as mothers are glorified, while women as sexual agents are vilified – underline the complex and sometimes contradictory nature of Chinese gender representations.

6 Freedman 1979: 290, emphasis added.

7 Indeed, Elizabeth Johnson reports that in the past, in the New Territories, when men arrived from the groom's village to take the bride away, her lineage sisters would fight with them (Johnson 1999).

8 Elizabeth Johnson points out that parental attitudes towards the marriages of daughters are not unambiguous: the mothers of brides also sang wedding laments in some parts of China (personal communication). See my discussion below.

9 Cited in Potter and Potter (1990: 193).

10 Elizabeth Johnson notes that the practice of singing bridal laments has declined in the New Territories in this century, and has now come to an end: 'Brides had few opportunities to learn laments, and felt less need to lament the fact that they

were marrying. They were no longer forced into blind marriages, and improved communication and changing economic opportunities meant that they were no long separated from their natal homes' (Johnson 1999).

7 DEVELOPING A SENSE OF HISTORY

1 As de Certeau (1988) and many others have noted, the category of 'history', and processes of 'making history', are subject to dramatic variation across cultures and through time. One influential anthropological account of this is found in Borofsky (1987).

2 Bloch 1991, Lave 1988, Sperber 1985, Toren 1993.

3 Feuchtwang (1992) discusses the importance of calendars and time-related rituals for various historical identifications in China. In *The Anthropology of Time*, Gell discusses (among many other things) the development of 'time-talk' during childhood (1992: 132–45). In spite of the cultural-specificity of this, note that Gell argues *against* the idea of time-relativism (cf. his discussion of ageing in relation to *universal* existential dilemmas – 'the fatefulness of human existence' (1992: 206–20)).

4 This girl's 'traditional' poetry-lesson deserves closer examination. In 'feudal society' (and to some extent still in practice), daughters married out (*chujia*), lived away from their natal homes, and were not heavily obligated to their parents. Teaching them verses related to filial obedience, or indeed teaching them at all, was perhaps not, strictly speaking, traditional. This girl's father, in 1993, was concerned with his daughter's education, in part because she is his only child and also because these days, as I was told, 'any child is useful' (*dou youyong*). Also note that until this century the majority of rural Chinese (male or female) were illiterate. The study of classical texts was an elite activity, not something for farmers, and the spread of literacy is now held up as a revolutionary achievement. In the post-reform era – with its bourgeois pretensions? – it has even become fashionable for youngsters to recite the classics for guests.

5 Sperber for example, argues that being able to process uncomprehended information in *some* way is part of the developmental process of understanding. He notes that 'meta-representational abilities [i.e. abilities to form representations of representations] allow humans to process information which they do not fully understand, information for which they are not able at the time to provide a well-formed representation ... Children use this ability all the time to process half-understood information ... The obvious function served by the ability to entertain half-understood concepts and ideas is to provide intermediate steps towards their full understanding' (1985: 85).

6 Children growing up in Dragon-head now were not alive, it goes without saying, during the Tang Dynasty, nor even during the Cultural Revolution. The oft-invoked 'time when Chairman Mao was alive' (*Mao Zhuxi huo de shihou*) is ancient history – the childhood of their parents – but nevertheless around them in images and ideas, including the still-ubiquitous portraits of Mao. And his 'attack on tradition' is also there, literally written on the walls around their family *kang*s, in letters, in carefully stored photographs of struggle sessions, in

the memories of their elders, and 'there' in the absence of those who died, and in the failures of those who were destroyed.

7 This part of my analysis obviously draws heavily on Bourdieu's notion of a primary *habitus* which is consciously and unconsciously 'inculcated' in children through various practices within a symbolic environment (Bourdieu 1977, Bourdieu 1990).

8 One woman told me – as her young son listened – that the reason for these first-month restrictions is that it is very easy to become ill during that time. Any exertion on the mother's part is thought likely to affect her own health both in the present and for the remainder of her life, and thus (indirectly) to harm her children. You should simply stay on the *kang*, feeding your baby and being fed (mostly on boiled eggs and rice). Even then, the woman told me, people (specifically your female in-laws) will criticise the way you sit. She often placed her feet on the floor and her mother-in-law said 'you will have soreness there later'. This had in fact happened, so some of the ideas were, she said, perhaps 'scientific' (*kexue*). She washed her hair and developed scalp problems; she ate something cold, and now cannot tolerate cold foods, and so on.

9 It is hard to imagine the negotiated process of 'making history', which Borofsky reports as taking place among the Pukapukans (Borofsky 1987), taking place in China, except as an activity of the few among the hundreds of millions. Even harder to imagine is what Astuti says of the Vezo of Madagascar, that far from being fixed by a non-negotiable history, they '*refused* to let the present be determined by the past' (1995: 77, emphasis added). For in China, by contrast, the past is seen to have had a great, and indeed inescapable, impact on the present.

10 This is somewhat ironic, given that population *growth* was encouraged not by traditionalists, but by various reformers and revolutionaries, including Sun Yat-sen.

11 During the Cultural Revolution, the most extreme manifestation of this much longer-term Chinese self-critique, the traditional family was once again held up as a force against change. Of course, fierce attacks were also made on a whole range of 'old' thoughts, thinkers, beliefs, practices, texts, and on 'the past' as a whole. This process (whatever else it may have been or done) engaged a vast number of people in explicit reflection on 'culture' as an object, and encouraged them to think about this 'culture' as a problem – again, the burden of the past. Historical over-determination (including the 'feudal thinking' which resulted from all those childhoods spent on *kangs*) was something to be resisted. And the Cultural Revolution may indeed have momentarily given Chinese young people a different sense of their historical agency vis-à-vis this cultural inheritance. This is what much of the rhetoric was about: the capacity of the young to 'smash' the historically over-determined, ancestor-focused world in which they lived, to throw firecrackers at the elders – and, by definition, to *halt* the centuries-long cycle of separations and reunions with ancestors and spirits.

8 CLASSICAL NARRATIVES OF SEPARATION AND REUNION

1 Translation by Charles Stafford and Yen Yueh-ping; cf. David Hawkes's translation in the Penguin edition of *Story of the Stone* (Cao 1973: 50).
2 Translation by Charles Stafford and Yen Yueh-ping; cf. the translation by Hawkes (Cao 1973: 287).
3 My translation.
4 My translation. For alternative translations see Hawkes 1967: 109ff and Hung 1952: 177.
5 Hawkes (1967: 72).
6 My translation. For a discussion of Meng Jiao see Owen 1975. For an alternative translation of this poem see Graham 1965: 63.
7 Birrell 1986: 38–9.
8 Translation by David Hawkes, *Ch'u Tz'u: The Songs of the South*, Oxford: Clarendon Press, 1959, p. 37.
9 'His sufferings and his concern for the hardships of others began as personal qualities in the poems before they were translated into moral values. Readers have found in Tu Fu qualities of unswerving loyalty, instinctive generosity, and unpretentiousness which have a moral dimension but which originate in human feeling. Intense participation in Tu Fu's difficult experiences ... and an empathy with him as a person are joined to an appreciation of his social conscience' (Chou 1995: 12).
10 Translated in Chou (1995: 193).
11 Translated in Hawkes (1967: 87–92); note also the translation of a second 'Dreaming of Li Po' verse (Hawkes 1967: 93–8).

9 THE POLITICS OF SEPARATION AND REUNION IN CHINA AND TAIWAN

1 Nor, as T'ien points out, is it unique to Chinese migrant communities to be more 'traditional' in outlook than those who stay at home. Of the Southeast Asian ('Nan Yang') Chinese he says:

> it is probably true to say that the richer the Nan Yang Chinese the more self-consciously he strives to adhere to a "Chinese" way of life. In many of the material details of everyday life these Nan Yang Chinese often appear more Chinese than the Chinese of China. Amid the alien corn they hark back to Chinese precedents all the more strongly, even tending to conserve what in China itself has been abandoned. A well-to-do Chinese wedding in the Nan Yang brings out replicas of all the old Ming costumes which are seldom seen in China to-day. (T'ian 1953: 9)

2 Shepherd notes of the Han Chinese groups settling Taiwan:

> social ties reinforced, rather than cross-cut, native-place ties and subethnicity. In Taiwan migrants tended to locate among and associate with other migrants from home – kin and fellow villagers. Chain migration reinforced this pattern. Fellow migrants formed associations such as brotherhoods and worship groups that rendered mutual aid and provided companionship and security. (Shepherd 1993: 315)

As a result, patterns of subethnic rivalry in Taiwan, which emerged during the Qing dynasty – in large part, Lamley suggests, due to weak Qing governance –

have been 'an enduring and deeply rooted phenomenon' (Lamley 1981: 315). Rivalries existed most prominently between three groups: two Hokkien-speaking subethnic groups (one each from Quanzhou and Zhangzhou, different prefectures in Fujian province), and the Taiwanese Hakka (primarily immigrants from Guangdong province). Interestingly, Lamley argues that Japanese colonial rule, by contrast with Qing rule, was relatively effective in controlling subethnic tension, thus hastening 'the growth of a more distinctively Taiwanese perspective among the island's Chinese inhabitants' (Lamley 1981: 314).

3 Matters have periodically escalated, e.g. in 1958, when China bombed for some days the Taiwanese-controlled islands near to the mainland on which many of Chiang Kai-shek's troops were stationed (Keith 1989: 108–10).

4 For example, in his discussion of various Hakka political constituencies in Taiwan, Howard Martin suggests that:

> The traditionalist view of [Hakka] ethnic unity leads many to support the [KMT] position on Taiwan's political reunification with the People's Republic of China. The deeply felt idea of Hakka unity is expressed as a blood relationship (*xueyuan guanxi*), which is temporarily in a state of disruption due to the bitter disputes between the Nationalists in Taiwan and the Communists in the People's Republic. Traditionalists hope that once the political questions are resolved, the *natural state* of unity will be restored. (1996: 180–1, emphasis added)

But other Hakka meanwhile argue that 'differences between the Hakka in Taiwan and those in mainland China are too great to bridge' (1996: 182). As one of Martin's informants put it: 'If I went back to Wuhan [*xian*, the ancestral home in Guangdong], it would only be to take a look around, to see what's there' (1996: 182). Radical Hakka reject entirely the idea that the mainland should be the source of Hakka ethic identity – but they are not, for all that, necessarily against reunification.

5 This phenomenon is discussed in an a recent article by Julian Baum and Andrew Sherry, 'Identity Crisis: "New Taiwanese" Concept Alarms Beijing', *Far Eastern Economic Review*, 4 March, 1999.

6 *People's Daily* (Overseas Edition), 21 August 1999.

7 *People's Liberation Army Daily*, 20 August 1999. My translation of this article draws on the official English language version posted on the *People's Daily* website under the headline 'China's PLA Daily Criticizes Lee Tung-hui's Divisiveness'.

8 'A Chinese Phase in Social Anthropology' (Freedman 1979: 384).

9 'Introduction', *The anthropology of Taiwanese Society* (1981: 7).

10 Stephen O. Murray and Keelung Hong have criticised anthropologists for their 'complicity' with the KMT in conflating Taiwan with China (see Murray and Hong 1994).

11 As Gates and Ahern put it, 'That the authorities in both parts of a politically divided China claim an essential unity for the nation is well known and need not divert us from the quite independent question of Taiwan's cultural connections with the present-day mainland and with China's past' (1981: 7).

12 Gates and Ahern suggest it may have been 'Taiwan's representativeness, not its special qualities' which attracted anthropologists to it in the first place (Gates

and Ahern 1981: 8); but they go on to explain that anthropologists have come to value Taiwan for its uniqueness rather than for its representativeness. In Murray and Hong (1994: 3), Keelung Hong remarks: 'I soon realized that American anthropologists and mainland Chinese on Taiwan were not interested in Taiwanese culture. They seemed to be looking at us, but were really *looking through us* to try to see some traditional Chinese culture without seeing our historical experiences and what we made of it (Taiwanese culture) . . . It was immediately obvious to me that publication of fieldwork on Taiwan obliterated Taiwanese culture to claim the higher-prestige object of study, Chinese culture.'

13 Sangren suggests that in Taiwan we can now observe the emergence of a distinctive 'min'nan' identity – i.e. one based on the links of many Taiwanese to their 'native places' in the 'min'nan' (Southern Min) area of Fujian Province. This identity is neither straightforwardly 'Taiwanese' nor 'Chinese'.

14 *People's Daily* (Overseas Edition), 20 June 1997.

15 *People's Daily* (Overseas Edition), 23 June 1997.

16 *People's Daily* (Overseas Edition), 2 July 1999.

17 I visited China in early 1996, i.e. a few months after the events surrounding the Taiwanese elections and the Chinese naval manoeuvres in the Straits. Many people there seemed genuinely infuriated by what had transpired – by the American intervention in particular – and several people spontaneously told me they were ready to fight the Americans in order to resist the division of China. I was somewhat surprised by these heartfelt outbursts, which in some cases came from complete strangers. People stressed to me that Taiwan absolutely could not have independence (*duli*), that a war would certainly be fought over any attempt at independence, and that Americans were being very *ba* (warlord-like) and *huai* (rotten) about something which was purely a matter for the Chinese people. Interestingly, similar positions on the inevitability and moral necessity of reunification with Hong Kong and Taiwan are expressed in the immensely popular neo-nationalist tract, 'China can say no' (*zhongguo keyi shuo bu*). On the Taiwan issue the authors reproduce almost exactly the official line:

To reunify with Taiwan is not to conduct an invasion, but rather to defend our sovereignty . . . And for this China is willing to pay the highest price. For whoever sits by and watches Taiwan become independent will surely be seen by history as having sinned against the Chinese people [*minzu zuiren*]. (Song 1996: 71–5)

18 I am very grateful to Yen Yueh-ping for bringing this fascinating article to my attention.

CONCLUSION: THE SEPARATION CONSTRAINT

1 Mauss 1979: 79.

2 From the *Odyssey*, by Homer, translated by Robert Fitzgerald, New York: Anchor Press (1963: 2).

3 Here he discusses one departure from home:

So long as I had been content to look from the warmth of my own bed in Paris at the Persian church of Balbec, shrouded in driving sleet, no sort of objection to this journey had been offered by my body. Its objections began only when it realised that it would be of the party, and that on the evening of my arrival I should be shown to 'my' room which would be unknown to it. Its revolt was all the more profound in that on the very eve of my departure I learned that my mother would not be coming with us. (Marcel Proust, *Remembrance of Things Past*, Volume 2, tr. C. K. Scott Moncrieff and Terence Kilmartin. Harmondsworth: Penguin Books, 1983, p. 694).

References

Ahern, Emily Martin 1973 *The Cult of the Dead in a Chinese village.* Stanford: Stanford University Press.
1975 'The Power and Pollution of Chinese Women', in Margery Wolf and Roxanne Witke (eds.), *Women in Chinese Society.* Stanford: Stanford University Press.
1981a *Chinese Ritual and Politics.* Cambridge: Cambridge University Press.
1981b 'The Thai Ti Kong Festival', in H. Gates and E. Ahern (eds.), *The Anthropology of Taiwanese Society.* Stanford: Stanford University Press.
Aijmer, Göran 1991 'Chong-yang and the Ceremonial Calendar in Central China', in Hugh Baker and Stephan Feuchtwang (eds.), *An Old State in New Settings: Studies in the Social Anthropology of China in Memory of Maurice Freedman.* Oxford: JASO Occasional Papers no. 8, pp. 178–196.
Ainsworth, Mary D. Salter, et al 1978 *Patterns of Attachment: a Psychological Study of the Strange Situation.* Hillsdale, N.J. Lawrence Erlbaum Associates.
Anderson, Eugene 1988   *The Food of China.* New Haven: Yale University Press.
Anthony, Sylvia 1971 *The Discovery of Death in Childhood and After.* London: Allen Lane.
Appadurai, Arjun 1996 *Modernity at Large: Cultural Dimensions of Globalization.* Minneapolis: University of Minnesota Press.
Astuti, Rita 1995 *People of the Sea: Identity and Descent Among the Vezo of Madagascar.* Cambridge: Cambridge University Press.
Basch, Linda Nina Glick Schiller and Christina Szanton Blanc. 1994 *Nations Unbound: Transnational Projects, Postcolonial Predicaments and Deterritorialized Nation-States.* Amsterdam: Gordon and Breach Publishers.
Benjamin, Jessica 1990 *The Bonds of Love: Psychoanalysis, Feminism and the Problem of Domination.* London: Virago Press.
Birrell, Anne 1986 *New Songs From a Jade Terrace: An Anthology of Early Chinese Love Poems.* Harmondsworth: Penguin (first published 1982).
Blake, Fred 1978 'Death and Abuse in Marriage Laments: The Curse of Chinese Brides', *Asian Folklore Studies* 37(1): 13–33.
Bloch, Maurice 1991 'Language, Anthropology and Cognitive Science', *Man* 26(2): 183–98.
1992 *Prey Into Hunter: The Politics of Religious Experience.* Cambridge: Cambridge University Press.
Borofsky, Robert 1987 *Making history: Pukapukan and Anthropological Constructions of Knowledge.* Cambridge: Cambridge University Press.

Bourdieu, Pierre 1977 *Outline of a Theory of Practice*. Cambridge: Cambridge University Press.

1990 *The Logic of Practice*. Cambridge: Polity Press.

Bowlby, John 1978 *Attachment and loss volume 2: Separation: Anxiety and Anger*, Harmondsworth: Penguin (first published 1973).

1989 *The Making and Breaking of Affectional Bonds*. London and New York: Routledge.

Bray, Francesca 1997 *Technology and Gender: Fabrics of Power in Late Imperial China*. Berkeley: University of California Press.

Brown, Donald E 1991 *Human Universals*. Philadelphia: Temple University Press.

Cao Xueqin. 1973 *The Story of the Stone*, vol.1, translated by David Hawkes. Harmondsworth, Middlesex: Penguin.

Carey, Susan 1985 *Conceptual Change in Childhood*. Cambridge, Mass.: The MIT Press.

de Certeau, Michel de 1988 *The Writing of History*. New York: Columbia University Press.

Chang, K. C. 1977 *Food in Chinese Culture: Anthropological and Historical Perspectives*. New Haven: Yale University Press.

1983 *Art, Myth and Ritual: the Path to Political Authority in Ancient China*. Cambridge, Mass.: Harvard University Press.

Chard, Robert 1990 'Folk Tales on the God of the Stove', *Chinese Studies*, 12(1): 149–82.

Cheung, Joseph 1984 *Hong Kong: In Search of a future*. Hong Kong: Oxford University Press.

Chi-cheung, Choi 1995 'Reinforcing Ethnicity: The Jiao Festival in Cheung Chau', in David Faure and Helen F. Siu (eds.), *Down to Earth: The Territorial Bond in South China*. Stanford: Stanford University Press, pp. 104–22.

Chou, Eva Shan 1995 *Reconsidering Tu Fu: Literary Greatness and Cultural Context*. Cambridge: Cambridge University Press.

Cohen, Myron L. 1976 *House United, House Divided: The Chinese Family in Taiwan*. New York: Columbia University Press.

1994 'Being Chinese: The Peripheralization of Traditional Identity', in Tu Weiming (ed.), *The Living Tree: The Changing Meaning of Being Chinese Today*. Stanford: Stanford University Press, pp. 88–108.

Constable, Nicole (ed.) 1996 *Guest People: Hakka Identity in China and Abroad*. Seattle: University of Washington Press.

Crissman, Lawrence W. 1981 'The Structure of Local and Regional Systems', in H. Gates and E. Ahern (eds.), *The Anthropology of Taiwanese Society*. Stanford: Stanford University Press. pp. 89–124.

Deng Xiaoping 1984 *Selected Works of Deng Xiaoping 1975–1982*. Beijing: Foreign Languages Press.

Doré, Henry S. J. 1987 *Chinese Customs*. Singapore: Graham Brash Publications (first published 1911).

Duara, Prasenjit 1997 *Rescuing History from the Nation: Questioning Narratives of Modern China*. Chicago: University of Chicago Press.

Eastman, Lloyd, Jerome Chen, Suzanne Pepper and Lyman Van Slyke. 1991 *The Nationalist Era in China: 1927–1949*. Cambridge: Cambridge University Press.

Eliade, Mircea 1965 *Rites and Symbols of Initiation: The Mysteries of Birth and Rebirth*. New York: Harper and Row.

Elliott, Alan J. A. 1990 *Chinese Spirit-Medium Cults in Singapore*. London: Athlone Press (first published 1955).

Erbaugh, Mary 1996 'The Hakka Paradox in the People's Republic of China', in N. Constable (ed.), *Guest People: Hakka Identity in China and Abroad*. Seattle: University of Washington Press, pp. 196–231.

Faure, David and Helen Siu (eds.) 1995 *Down to Earth: The Territorial Bond in South China*. Stanford: Stanford University Press.

Feuchtwang, Stephan 1974 'Domestic and Communal Worship in Taiwan', in Arthur P. Wolf (ed.), *Religion and Ritual in Chinese Society*. Stanford: Stanford University Press, pp. 105–29.

1992 *The Imperial Metaphor: Popular Religion in China*. London: Routledge.

Firth, Raymond 1972 'Verbal and Bodily Rituals of Greeting and Parting', in Jean S. LaFontaine (ed.), *The Interpretation of Rituals: Essays in Honour of A. I. Richards*. London: Tavistock Publications, pp. 1–38.

Fitzgerald, C. P. 1986 *China: A Short Cultural History*. London: The Cresset Library (first published 1935).

Fox. James 1979 'Forward', M. Mauss, *Seasonal Variations of the Eskimo: A Study in Social Morphology*, in collaboration with Henri Beuchat, translated by James J. Fox. London: Routledge and Kegan Paul (first published 1950).

Freedman, Maurice 1979 *The Study of Chinese Society*. Stanford: Stanford University Press.

Freud, Sigmund 1955 *The Standard Edition of the Complete Psychological Works of Sigmund Freud, Translated from the German Under the General Editorship of James Strachey in Collaboration with Anna Freud; Volume 18 (1920–1922): Beyond the Pleasure Principle, Group Psychology, and Other Works*. London: The Hogarth Press

Gates, Hill 1981 'Ethnicity and Social Class', in H. Gates and E. Ahern (eds.), *The Anthropology of Taiwanese Society*. Stanford: Stanford University Press, pp. 241–281.

1996 *China's Motor: A Thousand Years of Petty Capitalism*. Ithaca: Cornell University Press.

Gates, Hill and Emily Martin Ahern. 1981 'Introduction', in H. Gates and E. Ahern (eds.), *The Anthropology of Taiwanese Society*. Stanford: Stanford University Press, pp. 1–10.

Gell, Alfred 1992 *The Anthropology of Time*. Oxford: Berg.

Goodrich, Anne S. 1981   *Chinese Hells: The Peking Temple of Eighteen Hells and the Chinese Conception of Hell*. Taipei: Monumenta Serica.

Graham, A. C. 1965 *Poems of the Late T'ang*. Harmondsworth, Middlesex: Penguin.

Greenberg, Jay R. and Stephen A. Mitchell. 1983 *Object relations in psychoanalytic theory*. Cambridge, Mass: Harvard University Press.

Harrell, Stevan (ed.). 1995 *Encounters on China's Ethnic Frontiers*. Seattle: University of Washington Press.

Harrell, Stevan and Huang Chun-chieh (eds.). 1994 *Cultural Change in Post-War Taiwan*. Boulder, Colo.: Westview Press.

Hawkes, David 1959 *Ch 'u Tz 'u: The Songs of the South.* Oxford: Clarendon Press.
1967 *A Little Primer of Tu Fu.* Oxford: Clarendon Press.

Hay, John 1994 'Introduction', in J. Hay (ed.) *Boundaries in China.* London: Reaktion Books.

Hazan, Cindy and Phillip Shaver. 1987 'Romantic Love Conceptualized as an Attachment Process', *Journal of Personality and Social Psychology,* 52(3): 511–24.

Herdt, Gilbert 1990 'Sambia Nosebleeding Rites and Male Proximity to Women', in James W. Stigler et al. (eds.), *Cultural Psychology: Essays on Comparative Human Development.* Cambridge and New York: Cambridge University Press, pp. 366–400.

Hevia, James L. 1995 *Cherishing men from afar: Qing Guest Ritual and the Macartney Embassy of 1793.* Durham: Duke University Press.

Hewlett, Barry S. 1992 'The Parent-Infant Relationship and Social-Emotional Development Among Aka Pygmies', in Jaipaul L. Roopnarine and D. Bruce Carter (eds.), *Parent-Child Socialization in Diverse Cultures,* Annual Advances in Applied Developmental Psychology Volume 5. Norwood, N.J.: Ablex Publishing Corporation, pp. 223–43.

Hinde, R. A. and Y. Spencer-Booth. 1971 'Effects of Brief Separation From Mother in Rhesus Monkeys', *Science* 173: 111–18.

Holmes, Jeremy 1993 *John Bowlby and Attachment Theory.* London and New York: Routledge.

Hung, William 1952 *Tu Fu: China's Greatest Poet.* Cambridge, Mass: Harvard University Press.

Jenner, William 1992 *The Tyranny of History: The Roots of China's Crisis.* Harmondsworth: Penguin.

Jenness, Diamond 1964 *The People of Twilight.* Chicago: University of Chicago Press (first edition 1928).

Jing Jun 1996 *The Temple of Memories: History, Power, and Morality in a Chinese Village.* Stanford: Stanford University Press.

Johnson, Elizabeth 1988 'Grieving For the Dead, Grieving For The Living: Funeral Laments of Hakka Women', in J. Watson and E. Rawski (eds.), *Death Ritual in Late Imperial and Modern China.* Berkeley: University of California Press, pp. 135–63.
1999 'Singing of Separation, Lamenting Loss: Hakka Women's expressions of separation and reunion', paper presented at workshop on 'The anthropology of separation and reunion in China', London School of Economics, May.

Jordan, David K. 1985 *Gods, Ghosts and Ancestors: Folk Religion in a Taiwanese Village* (second edition). Taipei: Caves Books (first edition published in 1972 by the University of California Press, Berkeley).

Judd, Ellen R. 1989 'Niangjia: Chinese Women and Their Natal Families', *Journal of Asian Studies,* 48(3): 525–44.
1994a *Gender and Power in Rural North China.* Stanford: Stanford University Press.
1994b 'Mulian Saves his Mother in 1989', in R. Watson (ed.), *Memory, History, and Opposition Under State Socialism.* Sante Fe: School of American Research Press, pp. 105–27.

Keith, Ronald C. 1989 *The Diplomacy of Zhou Enlai*. London: Macmillan.

Kohut, Kohut 1977 *The Restoration of the Self*. Madison, Conn.: International Universities Press.

LaFontaine, Jean 1985 *Initiation*. Harmondsworth: Penguin.

Lamley, Harry J. 1981 'Subethnic Rivalry in the Ch'ing Period', in H. Gates and E. Ahern (eds), *The Anthropology of Taiwanese Society*. Stanford: Stanford University Press, pp. 282–318.

Lave, Lave 1988 *Cognition in Practice*. Cambridge: Cambridge University Press.

LeVine, Robert A. 1990 'Infant Environments in Psychoanalysis: a Cross-Cultural View', in James W. Stigler et al. (eds.), *Cultural Psychology: Essays on Comparative Human Development*. Cambridge and New York: Cambridge University Press, pp. 454–74.

Loizos, Peter 1981 *The Heart Grown Bitter: a chronicle of Cypriot War Refugees*. Cambridge: Cambridge University Press.

Mahler, Margaret S. 1969 *On Human Symbiosis and the Vicissitudes of Individuation, Vol I: Infantile Psychosis*. London: The Hogarth Press and the Institute of Psycho-analysis.

Martin, Emily 1988 'Gender and Ideological Differences in Representations of Life and Death', in J. Watson and E. Rawski (eds.), *Death Ritual in Late Imperial and Modern China*. Berkeley: University of California Press, pp. 164–79.

Martin, Howard J. 1996 'The Hakka Ethnic Movement in Taiwan', in N. Constable (ed.), *Guest People: Hakka Identity in China and Abroad*. Seattle: University of Washington Press, pp. 176–95.

Mauss, Marcel 1979 *Seasonal Variations of the Eskimo: a Study in Social Morphology*, in collaboration with Henri Beuchat, translated by James J. Fox. London: Routledge and Kegan Paul (first published 1950).

Murray, Stephen O. and Keelung Hong. 1994 *Taiwanese culture, Taiwanese society: A Critical Review of Social Science Research Done on Taiwan*. Lanham, Md.: University Press of America.

Myers, Fred R. 1986 *Pintupi Country, Pintupi Self: Sentiment, Place, and Politics Among Western Desert Aborigines*. Washington and Canberra: Smithsonian Institution and Australian Institute of Aboriginal Studies.

1988 'The Logic and Meaning of Anger Among Pintupi Aborigines', *Man* 23(4): 589–610.

Obata, Shigeyoshi 1922 *The Works of Li Po, the Chinese Poet*. New York: E. P. Dutton.

Ong, Aihwa and Donald Nonini 1997 *Ungrounded Empires: The Cultural Politics of Modern Chinese Transnationalism*. New York: Routledge.

Oxfeld, Ellen 1993 *Blood, Sweat and Mahjong: Family and Enterprise in an Overseas Chinese Community*. Ithaca: Cornell University Press.

Owen, Stephen 1975 *The Poetry of Meng Chiao and Han Yu*. New Haven: Yale University Press.

Parkes, Colin M., Joan Stevenson-Hinde and Pater Marris (eds.) 1991 *Attachment Across the Life Cycle*. London and New York: Routledge.

Parkin, David 1997 'Mementos as Transitional Objects in Human Displacement', the 1997 Colson Lecture (also forthcoming in *Journal of Material Culture*).

Pieke, Frank N. and Hein Mallee (eds.) 1999 *Internal and International Migration:*

Chinese Perspectives. Richmond, Surrey: Curzon Press.

Plaks, Andrew H. 1976 *Archetype and allegory in the Dream of the Red Chamber.* Princeton: Princeton University Press.

Potter, Sulamith H. and Jack M. Potter 1990 *China's Peasants: The Anthropology of a Revolution.* Cambridge: Cambridge University Press.

Radcliffe-Brown, A. R. 1933 *The Andaman Islanders.* Cambridge: Cambridge University Press.

Rosaldo, Renato 1993 *Culture and Truth: The Remaking of Social Analysis.* London: Routledge (first published 1989).

Sangren, P. Steven 1983 'Female Gender in Chinese Religious Symbols: Kuan Yin, Ma Tsu, and the "Eternal Mother"', *Signs.* 9(1): 4–25.

1987 *History and Magical Power in a Chinese community.* Stanford: Stanford University Press.

1991 'Dialectics of Alienation: Individuals and Collectivities in Chinese religion', *Man* (n.s.) 26: 67–86.

1998 'Anthropology and Identity Politics in Taiwan: The Relevance of Local Religion', *Harvard Studies on Taiwan: Papers of the Taiwan Studies Workshop* 2: 161–91. Also published in Chinese as 'Renleixue yu taiwan di rentong zhengzhi: Lun difang congjiao di yingxiang', *Xianggang shehui kexue xuebao* 11: 41–72.

1999 'Recognition and Autonomy; Mythic Reflections on Individual and Collective Self-Production', paper given at workshop on 'The Anthropology of Separation and Reunion in China', held at the London School of Economics, May.

Seaman, Gary 1981 'The Sexual Politics of Karmic Retribution', in H. Gates and E. Ahern (eds.), *The Anthropology of Taiwanese Society*, Stanford: Stanford University Press.

Shepherd, John Robert 1993 *Statecraft and Political Economy on the Taiwan Frontier 1600–1800.* Stanford: Stanford University Press.

Silber, Cathy 1994 'From Daughter to Daughter-in-law in the Women's Script of Southern Hunan', in C. K. Gilmartin et al. (eds.), *Engendering China: Women, Culture and the State.* Cambridge, Mass.: Harvard University Press, pp. 47–68.

Slaughter, Virginia, Raquel Jaakkola and Susan Carey 1999 'Constructing a Coherent Theory: Children's Biological Understanding of Life and Death', forthcoming in M. Siegal and C. Peterson (eds), *Children's Understanding of Biology and Health.* Cambridge: Cambridge University Press.

Song Qiang, Zhang Zangzang and Qiao Bian 1996 *Zhongguo keyi shuo bu* [*China Can Say No*]. Beijing: Zhonghua Gongshang Lianhe Chubanshe.

Sperber, Dan 1985 'Anthropology and Psychology: Towards an Epidemiology of Representations', *Man* 20: 73–89.

Spiro, Melford E. 1982 *Oedipus in the Trobriands.* Chicago and London: University of Chicago Press.

Stafford, Charles 1992 'Good Sons and Virtuous Mothers: Kinship and Chinese Nationalism in Taiwan', *Man* 27: 363–78.

1995 *The Roads of Chinese Childhood.* Cambridge: Cambridge University Press.

2000 'Chinese Patriliny and the Cycles of *yang* and *laiwang*', in Janet Carsten (ed.), *Cultures of Relatedness.* Cambridge: Cambridge University Press.

Stern, Daniel N. 1985 *The Interpersonal World of the Infant: A View From Psychoanalysis and Developmental Psychology*. New York: Basic Books.

Thompson, Stuart 1988 'Death, Food and Fertility', in James L. Watson and Evelyn S. Rawski (eds.), *Death Ritual in Late Imperial and Modern China*. Berkeley: University of California Press, pp. 71–108.

T'ien Ju K'ang 1953 *The Chinese of Sarawak: A Study of Social Structure*. London: London School of Economics Monographs on Social Anthropology (no. 12).

Topley, Marjorie 1975 'Marriage Resistance in Rural Kwangtung', in M. Wolfe and R. Witke (eds.), *Women in Chinese Society*. Stanford: Stanford University Press.

Toren, Christina 1993 'Making History: The Significance of Childhood Cognition for a Comparative Anthropology of Mind', *Man* 28: 461–78.

Tu Wei-ming 1994 'Cultural China: the Periphery as the Centre', in W Tu (ed.), *The Living Tree: The Changing Meaning of Being Chinese Today*. Stanford: Stanford University Press.

Turner, Terence S. 1977 'Transformation, Hierarchy and Transcendence: A Reformulation of Van Gennep's Model of the Structure of *rites de passage*', in S. F. Moore and B. G. Myerhoff (eds.), *Secular Rituals*. Amsterdam: Van Gorcum, pp. 53–70.

Turner, Victor 1977a *The Ritual Process*. Ithaca: Cornell University Press (first published 1969).

1977b 'Variations on the Theme of Liminality', in S. F. Moore and B. G. Myerhoff (eds.), *Secular Rituals*. Amsterdam: Van Gorcum, pp. 36–52.

Turton, David 1996 'Migrants and Refugees: A Mursi Case Study', in Tim Allen (ed.), *In Search of Cool Ground: War, Flight and Homecoming in Northeast Africa*. London: James Currey Ltd, pp. 96–110.

van Gennep, Arnold 1960 *The Rites of Passage*. London: Routledge and Kegan Paul (first published 1909).

Watson, James L. 1982 'Of Flesh and Bones: The Management of Death Pollution in Cantonese Society', in M. Bloch and J. Parry (eds.), *Death and the Regeneration of Life*. Cambridge: Cambridge University Press, pp. 155–86.

1987 'From the Common Pot: Feasting With Equals in Chinese society', *Anthropos* 82: 389–401.

1988 'The Structure of Chinese Funerary Rites: Elementary Forms, Ritual Sequence, and the Primacy of Performance', in J. Watson and E. Rawski (eds.), *Death Ritual in Late Imperial and Modern China*. Berkeley: University of California Press, pp. 3–19.

1992 'The Renegotiation of Chinese Cultural Identity in the Post-Mao Era', in J. Wasserstrom and E. Perry (eds.), *Popular Protest and Political Culture in Modern China*. Boulder, Colo.: Westview Press.

Watson, James L. and Evelyn S. Rawski (eds.) 1988 *Death Ritual in Late Imperial and Modern China*. Berkeley: University of California Press.

Watson, Rubie S. 1985 *Inequality Among Brothers: Class and Kinship in South China*. Cambridge: Cambridge University Press.

1994 'Introduction' and 'Making Secret Histories: Memory and Mourning in Post-Mao China', in R. Watson (ed), *Memory, History, and Opposition Under State Socialism*. Sante Fe: School of American Research Press.

Watson, Rubie S. and Patricia Buckley Ebrey (eds.) 1991 *Marriage and Inequality in Chinese Society*. Berkeley: University of California Press.

Weller, Robert P. 1987 *Unities and Diversities in Chinese Religion*. Houndmills, Basingstoke: Macmillan.

Whiting, John M. W. 1981 'Environmental Constraints on Infant Care Practices', in R. L. Munroe et al. (eds.), *Handbook of Cross-Cultural Human Development*. New York: Garland.

1990 'Adolescent Rituals and Identity Conflicts', in James W. Stigler et al. (eds.), *Cultural Psychology: Essays on Comparative Human Development*. Cambridge and New York: Cambridge University Press, pp. 357–365.

Wolf, Arthur 1974 'Gods, Ghosts and Ancestors', in A. Wolf (ed.), *Religion and Ritual in Chinese Society*. Stanford: Stanford University Press, pp. 131–82.

Wolf, Margery 1968 *The House of Lim: A Study of a Chinese Farm Family*. New York: Appleton- Century-Crofts.

1972 *Women and the Family in Rural Taiwan*. Stanford: Stanford University Press.

1987 *Revolution Postponed: Women in Contemporary China*. London: Methuen (first published 1985).

1990 'The Woman Who Didn't become a Shaman', *American Ethnologist* 17(3): 419–30.

Wollheim, Richard 1991 *Freud*, second edition. London: Fontana Press.

Wu Hung 1994 'Beyond the Great Boundary: Funerary Narrative in the Cangshan Tomb', in John Hay (ed.), *Boundaries in China*. London: Reaktion Books.

Yunxiang Yan 1996 *The Flow of Gifts: Reciprocity and Social Networks in a Chinese Village*. Stanford: Stanford University Press.

Yang, Mayfair Mei-hui 1994 *Gifts, Favors and Banquets: The Art of Social Relationships in China*. Ithaca: Cornell University Press.

Zito, Angela 1997 *Of Body and Brush: Grand Sacrifice as Text/Performance in Eighteenth Century China*. Chicago: University of Chicago Press.

Index